*Everyman, I will go with thee,
and be thy guide*

THE EVERYMAN LIBRARY

The Everyman Library was founded by J. M. Dent in 1906. He chose the name Everyman because he wanted to make available the best books ever written in every field to the greatest number of people at the cheapest possible price. He began with Boswell's Life of Johnson; *his one thousandth title was Aristotle's* Metaphysics, *by which time sales exceeded 40 million.*

Today Everyman paperbacks remain true to J. M. Dent's aims and high standards, with a wide range of titles at affordable prices in editions which address the needs of today's readers. Each new text is reset to give a clear, elegant page and to incorporate the latest thinking and scholarship. Each book carries the pilgrim logo, the character in Everyman, *a medieval mystery play, a proud link between Everyman past and present.*

Edgar Allan Poe

COMPLETE POEMS AND SELECTED ESSAYS

Edited by
RICHARD GRAY
University of Essex

Consultant Editor for this volume
CHRISTOPHER BIGSBY
University of East Anglia

EVERYMAN
J. M. DENT · LONDON
CHARLES E. TUTTLE
VERMONT

Poems and Essays of Poe first included in
Everyman's Library 1927

This edition of *Complete Poems and Selected Essays*
first published by J. M. Dent 1993

Typeset at The Spartan Press Ltd, Lymington, Hants

Printed in Great Britain by The Guernsey Press Co. Ltd, Guernsey, C.I.

for
J. M. Dent
Orion Publishing Group
Orion House
5 Upper St Martin's Lane, London, WC2H 9EA

and
Charles E. Tuttle Co. Inc
28 South Main Street, Rutland, Vermont,
05701, USA

British Library Cataloguing-in-Publication Data
available upon request.

ISBN 0 460 87261 3

CONTENTS

ESSAYS AND REVIEWS

NOTE ON THE AUTHOR

Born in Boston, Massachusetts in 1809 to travelling actors, Edgar Allan Poe had lost both his parents by the time he was two. He was brought up by foster-parents, Mr and Mrs John Allan, in Richmond, Virginia; and in 1815 he went with them to England, where he attended school. On returning home, he was sent to the University of Virginia only to be expelled within the year. Mr Allan then wanted Poe to start a commercial career; but Poe was unwilling. He ran away from home and enlisted in the army under a pseudonym. In 1830 he was enrolled at West Point but, in a short while, he was again expelled. Relations with Mr Allan soon broke down completely, and Poe subsequently tried to make his way as an editor, critic, and creative writer. His responsibilities were increased when in 1836 he married his cousin Virginia Clemm, a girl of thirteen. He enjoyed some success with his collection of short stories, *Tales of the Grotesque and Arabesque*, which appeared in 1840; and his poem 'The Raven' caused a sensation when it was published in 1844. However, he was always on the move from one position to another and his financial circumstances were never good. Virginia died in 1847, after a long and painful illness; and Poe turned increasingly to alcohol for support, and to the companionship of older women. He died in Baltimore in 1849 in mysterious circumstances, while travelling from Richmond to New York.

NOTE ON THE EDITOR

Richard Gray is Professor in the Department of Literature at the University of Essex. He is the author of *The Literature of Memory: Modern Writers of the American South*, *Writing the South: Ideas of an American Region* (which won the C. Hugh Holman Award from the Society for the Study of Southern Literature for the most distinguished book on the American South published in 1986), and *American Poetry of the Twentieth Century*. He has edited two anthologies of American poetry, a collection of original essays on American fiction, and a collection of essays on Robert Penn Warren; and he has written a large number of essays and articles on American literature of the last two centuries. Currently writing a critical biography of William Faulkner, he is a regular reviewer for *The Higher* (formerly *The Times Higher Education Supplement*), *Notes and Queries*, *Modern Language Review*, and other journals. He is Associate Editor of the *Journal of American Studies* (published by Cambridge UP) and Consulting Editor for *American Literary History* (published by Oxford UP).

CHRONOLOGY OF POE'S LIFE

Year	*Age*	*Life*
1809		Born 19 January in Boston to Elizabeth Arnold Poe and David Poe, Jr.
1811		Following disappearance of his father and the death of his mother, Poe taken into house of merchant in Richmond, Virginia, John Allan.
1815	6	Travels to England with Allan family and attends school in Stoke Newington.
1820	11	Returns to Richmond, Virginia.
1826	17	Engaged to Sarah Elmira Royster. Enters University of Virginia but leaves after incurring heavy debts. Estrangement from John Allan because of this.
1827	18	Assumes the name Henri Le Rennet and travels to Boston. Enlists under the name of Edgar S. Perry in the United States Army. Publishes *Tamerlane and Other Poems* 'by a Bostonian'.
1829	20	Death of Frances Allan, his foster-mother. Receives honourable discharge from army. *Al Aaraaf, Tamerlane, and Minor Poems* published in Baltimore.

CHRONOLOGY OF HIS TIMES

Year	*Literary context*	*Historical events*
1809	Washington Irving, *A History of New York*	James Madison President Sequoya begins to develop writing system for the Cherokees
1812		Naval war between USA and Britain until 1814
1814	Francis Scott Key, 'The Star-Spangled Banner'	Washington DC burned by British troops
1817		James Monroe President
1820	Washington Irving, *The Sketch Book*	Purchase of Florida from Spain Missouri Compromise outlaws slavery north of latitude 36 30°
1826	James Fenimore Cooper, *The Last of the Mohicans*	Robert Owen founds community at New Harmony, Indiana
1827	James Fenimore Cooper, *The Prairie* John James Audubon, *The Birds of America* (first section; completed 1838)	Disciples of Christ founded by Alexander Campbell.
1828	Noah Webster, *An American Dictionary of the English Language.*	
1829		Andrew Jackson President

Year	Age	Life
1830		Brief reconciliation with John Allan, during which Poe returns to Richmond. Writes 'To Helen' (p). Enrols in West Point Military Academy.
1831		Contrives dismissal from West Point. Other cadets help to publish *Poems* by subscription. Writes 'Israfel' (p). First stories written, intended as parodies of *Blackwood's Magazine* Gothic fiction. *Tales of the Folio Club* published.
1833	24	Wins prize from *Baltimore Saturday Visitor* with story, 'Ms. Found in a Bottle' (s). Final estrangement from John Allan.
1834		John Allan dies, leaving Poe nothing.
1835		Editor of *Southern Literary Messenger*, a magazine published in Richmond.
1836		Marries Virginia Clemm, his cousin aged thirteen. Discharged from *Southern Literary Messenger*.
1837	28	Moves to New York. Writes his only completed long fiction, 'The Narrative of Arthur Gordon Pym'.
1838		Moves to Philadelphia
1839		Writes 'The Fall of the House of Usher' (s). Associate Editor of *Burton's Gentleman's Magazine*. Publishes *Tales of the Grotesque and Arabesque*.
1840	31	Leaves *Burton's Gentleman's Magazine*.
1841		Writes 'The Murders of the Rue Morgue' (s) and 'A Descent into the Maelstrom' (s). Editor of

Year	*Literary context*	*Historical events*
1830	Joseph Smith, *Book of Mormon*	Debate in Congress between Daniel Webster and Robert Y. Hayne on the nature of the Union
1831	Robert Montgomery Bird, *The Gladiator*	Nat Turner's slave insurrection in Virginia William Lloyd Garrison founds anti-slavery journal *The Liberator* in Boston
1833		American Anti Slavery Society founded Oberlin College founded as the first co-educational institution of higher learning
1835	Alexis de Tocqueville, *Democracy in America* (vol. 1; vol. 2 1840)	New York *Herald* founded Samuel Colt patents his revolver
1836	Ralph Waldo Emerson, *Nature*	Texas declares independence from Mexico and establishes the 'Lone Star Republic' Battle of the Alamo
1837	Ralph Waldo Emerson, 'The American Scholar' Nathaniel Hawthorne, *Twice-Told Tales*	Martin Van Buren President
1838		Regular steam travel across the Atlantic begins with arrival of British *Sirius and Great Western* (journey of sixteen days) 'Underground railway' for escaped slaves organized by abolitionists
1839	Henry Wadsworth Longfellow, *Voices of the Night*	Abolitionists found the Liberty Party
1840	James Fenimore Cooper, *The Pathfinder*	Transcendentalist magazine, *The Dial*, founded under the editorship of Margaret Fuller
1841	James Fenimore Cooper, *The Deerslayer*	New York *Tribune* founded by Horace Greeley

Year	*Age*	*Life*
1841 *(cont.)*		*Graham's Magazine*. Increasing health and financial problems.
1842	33	Virginia haemorrhages, the first signs of a painful illness that eventually kills her. Writes 'The Oval Portrait' (s), 'The Mystery of Marie Roget' (s), and 'The Masque of the Red Death' (s). Publishes 'The Tell-Tale Heart' (s). Leaves *Graham's Magazine*.
1843		Wins prize for 'The Gold Bug' (s). Publishes 'The Conqueror Worm' (p). Attempts to publish *The Prose Romances of Edgar A. Poe* in serial form, but first issue fails to sell.
1844		Writes 'The Purloined Letter' (s). Moves to New York. Joins N. P. Willis's *Mirror* magazine. Publishes 'The Raven' (p) which is an immediate success and is reprinted across the country.
1845	36	Co-editor of *Broadway Journal*. Publishes *Tales* and *The Raven and Other Poems*. Writes 'Eulalie' (p). *Broadway Journal* fails. Begins writing a series of articles on 'Literary America'.
1846		Writes 'The Cask of Amontillado' (s) and 'Ulalume' (p). Moves to Fordham, New York State. Both Poe and Virginia ill.
1847		Virginia dies.
1848		Publishes *Eureka*, a long prose account of his 'philosophy'. Moves to Richmond. Engaged to Sarah Helen Whitman.
1849	40	Writes 'For Annie' (p) and 'Annabel Lee' (p). Engaged to Sarah Elmira (Royster) Shelton, to whom he was engaged in 1826. Dies on 7 October in Baltimore, Maryland.

(p) = poem (s) = story

Year	*Literary context*	*Historical events*
1841 *(cont.)*	Ralph Waldo Emerson, *Essays*	William Henry Harrison President. Dies after one month in office and succeeded by John Tyler
1843	William Hickling Prescott, *History of the Conquest of Mexico*	John Smith authorizes Mormon polygamy
1844		Telegraph line from Washington to Baltimore opens
1845	Anna Cora Mowatt, *Fashion; or, Life in New York*	James K. Polk President USA annexes Texas *Scientific American* begins publication
1846	Nathaniel Hawthorne, *Mosses from an Old Manse* Herman Melville, *Typee*	War between USA and Mexico Mormons under Brigham Young set out for Utah USA acquires Oregon Territory
1847	Ralph Waldo Emerson, *Poems* Henry Wadsworth Longfellow, *Evangeline* Herman Melville, *Omoo* William Hickling Prescott, *History of the Conquest of Peru*	USA captures Mexico City Salt Lake City founded by Mormons Gold discovered in California More than 200,000 leave Ireland for USA
1848	James Russell Lowell, *The Biglow Papers* (first series)	War between USA and Mexico ends; USA acquires territory between Rocky Mountains and Pacific Free Soil Party founded
1849	Francis Parkman, *The California and Oregon Trail* Henry David Thoreau, 'Civil Disobedience' and *A Week on the Concord and Merrimack Rivers*	Zachary Taylor President William Hunt invents safety pin 'Bloomers' invented by Amelia Jenks Bloomer

INTRODUCTION

According to the critic Leslie Fiedler, Edgar Allan Poe's greatest creation was himself. Like many Romantic artists, such as Byron or Baudelaire, Poe turned his own life into drama by playing roles that he thought suited him, or by telling colourful lies about himself when the truth seemed too dull. Poe even ensured that the lies would continue after his death because, with typically sardonic humour, he made a personal enemy, a hack named Rufus Griswold, his official biographer. Griswold immediately seized the chance Poe had given him to fabricate lurid stories about his subject's life. The result is that Edgar Allan Poe as we now know him – through tales and biographies, film portraits, and by way of collective myth – is as much an invention of Poe himself, working directly or through the agency of Griswold, as he is a product of anything remotely resembling fact. In this sense, as in so many others, Poe is like one of his own heroes of poetic *personæ*, using his mind and will in an effort to reinvent his life.

All this is by way of saying that Poe's life, strange though it was, has been rendered even stranger by various fabrications, and it is only recently that biographers and historians have managed to separate fantasy from fact. Poe, we now know, was born in Boston – something he preferred to conceal later, when he chose to play the part of Southern gentleman. And he was born not, as he later claimed, to two members of the English nobility, but to two travelling actors: Elizabeth Arnold, an Englishwoman, and David Poe, her second husband, who was of Irish descent. David Poe had two habits that were to be inherited by his son – drinking and falling into debt; and soon after Edgar's birth he deserted his wife and was never heard of again. Two years later, in 1811, Elizabeth Arnold Poe died while staying in Richmond, Virginia; and Poe, now to all intents and purposes an orphan, was taken as a foster-child into the home of John Allan, a wealthy Richmond tobacco merchant, and his wife Frances. Naturally, this early loss of both his parents, and particularly his mother, had a profound effect on Poe, as his later writing bears painful witness. Time after time we are confronted with the same situation in Poe's work: the hero, the protagonist or speaker of the poem, loses a strange, distant, loved woman, a creature part-woman, part-statue and part-goddess. And he spends his time trying to reach her, trying to recover her somehow, by crossing the abyss between life and death.

Poe was brought up by his foster-parents first in Richmond and then, for five years between 1815 and 1820, in England where he attended Manor House School in Stoke Newington. Returning to Richmond with the Allans and to school there, he proceeded to fall in love with the mother of one of his fellow pupils, a Mrs Jane Stanard. Poe later described Mrs Stanard as 'the first, purely ideal love of my soul'. His pet name for her was Helen, and she later became one of the models for his poems to a woman of that name. Probably, this affection for a woman much older than himself had been initiated by Poe's early loss of his mother; so it was a cruel irony that, shortly after Poe met her, Mrs Stanard too suddenly died after a brief illness. The association of death and beauty, and more specifically death and a beautiful woman, that was to haunt so much of Poe's poetic practice and theory was consquently confirmed in the most painful way.

Shortly after this traumatic event, Poe entered the University of Virginia. Evidently, he was a good student, but life at university was made difficult for Poe by the fact that his foster-father, a hard-headed businessman, was reluctant to give the young man much financial support. In a typically self-destructive move, Poe then took to gambling to supplement his income. The predictable occurred: Poe lost heavily and fell further into debt and so, after only one year as a student, he was forced to leave. Looking for another world to enter, Poe now enlisted in the army under the assumed name of Edgar S. Perry. Poe apparently began by liking this new career, even rising to the rank of sergeant-major. Eventually, however, the routine of army life began to oppress him and he managed to persuade John Allan to buy him out of army service. Allan was reluctant to do so, partly because he was mean by nature and partly because he considered the army a respectable career. But Poe was adamant, since by this time he had found a new and, as it turned out, lifelong focus for his attention and for the realization of his needs in writing, the world of the word. He had been composing poetry, on and off, since he was an adolescent. It was only after leaving the University of Virginia, however, that he gave it detailed, concentrated attention.

With this, his work quickly bore fruit. His first book of poems was published privately in Boston in 1827. Entitled simply *Tamerlane and Other Poems* by 'A Bostonian', it contained the first versions of some of his most famous pieces, like 'Tamerlane', 'A Dream Within a Dream' and ' Spirits of the Dead'; but it excited little notice among the public and critics and there are few copies of it extant.

Undiscouraged, Poe continued writing new poems and revising old ones; and he decided that he would try to make a career out of literature. This was a brave course to follow – and one unusual in the America of that time. There were successful writers, of course, such as Washington Irving and William Cullen Bryant, but they had other means by which to support themselves. America was still a young, underpopulated country with an appetite for good writing that could hardly be called voracious. There was no tradition of patronage to make up for the relative indifference of the public. Worse still, the absence of international copyright laws meant that American publishers could satisfy what audience there was for literature with the work of famous European novelists and poets whom they did not even have to pay for the privilege.

Poe's ambition to be a full-time writer seems all the bolder because by this time he had lost all hope that his foster-parents would help him if necessary. His foster-mother, who seems to have been responsible for taking Poe into the house in the first place, died in 1829. John Allan, a practical man never very fond of Poe, grew tired of trying to turn his foster-son into a soldier or businessman, and by 1830 their relationship consisted of little more than an exchange of the occasional curt letter. Poe made one more attempt to satisfy Allan's expectations of him by entering West Point that year to train as an army officer. Almost as soon as he arrived, though, Poe wanted to leave again; and he did so by deliberately neglecting his duties in order to be court-martialled and expelled. Unsurprisingly, this did not endear him to Allan; and the only result of this curious re-entry into army life was the even more curious fact that Poe's third volume of poems, published in 1831, was paid for by subscription among his colleagues at West Point and dedicated to 'The US Corps of Cadets'. What his fellow soldiers were expecting from this volume is hard to say, although they probably anticipated a few joky pieces about army life. What they received for their money was a series of strange, intangible and often hallucinatory pieces, like 'To Helen', 'The City in the Sea' and 'The Sleeper', which seemed to inhabit some borderland between sleep and waking.

Pursuing his literary ambitions, Poe first set up home in Baltimore, Maryland, where he took lodgings with Mrs Maria Clemm, an aunt on his father's side. He began writing for the popular magazines of the time: periodicals such as *Harper's* and *Saturday Evening Post* which were often people's only contact with the world outside their farm or village. Most of the work he produced for them was prose: tales of terror or detection, macabre humour or bizarre fantasy. But he continued writing poetry, too, and criticism, for the major magazines. Several more volumes of his poetry were published; and, moving between Baltimore, New York and Philadelphia, the three major publishing centres in America at the time, he added to his income by taking a number of posts as editor of various journals and magazines. He even created something of a sensation when his poem 'The Raven' was published in 1844 and then reprinted in newspapers all over the United States and Europe. After this, Poe was invariably described as 'The author of "The Raven"' whenever his name appeared in print – something he began by enjoying but soon came to regard as a burden and a curse.

Despite apparent success, however, Poe's life was still far from happy. He was haunted by feelings of insecurity and inadequacy, reasonless fears that nothing seemed to diminish. He courted dislike, by playing the role of aristocratic dandy in a largely materialistic, utilitarian society; yet he was always profoundly hurt and resentful when he met with the slightest rebuff. He had tried to give his life a semblance of domestic normality in 1836 by marrying his cousin Virginia Clemm, a girl of thirteen; but Virginia contracted a painful, debilitating illness that ended eventually in her death in 1847. At the same time, Poe was finding it more and more difficult to place his work, or to find adequate financial support, and suffering from periodic attacks of what he termed 'brain fever': a temporary mental instability. In the face of all these pressures, Poe turned increasingly for comfort to a series of relationships with women much older than himself – and to the simpler chemical comfort offered by alcohol and opium.

This went on for several years, with Poe still writing but deteriorating rapidly and with stories, sometimes fanciful, of his erratic behaviour and wretched circumstances circulating through literary America. His end, when it came, was equally and darkly melodramatic. One day, in September 1849, Poe left Richmond, where he was living at the time, for New York. Nothing was heard of him for over a week; he never arrived in New York. Then, some time in October, one of Poe's friends received a letter from a man in Baltimore, Maryland, called Joseph Walker. In the letter Walker explained that he had found, as he put it, 'a gentleman rather the worse for wear' dressed in a poor, thin suit that was not his own and wandering about Ryan's Fourth Ward Polls – a local polling-booth located, rather conveniently, in a public house. The 'gentleman' was, of course, Poe. He was taken to Washington College Hospital in Baltimore, where only a distant relative came to see him. According to report, he never explained why he was in Baltimore, why he was at Ryan's Fourth Ward Polls, or why he was dressed in someone else's clothes. He just lay on his bed for a few days, talking coherently but at random, and then, on 7 October, he died, calling out the name 'Reynolds'. His friends, when told this, were puzzled about the identity of the man Reynolds since, as far as they knew, Poe had never known a person of that name. Then, finally, someone remembered that Reynolds was the name of an explorer who had embarked on a cruise from which he had never returned – and that Reynolds' life and writings had formed a basis for Poe's one long, completed work of fiction, *The Narrative of Arthur Gordon Pym*, in which the hero, Pym, makes his own journey of exploration to an undiscovered country: a journey, that turns out to be an elaborate metaphor for death.

Which brings us back to the poetry. Exactly what happened in the last week or so of Poe's life remains a mystery, but one thing is clear: Poe seems to have seen his passing away as a voyage of exploration – to a place 'from whose bourn' (to borrow from *Hamlet*) 'no traveller returns'. Similarly, what happens in Poe's poems remains a mystery to the extent that they are not simple allegories, to be given straightforward, prosaic interpretations. But, again, one thing is fairly clear: on one level Poe seems to have seen his poetry as a voyage of exploration, as an attempt to conjure up, dramatize and discover the world that exists beyond death. All his poetic output is, in fact, based on one simple but radical premise: that reality does not lie here, in this life. The real is not the physical, the material, but its contrary: the spiritual, the intangible. It is the reverse of all that our senses can conceive or our reason can encompass; and it lies beyond life, something we can discover only in sleep, in madness and trance, or above all in death. The real world, as Poe puts it in 'Dreamland', exists 'out of SPACE – out of TIME'; and his intention in his poetry is to explore this world and convince the reader of its reality.

The pressures that led Poe towards this notion of poetry are, perhaps, to be found in his life: the early loss of his mother was certainly crucial, as was his lifelong sense that he was born out of his due time into a society that was, at the very best, indifferent to him. But, whatever the pressures, this notion is most fully articulated in his two essays 'The Poetic Principle' and 'The Philosophy of Composition', where Poe makes it abundantly clear that the poet should be concerned, first and last, with the 'circumscribed Eden' of his own dreams. 'It is the desire of the moth for the star,' Poe says of the poetic impulse in 'The Poetic Principle': 'Inspired by an ecstatic prescience of the glories beyond the grave, we struggle, by multiform combinations among the things and thoughts of Time, to attain a portion of that Loveliness whose very elements, perhaps, appertain to eternity alone.' The poet's task, in effect, is to weave a tapestry of talismanic signs and sounds designed to draw, or rather subdue, the reader into sharing the world beyond phenomenal experience. Poems make nothing happen in any practical, immediate sense, according to this view. On the contrary, the ideal poem becomes one in which the words efface themselves, disappear as they are read, leaving only a feeling of significant absence, of no-thing.

Clearly, Poe drew elements of this visionary, even cabalistic notion of poetry from some of the English Romantics – particularly Coleridge, whose work he was not above plagiarizing. What is remarkable, however, is just how far he pushed this notion – so that, in his critical hands, the poet becomes a prophet who has somehow seen the promised land and is now trying to lead others there. Or, it could be added, Poe sees the poet as a priest or shaman, using his arts to entice us into rejection of the here and now – even a kind of magician who is attempting in effect to enchant us, or simply trick us into forgetting the laws of the ordinary world. Seen from this perspective, it is easy to understand why Poe became such an influential figure for Baudelaire and the French Symbolist poets, who learned, in part, from their American cousin to regard the poet as a person with arcane, almost divine knowledge and the poem as a magic document resisting the heresy of paraphrase. 'The poet makes himself a seer,' Rimbaud declared, 'by a long, prodigious, and rational disordering of all the senses.' Poe would undoubtedly have agreed, not least because he would have recognized the echoes of his own essays in these words.

Just how Poe's ideas of poetry shaped his poetic practice is suggested in his essay 'The Philosophy of Composition', where he claims to describe how he came to write his most famous poem, 'The Raven'. The whole piece, he insists, 'proceeded, step by step, with the precision and rigid consequence of a mathematical problem'. Beginning with a decision about length (the poem, he decided, would have to be short enough to create 'unity of impression'), and following this with a choice of 'province' or effect and decisions about the poem's tone and 'key-note' or refrain, Poe claimed that only at a late stage in the process of composition did he consider what, in a narrative sense, 'The Raven' should be 'about'. And, having decided this, he tells us that he then wrote the third stanza from the end before anything else. Poe loved tricks and hoaxes; it was one of the few ways in which his sense of humour found free play (not least because it could work there in conjuction with his ever-present preoccupation with power). And 'The Philosophy of Composition' should be read as a sort of critical hoax, in which the author conceals the literal truth (how he actually wrote 'The Raven') in order to strike at a deeper, symbolic truth (the true genesis of poetry and the proper way in which, in his view, poetry should be read). What matters about 'The Raven', Poe is telling us, is what matters about all his poetry and *all* poetry for that matter: not what is commonly called its 'content' or 'subject' but the elusive, intangible, magical effects the poem creates partly through the *use* of content or subject. Content, narrative or argument or whatever, is merely a means, a device the poet uses while he attempts, coolly and deliberately, to manoeuvre the reader into a state of suspended animation, a sense of the 'glories beyond the grave'. The subject of 'The Raven' did not really matter to me the author, Poe is saying, and it should not really matter to you the reader, either.

Subjects, however, are not neutral elements, even if they are means rather than ends. It matters, after all, what 'wheels and pinions' or 'tackle for scene shifting' the poet adopts to entrance or enchant the reader. Which is all by way of saying that certain poetic scenes and subjects are favourites with Poe precisely because they reinforce his ultimately visionary aims. Unsurprisingly, life after death is a favourite topic, in poems like 'Annabel Lee' or 'The Sleeper'. So, too, is the theme of a strange, shadowy region beyond the borders of normal consciousness: places such as those described in 'The City in the Sea' or 'Eldorado' which are, in effect, elaborate figures for death. As Poe himself explains in 'The Philosophy of Composition', 'the death . . . of a beautiful woman is unquestionably the most poetical topic in the world', precisely because it enhances the seductive nature of death, transforming annihilation into erotic fulfilment. 'O!

nothing earthly' begins 'Al Aaraaf', one of Poe' earliest poems – and that captures Poe's narrative thrust precisely: whatever the apparent subject, the movement is always away from the world of things and towards 'nothing'. The sights and sounds of a realizable world may be there in a poem like 'The Raven', but their presence is only fleeting, ephemeral; Poe's scenes are always shadowy and insubstantial, the colours dim, the lighting dusky. In the final instance, the things of the real world are there only to be discarded – as signposts to another country that is, strictly speaking, imperceptible, unrealizable by the waking consciousness.

'Poe's aesthetic, Poe's theory of art,' the contemporary American poet Richard Wilbur has said, 'seems to me insane. To say that art should repudiate everything human and earthly . . . is hopelessly to narrow [its] scope and function.' That is, certainly, arguable. What is surely unarguable is that this theory has profoundly affected the way in which not only poetry but art generally has been perceived in the modern world. A brief anecdote can be cited in evidence. Just before the painter Gauguin left Paris for the South Seas, a farewell dinner was held for him. At the dinner, the poet Mallarmé recited 'The Raven' in Gauguin's honour. So struck was Gauguin by the poem that, just a year later, he produced one of his most famous paintings, 'Nevermore', the title of which is borrowed from Poe's haunting refrain. There are a number of visual similarities between poem and painting; but what is far more important is the fact that Gauguin is clearly striving for the same *effect* as the one he received from Poe's lines, the same mysterious feelings. 'I obtain,' Gauguin said,

> by arrangement of lines and colours, using as a pretext some subject borrowed from human life or nature, symphonies, harmonies which represent nothing real in the vulgar sense of the word and which express no idea directly, but which should provoke you to think as music does, without help of ideas or images, simply by the mysterious relationship which exists between our brains and such arrangements of colours and lines.

To this extent, Poe's emphasis on the single and singular state of death is misleading. It obsessed him, of course. But it is worth saying that this obsession led him in the direction that so impressed Gauguin, or for that matter Baudelaire, Mallarmé, Rimbaud and many others: away from the idea of representational art and towards the idea of art as an absolute, purely aesthetic experience. Poetry, writing generally in this context, becomes just one among many possible mediums for realizing and communicating feeling, states of consciousness. The work of art, as Gauguin loftily claims, is not 'about' anything at all; it simply 'is'. It is nature, not physics; a state of being rather than knowing; an experiential process instead of instruction or argument. 'Nevermore' and 'The Raven' have this in common, finally: that they are anti-representational. This, of course, they share with so much art of the late nineteenth and twentieth centuries. It is Poe's peculiar narrowness of focus, on 'nothing earthly', that strikes the reader at first and tends to alienate people like Wilbur. That very narrowness, however, also endows his poetry with a strange, hypnotic quality, making Poe the poet, for all his occasional absurdities, a charismatic figure for so many readers. Closely related to this, it has given Poe a central place in the story of modern poetry, making him one of the founding fathers of Symbolist, Surrealist and Modernist aesthetics.

Poe's American contemporary, Ralph Waldo Emerson, referred to him contemptuously as 'the jingle-man', by which he clearly had in mind Poe's almost obsessive use of repetition, internal and recurring rhyme, drum-beat rhythms and verbal melody all to produce a hypnotic, incantatory effect. The French writer Victor Hugo, by contrast, claimed that he had discovered '*un frisson nouveau*' in Poe's writing; and perhaps when he said this he had in mind not only the elaborate verbal effects that Emerson so disliked but also Poe's tendency to choose words for their mystery or melody rather than their meaning, his use of synaesthetic effects, and his preference for imagery of dream or nightmare. In a way, they were and are both right: a single poem, like 'The City in the Sea', can swing between the obvious and the elusive, the banal and the hauntingly unforgettable, in the space of a few lines. Some of the effects Poe strives for in this poem are both mechanical and obtrusive: the rhetorical building ('Up . . . Up . . . Up'), for instance, and the repetitive rhythms seem to be demanding a response rather than evoking one. Others are simply bad: a line like 'The viol, the violet, and the vine' reads like a pastiche of early Romantic poetry while the use of words such as 'lurid' and 'marvellous' merely points to the reaction Poe wants to elicit from the reader rather than creating the effect itself. And yet, and yet . . . there are lines that haunt the imagination and stay in the memory, and make it clear why Baudelaire, for instance, 'experienced a strange commotion', as he put it, when he first encountered this kind of writing. The description of death looking 'gigantically down' from 'a proud tower', for example, depends precisely on not referring to death directly as proud or gigantic: the transferred epithet adds distance, mystery and fear. Similarly, the portrait of 'turrets and shadows' that 'seem pendulous in air' recollects or anticipates other dream cities, suspended, like Thomas Mann's Venice, in an insubstantial atmosphere of magic. Most notable of all, perhaps, lines such as 'But light from out the lurid sea / Streams up the turrets silently' work by challenging logic. Strictly speaking, light cannot be anything other than silent, so the reference to its silence is at best superfluous. Nevertheless, its very strangeness renders it imaginatively striking: we are being asked, or rather compelled, to look again at the familiar, to gaze on the customarily accepted with wonder and fear. The sense, quietly communicated, is of an impalpable, irresistible force taking over this dream city: a force the very intangibility of which makes it impossible to comprehend, let alone stop.

'Streams up the turrets silently': mystery is the key quality of a phrase like this. At his best Poe *does* achieve an ordered derangement of our senses: he detaches us from the world of phenomenal experience and persuades us of the possibility of other dimensions. To an extent, the absurdities of rhythm, phrasing or whatever are all part of it, since they too can often help to discompose the reader, calling into question or even subverting our customary standards of good taste. In his art, as in his life, Poe challenges and unnerves. He reinvents, jettisoning the literal in favour of the imagined, the carefully moulded and mundane in favour of the magical, bare fact in favour of mysterious fantasy. As we look at the story of Poe's forty years, we see certain experiences and obsessions emerging to haunt his writing and aesthetic: death and beauty, alienation and subterfuge, loss and despair. What is perhaps most marked, however, is not this or that particular theme but a guiding impulse; the living and the writing show us someone who by sheer effort of will transforms everything he inhabits, who dissolves the sights and signs of the world just as he touches them. Poe re-created himself; and his poetry shows a strenuous effort to re-create reality so that, in his hands, art is not so much a mirror as a series of masks. Other writers, American and European, were to feel his influence or even follow his example; or, more simply and disturbingly, they have been haunted by him. But none has gone quite so far in the devising of a character and a craft that thrive on magic and mystery. Poe turned personality into shadow play, and poetry into a series of ghostly gestures; in the process, he marked out boundaries for Romanticism and its succeeding movements that few writers have been able, or even perhaps dared, to cross.

Richard Gray
Colchester, 1993

NOTE ON THE TEXT

The order of the poems in this edition is that of the first periodical publication according to the Poe scholar Killis Campbell. Poe was constantly revising his poems and presenting them in different published forms. In each case, the aim here has been to offer the best version of the poem in question, bearing in mind the different available versions.

COMPLETE POEMS

TAMERLANE

Kind solace in a dying hour!
  Such, father, is not (now) my theme –
I will not madly deem that power
    Of Earth may shrive me of the sin
    Unearthly pride hath revell'd in –
  I have no time to dote or dream:
You call it hope – that fire of fire!
It is but agony of desire:
If I *can* hope – Oh God! I can –
  Its fount is holier – more divine –
I would not call thee fool, old man,
  But such is not a gift of thine.

Know thou the secret of a spirit
  Bow'd from its wild pride into shame.
O yearning heart! I did inherit
  Thy withering portion with the fame,
The searing glory which hath shone
Amid the Jewels of my throne,
Halo of Hell! and with a pain
Not Hell shall make me fear again –
O craving heart, for the lost flowers
And sunshine of my summer hours!
The undying voice of that dead time,
With its interminable chime,
Rings, in the spirit of a spell,
Upon thy emptiness – a knell.

I have not always been as now:
The fever'd diadem on my brow
  I claim'd and won usurpingly –
Hath not the same fierce heirdom given
  Rome to the Cæsar – this to me?
    The heritage of a kingly mind,
And a proud spirit which hath striven
    Triumphantly with human kind.

On mountain soil I first drew life:
  The mists of the Taglay have shed
  Nightly their dews upon my head,
And, I believe, the winged strife
And tumult of the headlong air
Have nestled in my very hair.

So late from Heaven – that dew – it fell
  ('Mid dreams of an unholy night)
Upon me with the touch of Hell,
  While the red flashing of the light
From clouds that hung, like banners, o'er,
  Appeared to my half-closing eye
  The pageantry of monarchy,
And the deep trumpet-thunder's roar
  Came hurriedly upon me, telling
    Of human battle, where my voice,
  My own voice, silly child! – was swelling
    (O! how my spirit would rejoice,
And leap within me at the cry)
The battle-cry of Victory!

The rain came down upon my head
  Unshelter'd – and the heavy wind
  Rendered me mad and deaf and blind.
It was but man, I thought, who shed
  Laurels upon me: and the rush –
The torrent of the chilly air
Gurgled within my ear the crush
  Of empires – with the captive's prayer –
The hum of suitors – and the tone
Of flattery 'round a sovereign's throne.

My passions, from that hapless hour,
  Usurp'd a tyranny which men
Have deem'd, since I have reach'd to power,
    My innate nature – be it so:
  But, father, there liv'd one who, then,
Then – in my boyhood – when their fire
    Burn'd with a still intenser glow
(For passion must, with youth, expire)
  E'en *then* who knew this iron heart
  In woman's weakness had a part.

I have no words – alas! – to tell
The loveliness of loving well!
Nor would I now attempt to trace
The more than beauty of a face
Whose lineaments, upon my mind,
Are — shadows on th' unstable wind:
Thus I remember having dwelt
   Some page of early lore upon,
With loitering eye, till I have felt
The letters – with their meaning – melt
   To fantasies – with none.

O, she was worthy of all love!
   Love – as in infancy was mine –
'Twas such as angel minds above
   Might envy; her young heart the shrine
On which my every hope and thought
   Were incense – then a goodly gift,
      For they were childish and upright –
Pure — as her young example taught:
   Why did I leave it, and, adrift,
      Trust to the fire within, for light?

We grew in age – and love – together –
   Roaming the forest, and the wild;
My breast her shield in wintry weather –
   And, when the friendly sunshine smil'd,
And she would mark the opening skies,
I saw no Heaven – but in her eyes.

Young Love's first lesson is — the heart:
   For 'mid that sunshine, and those smiles,
When, from our little cares apart,
   And laughing at her girlish wiles,
I'd throw me on her throbbing breast,
   And pour my spirit out in tears –
There was no need to speak the rest –
   No need to quiet any fears
Of her – who ask'd no reason why,
But turn'd on me her quiet eye!

Yet *more* than worthy of the love
My spirit struggled with, and strove,

When, on the mountain peak, alone,
Ambition lent it a new tone –
I had no being – but in thee:
  The world, and all it did contain
In the earth – the air – the sea –
  Its joy – its little lot of pain
That was new pleasure — the ideal,
  Dim, vanities of dreams by night –
And dimmer nothings which were real –
  (Shadows – and a more shadowy light!)
Parted upon their misty wings,
    And, so, confusedly, became
    Thine image and – a name – a name!
Two separate – yet most intimate things.

I was ambitious – have you known
    The passion, father? You have not:
A cottager, I mark'd a throne
Of half the world as all my own,
    And murmur'd at such lowly lot –
But, just like any other dream,
    Upon the vapour of the dew
My own had past, did not the beam
    Of beauty which did while it thro'
The minute – the hour – the day – oppress
My mind with double loveliness.

We walk'd together on the crown
Of a high mountain which look'd down
Afar from its proud natural towers
  Of rock and forest, on the hills –
The dwindled hills! begirt with bowers
And shouting with a thousand rills.

I spoke to her of power and pride,
  But mystically – in such guise
That she might deem it nought beside
  The moment's converse; in her eyes
I read, perhaps too carelessly –
  A mingled feeling with my own –
The flush on her bright cheek, to me
  Seem'd to become a queenly throne

Too well that I should let it be
  Light in the wilderness alone.

I wrapp'd myself in grandeur then
  And donn'd a visionary crown —
    Yet it was not that Fantasy
    Had thrown her mantle over me –
But that, among the rabble – men,
    Lion ambition is chain'd down –
And crouches to a keeper's hand –
Not so in deserts where the grand –
The wild – the terrible conspire
With their own breath to fan his fire.

Look 'round thee now on Samarcand! –
  Is she not queen of Earth? her pride
Above all cities? in her hand
  Their destinies? in all beside
Of glory which the world hath known
Stands she not nobly and alone?
Falling – her veriest stepping-stone
Shall form the pedestal of a throne –
And who her sovereign? Timour – he
  Whom the astonished people saw
Striding o'er empires haughtily
  A diadem'd outlaw!

O, human love! thou spirit given,
On Earth, of all we hope in Heaven!
Which fall'st into the soul like rain
Upon the Siroc-wither'd plain,
And, failing in thy power to bless,
But leav'st the heart a wilderness!
Idea! which bindest life around
With music of so strange a sound
And beauty of so wild a birth –
Farewell! for I have won the Earth.

When Hope, the eagle that tower'd, could see
  No cliff beyond him in the sky,
His pinions were bent droopingly –
  And homeward turn'd his soften'd eye.

'Twas sunset: when the sun will part
There comes a sullenness of heart
To him who still would look upon
The glory of the summer sun.
That soul will hate the ev'ning mist
So often lovely, and will list
To the sound of the coming darkness (known
To those whose spirits harken) as one
Who, in a dream of night, *would* fly
But *cannot* from a danger nigh.

What tho' the moon – the white moon
Shed all the splendour of her noon,
Her smile is chilly – and *her* beam,
In that time of dreariness, will seem
(So like you gather in your breath)
A portrait taken after death.
And boyhood is a summer sun
Whose waning is the dreariest one –
For all we live to know is known
And all we seek to keep hath flown –
Let life, then, as the day-flower, fall
With the noon-day beauty – which is all.

I reach'd my home – my home no more –
  For all had flown who made it so.
I pass'd from out its mossy door,
  And, tho' my tread was soft and low,
A voice came from the threshold stone
Of one whom I had earlier known –
  O, I defy thee, Hell, to show
  On beds of fire that burn below,
  An humbler heart – a deeper wo.

Father, I firmly do believe –
  I *know* – for Death who comes for me
    From regions of the blest afar,
Where there is nothing to deceive,
    Hath left his iron gate ajar,
  And rays of truth you cannot see
  Are flashing thro' Eternity —

I do believe that Eblis hath
A snare in every human path –
Else how, when in the holy grove
I wandered of the idol, Love,
Who daily scents his snowy wings
With incense of burnt offerings
From the most unpolluted things,
Whose pleasant bowers are yet so riven
Above with trellic'd rays from Heaven
No mote may shun – no tiniest fly –
The light'ning of his eagle eye –
How was it that Ambition crept,
  Unseen, amid the revels there,
Till growing bold, he laughed and leapt
  In the tangles of Love's very hair?

TO — —

I saw thee on thy bridal day –
  When a burning blush came o'er thee,
Though happiness around thee lay,
  The world all love before thee:

And in thine eye a kindling light
  (Whatever it might be)
Was all on Earth my aching sight
  Of Loveliness could see.

That blush, perhaps, was maiden shame –
  As such it well may pass –
Though its glow hath raised a fiercer flame
  In the breast of him, alas!

Who saw thee on that bridal day,
  When that deep blush *would* come o'er thee,
Though happiness around thee lay,
  The world all love before thee.

DREAMS

Oh! that my young life were a lasting dream!
My spirit not awakening, till the beam
Of an Eternity should bring the morrow.
Yes! tho' that long dream were of hopeless sorrow,
'Twere better than the cold reality
Of waking life, to him whose heart must be,
And hath been still, upon the lovely earth,
A chaos of deep passion, from his birth.

But should it be – that dream eternally
Continuing – as dreams have been to me
In my young boyhood – should it thus be given,
'Twere folly still to hope for higher Heaven.
For I have revell'd when the sun was bright
I' the summer sky, in dreams of living light,
And loveliness, – have left my very heart
In climes of mine imagining, apart
From mine own home, with beings that have been
Of mine own thought – what more could I have seen?

'Twas once – and only once – and the wild hour
From my remembrance shall not pass – some power
Or spell had bound me – 'twas the chilly wind
Came o'er me in the night, and left behind
Its image on my spirit – or the moon
Shone on my slumbers in her lofty noon
Too coldly – or the stars – howe'er it was
That dream was as that night-wind – let it pass.

I *have been* happy, tho' but in a dream.
I have been happy – and I love the theme:
Dreams! in their vivid colouring of life
As in that fleeting, shadowy, misty strife
Of semblance with reality which brings
To the delirious eye, more lovely things
Of Paradise and Love – and all our own!
Than young Hope in his sunniest hour hath known.

SPIRITS OF THE DEAD

I

Thy soul shall find itself alone
'Mid dark thoughts of the grey tomb-stone –
Not one, of all the crowd, to pry
Into thine hour of secrecy:

II

Be silent in that solitude,
  Which is not loneliness – for then
The spirits of the dead who stood
  In life before thee, are again
In death around thee – and their will
Shall overshadow thee: be still.

III

The night – tho' clear – shall frown –
And the stars shall look not down,
From their high thrones in the heaven,
With light like Hope to mortals given –
But their red orbs, without beam,
To thy weariness shall seem
As a burning and a fever
Which would cling to thee for ever.

IV

Now are thoughts thou shalt not banish –
Now are visions ne'er to vanish –
From thy spirit shall they pass
No more – like dew-drops from the grass.

V

The breeze – the breath of God – is still –
And the mist upon the hill

Shadowy – shadowy – yet unbroken,
Is a symbol and a token –
How it hangs upon the trees,
A mystery of mysteries! –

EVENING STAR

'Twas noontide of summer,
  And mid-time of night;
And stars, in their orbits,
  Shone pale, thro' the light
Of the brighter, cold moon,
  'Mid planets her slaves,
Herself in the Heavens,
  Her beam on the waves.
    I gazed awhile
    On her cold smile;
Too cold – too cold for me –
    There pass'd, as a shroud,
    A fleecy cloud,
And I turn'd away to thee,
    Proud Evening Star,
    In thy glory afar,
And dearer thy beam shall be;
    For joy to my heart
    Is the proud part
Thou bearest in Heaven at night,
    And more I admire
    Thy distant fire,
Than that colder, lowly light.

A DREAM WITHIN A DREAM

Take this kiss upon the brow!
And, in parting from you now,
Thus much let me avow –
You are not wrong, who deem
That my days have been a dream;
Yet if hope has flown away
In a night, or in a day,
In a vision, or in none,
Is it therefore the less *gone*?
All that we see or seem
Is but a dream within a dream.

I stand amid the roar
Of a surf-tormented shore,
And I hold within my hand
Grains of the golden sand –
How few! yet how they creep
Through my fingers to the deep,
While I weep – while I weep!
O God! can I not grasp
Them with a tighter clasp?
O God! can I not save
One from the pitiless wave?
Is *all* that we see or seem
But a dream within a dream?

STANZAS

How often we forget all time, when lone
Admiring Nature's universal throne;
Her woods – her wilds – her mountains – the intense
Reply of HERS to OUR intelligence!

1

In youth have I known one with whom the Earth
In secret communing held – as he with it,
In daylight, and in beauty from his birth:
Whose fervid, flickering torch of life was lit
From the sun and stars, whence he had drawn forth
A passionate light – such for his spirit was fit –
And yet that spirit knew not, in the hour
Of its own fervour, what had o'er it power.

2

Perhaps it may be that my mind is wrought
To a fever by the moonbeam that hangs o'er,
But I will half believe that wild light fraught
With more of sovereignty than ancient lore
Hath ever told; – or is it of a thought
The unembodied essence, and no more,
That with a quickening spell doth o'er us pass
As dew of the night-time o'er the summer grass?

3

Doth o'er us pass, when, as th' expanding eye
To the loved object, – so the tear to the lid
Will start, which lately slept in apathy?
And yet it need not be – (that object) hid
From us in life – but common – which doth lie
Each hour before us – but *then* only, bid
With a strange sound, as of a harp-string broken,
To awake us – 'Tis a symbol and a token

4

Of what in other worlds shall be – and given
In beauty by our God, to those alone
Who otherwise would fall from life and Heaven
Drawn by their heart's passion, and that tone,
That high tone of the spirit which hath striven,
Tho' not with Faith – with godliness – whose throne
With desperate energy 't hath beaten down;
Wearing its own deep feeling as a crown.

A DREAM

In visions of the dark night
  I have dreamed of joy departed –
But a waking dream of life and light
  Hath left me broken-hearted.

Ah! what is not a dream by day
  To him whose eyes are cast
On things around him with a ray
  Turned back upon the past?

That holy dream – that holy dream,
  While all the world were chiding,
Hath cheered me as a lovely beam
  A lonely spirit guiding.

What though that light, thro' storm and night,
  So trembled from afar –
What could there be more purely bright
  In Truth's day-star?

'THE HAPPIEST DAY, THE HAPPIEST HOUR'

The happiest day – the happiest hour
  My seared and blighted heart hath known,
The highest hope of pride and power,
  I feel hath flown.

Of power! said I? yes! such I ween;
  But they have vanish'd long, alas!
The visions of my youth have been –
  But let them pass.

And, pride, what have I now with thee?
  Another brow may even inherit
The venom thou hast pour'd on me –
  Be still, my spirit!

The happiest day – the happiest hour
  Mine eyes shall see – have ever seen,
The brightest glance of pride and power,
  I feel – have been:

But were that hope of pride and power
  Now offer'd, with the pain
Even *then* I felt – that brightest hour
  I would not live again:

For on its wing was dark alloy,
  And as it flutter'd – fell
An essence – powerful to destroy
  A soul that knew it well.

THE LAKE: TO —

In spring of youth it was my lot
To haunt of the wide world a spot
The which I could not love the less –
So lovely was the loneliness
Of a wild lake, with black rock bound,
And the tall pines that towered around.

But when the Night had thrown her pall
Upon that spot, as upon all,
And the mystic wind went by
Murmuring in melody –
Then – ah then I would awake
To the terror of the lone lake.

Yet the terror was not fright,
But a tremulous delight –
A feeling not the jewelled mine
Could teach or bribe me to define –
Nor Love – although the Love were thine.

Death was in that poisonous wave,
And in its gulf a fitting grave
For him who thence could solace bring
To his lone imagining –
Whose solitary soul could make
An Eden of that dim lake.

SONNET – TO SCIENCE

Science! true daughter of Old Time thou art!
   Who alterest all things with thy peering eyes.
Why preyest thou thus upon the poet's heart,
   Vulture, whose wings are dull realities?
How should he love thee? or how deem thee wise,
   Who wouldst not leave him in his wandering
To seek for treasure in the jewelled skies,
   Albeit he soared with an undaunted wing?
Hast thou not dragged Diana from her car?
   And driven the Hamadryad from the wood
To seek a shelter in some happier star?
   Hast thou not torn the Naiad from her flood,
The Elfin from the green grass, and from me
The summer dream beneath the tamarind tree?

AL AARAAF

PART I

O! nothing earthly save the ray
(Thrown back from flowers) of Beauty's eye,
As in those gardens where the day
Springs from the gems of Circassy –
O! nothing earthly save the thrill
Of melody in woodland rill –
Or (music of the passion-hearted)
Joy's voice so peacefully departed
That like the murmur in the shell,
Its echo dwelleth and will dwell –
Oh, nothing of the dross of ours –
Yet all the beauty – all the flowers
That list our Love, and deck our bowers –
Adorn yon world afar, afar –
The wandering star.

'Twas a sweet time for Nesace – for there
Her world lay lolling on the golden air,
Near four bright suns – a temporary rest –
An oasis in desert of the blest.
Away – away – 'mid seas of rays that roll
Empyrean splendour o'er th' unchained soul –
The soul that scarce (the billows are so dense)
Can struggle to its destin'd eminence –
To distant spheres, from time to time, she rode,
And late to ours, the favour'd one of God –
But, now, the ruler of an anchor'd realm,
She throws aside the sceptre – leaves the helm,
And, amid incense and high spiritual hymns,
Laves in quadruple light her angel limbs.

Now happiest, loveliest in yon lovely Earth,
Whence sprang the 'Idea of Beauty' into birth,
(Falling in wreaths thro' many a startled star,
Like woman's hair 'mid pearls, until, afar,
It lit on hills Achaian, and there dwelt)

She look'd into Infinity – and knelt.
Rich clouds, for canopies, about her curled –
Fit emblems of the model of her world –
Seen but in beauty – not impeding sight
Of other beauty glittering thro' the light –
A wreath that twined each starry form around,
And all the opal'd air in colour bound.

All hurriedly she knelt upon a bed
Of flowers: of lilies such as rear'd the head
On the fair Capo Deucato, and sprang
So eagerly around about to hang
Upon the flying footsteps of — deep pride –
Of her who lov'd a mortal – and so died.
The Sephalica, budding with young bees,
Uprear'd its purple stem around her knees:
And gemmy flower, of Trebizond misnam'd –
Inmate of highest stars, where erst it sham'd
All other loveliness: its honied dew
(The fabled nectar that the heathen knew)
Deliriously sweet, was dropp'd from Heaven,
And fell on gardens of the unforgiven
In Trebizond – and on a sunny flower
So like its own above that, to this hour,
It still remaineth, torturing the bee
With madness, and unwonted reverie:
In Heaven, and all its environs, the leaf
And blossom of the fairy plant, in grief
Disconsolate linger – grief that hangs her head,
Repenting follies that full long have fled,
Heaving her white breast to the balmy air,
Like guilty beauty, chasten'd, and more fair:
Nyctanthes too, as sacred as the light
She fears to perfume, perfuming the night:
And Clytia pondering between many a sun,
While pettish tears adown her petals run:
And that aspiring flower that sprang on Earth –
And died, ere scarce exalted into birth,
Bursting its odorous heart in spirit to wing
Its way to Heaven, from garden of a king:

And Valisnerian lotus thither flown
From struggling with the waters of the Rhone:
And thy most lovely purple perfume, Zante!
Isola d'oro – Fior di Levante!
And the Nelumbo bud that floats for ever
With Indian Cupid down the holy river –
Fair flowers, and fairy! to whose care is given
To bear the Goddess' song, in odours, up to Heaven:

'Spirit! that dwellest where,
  In the deep sky,
The terrible and fair,
  In beauty vie!
Beyond the line of blue –
  The boundary of the star
Which turneth at the view
  Of thy barrier and thy bar –
Of the barrier overgone
  By the comets who were cast
From their pride, and from their throne
  To be drudges till the last –
To be carriers of fire
  (The red fire of their heart)
With speed that may not tire
  And with pain that shall not part –
Who livest – *that* we know –
  In Eternity – we feel –
But the shadow of whose brow
  What spirit shall reveal?
Tho' the beings whom thy Nesace,
  Thy messenger hath known
Have dream'd for thy Infinity
  A model of their own –
Thy will is done, Oh, God!
  The star hath ridden high
Thro' many a tempest, but she rode
  Beneath thy burning eye;
And here, in thought, to thee –
  In thought that can alone
Ascend thy empire and so be
  A partner of thy throne –

By winged Fantasy,
 My embassy is given,
Till secrecy shall knowledge be
 In the environs of Heaven.'

She ceas'd – and buried then her burning cheek
Abash'd, amid the lilies there, to seek
A shelter from the fervour of His eye;
For the stars trembled at the Deity.
She stirr'd not – breath'd not – for a voice was there
How solemnly pervading the calm air!
A sound of silence on the startled ear
Which dreamy poets name 'the music of the sphere.'
Ours is a world of words: Quiet we call
'Silence' – which is the merest word of all.
All Nature speaks, and ev'n ideal things
Flap shadowy sounds from visionary wings –
But ah! not so when, thus, in realms on high
The eternal voice of God is passing by,
And the red winds are withering in the sky!

'What tho' in worlds which sightless cycles run,
Link'd to a little system, and one sun –
Where all my love is folly and the crowd
Still think my terrors but the thunder cloud,
The storm, the earthquake, and the ocean-wrath –
(Ah! will they cross me in my angrier path?)
What tho' in worlds which own a single sun
The sands of Time grow dimmer as they run,
Yet thine is my resplendency, so given
To bear my secrets thro' the upper Heaven.
Leave tenantless thy crystal home, and fly,
With all thy train, athwart the moony sky –
Apart – like fire-flies in Sicilian night,
And wing to other worlds another light!
Divulge the secrets of thy embassy
To the proud orbs that twinkle – and so be
To ev'ry heart a barrier and a ban
Lest the stars totter in the guilt of man!'

Up rose the maiden in the yellow night,
The single-mooned eve! – on Earth we plight

Our faith to one love – and one moon adore –
The birthplace of young Beauty had no more.
As sprang that yellow star from downy hours
Up rose the maiden from her shrine of flowers,
And bent o'er sheeny mountains and dim plain
Her way – but left not yet her Therasæan reign.

PART II

High on a mountain of enamell'd head –
Such as the drowsy shepherd on his bed
Of giant pasturage lying at his ease,
Raising his heavy eyelid, starts and sees
With many a mutter'd 'hope to be forgiven'
What time the moon is quadrated in Heaven –
Of rosy head, that towering far away
Into the sunlit ether, caught the ray
Of sunken suns at eve – at noon of night,
While the moon danc'd with the fair stranger light –
Uprear'd upon such height arose a pile
Of gorgeous columns on th' unburthen'd air,
Flashing from Parian marble that twin smile
Far down upon the wave that sparkled there,
And nursled the young mountain in its lair.
Of molten stars their pavement, such as fall
Thro' the ebon air, besilvering the pall
Of their own dissolution, while they die –
Adorning then the dwellings of the sky.
A dome, by linked light from Heaven let down,
Sat gently on these columns as a crown –
A window of one circular diamond, there,
Look'd out above into the purple air,
And rays from God shot down that meteor chain
And hallow'd all the beauty twice again,
Save when, between th' Empyrean and that ring,
Some eager spirit flapp'd his dusky wing.
But on the pillars Seraph eyes have seen
The dimness of this world: that greyish green
That Nature loves the best for Beauty's grave
Lurk'd in each cornice, round each architrave –

And every sculptur'd cherub thereabout
That from his marble dwelling peeréd out,
Seem'd earthly in the shadow of his niche –
Achaian statues in a world so rich?
Friezes from Tadmor and Persepolis –
From Balbec, and the stilly, clear abyss
Of beautiful Gomorrah! O, the wave
Is now upon thee – but too late to save!

Sound loves to revel in a summer night:
Witness the murmur of the grey twilight
That stole upon the ear, in Eyraco,
Of many a wild star-gazer long ago –
That stealeth ever on the ear of him
Who, musing, gazeth on the distance dim,
And sees the darkness coming as a cloud –
Is not its form – its voice – most palpable and loud?

But what is this? – it cometh – and it brings
A music with it – 'tis the rush of wings –
A pause – and then a sweeping, falling strain
And Nesace is in her halls again.
From the wild energy of wanton haste
Her cheeks were flushing, and her lips apart;
And zone that clung around her gentle waist
Had burst beneath the heaving of her heart.
Within the centre of that hall to breathe
She paus'd and panted, Zanthe! all beneath,
The fairy light that kiss'd her golden hair
And long'd to rest, yet could but sparkle there!

Young flowers were whispering in melody
To happy flowers that night – and tree to tree;
Fountains were gushing music as they fell
In many a star-lit grove, or moon-lit dell;
Yet silence came upon material things –
Fair flowers, bright waterfalls and angel wings –
And sound alone that from the spirit sprang
Bore burthen to the charm the maiden sang:

"'Neath blue-bell or streamer –
Or tufted wild spray
That keeps, from the dreamer,
The moonbeam away –

Bright beings! that ponder,
  With half closing eyes,
On the stars which your wonder
  Hath drawn from the skies,
'Till they glance thro' the shade, and
  Come down to your brow
Like — eyes of the maiden
  Who calls on you now –
Arise! from your dreaming
  In violet bowers,
To duty beseeming
  These star-litten hours –
And shake from your tresses
  Encumber'd with dew
The breath of those kisses
  That cumber them too –
(O! how, without you, Love!
  Could angels be blest?)
Those kisses of true love
  That lull'd ye to rest!
Up! – shake from your wing
  Each hindering thing:
The dew of the night –
  It would weigh down your flight;
And true love caresses –
  O! leave them apart!
They are light on the tresses,
  But lead on the heart.

Ligeia! Ligeia!
  My beautiful one!
Whose harshest idea
  Will to melody run,
O! is it thy will
  On the breezes to toss?
Or, capriciously still,
  Like the lone Albatross,
Incumbent on night
  (As she on the air)
To keep watch with delight
  On the harmony there?

Ligeia! wherever
  Thy image may be,
No magic shall sever
  Thy music from thee.
Thou hast bound many eyes
  In a dreamy sleep –
But the strains still arise
  Which *thy* vigilance keep –
The sound of the rain
  Which leaps down to the flower,
And dances again
  In the rhythm of the shower –
The murmur that springs
  From the growing of grass
Are the music of things –
  But are modell'd, alas! –
Away, then my dearest,
  O! hie thee away
To springs that lie clearest,
  Beneath the moon-ray –
To lone lake that smiles,
  In its dream of deep rest,
At the many star-isles
  That enjewel its breast –
Where wild flowers, creeping,
  Have mingled their shade,
On its margin is sleeping
  Full many a maid –
Some have left the cool glade, and
  Have slept with the bee –
Arouse them my maiden,
  On moorland and lea –
Go! breathe on their slumber,
  All softly in ear,
The musical number
  They slumber'd to hear –
For what can awaken
  An angel so soon
Whose sleep hath been taken
  Beneath the cold moon,

As the spell which no slumber
  Of witchery may test,
The rhythmical number
  Which lull'd him to rest?'

Spirits in wing, and angels to the view,
A thousand seraphs burst th' Empyrean thro',
Young dreams still hovering on their drowsy flight –
Seraphs in all but 'Knowledge,' the keen light
That fell, refracted thro' thy bounds, afar
O Death! from eye of God upon that star:
Sweet was that error – sweeter still that death –
Sweet was that error – ev'n with *us* the breath
Of Science dims the mirror of our joy –
To them 'twere the Simoom, and would destroy –
For what (to them) availeth it to know
That Truth is Falsehood – or that Bliss is Woe?
Sweet was their death – with them to die was rife
With the last ecstasy of satiate life –
Beyond that death no immortality –
But sleep that pondereth and is not 'to be' –
And there – oh! may my weary spirit dwell –
Apart from Heaven's Eternity – and yet how far from Hell!
What guilty spirit, in what shrubbery dim,
Heard not the stirring summons of that hymn?
But two: they fell: for Heaven no grace imparts
To those who hear not for their beating hearts.
A maiden-angel and her seraph-lover –
O! where (and ye may seek the wide skies over)
Was Love, the blind, near sober Duty known?
Unguided Love hath fallen – 'mid 'tears of perfect moan.'

He was a goodly spirit – he who fell:
A wanderer by moss-y-mantled well –
A gazer on the lights that shine above –
A dreamer in the moonbeam by his love:
What wonder? for each star is eye-like there,
And looks so sweetly down on Beauty's hair –
And they, and ev'ry mossy spring were holy
To his love-haunted heart and melancholy.
The night had found (to him a night of wo)
Upon a mountain crag, young Angelo –

Beetling it bends athwart the solemn sky,
And scowls on starry worlds that down beneath it lie.
Here sate he with his love – his dark eye bent
With eagle gaze along the firmament:
Now turn'd it upon her – but ever then
It trembled to the orb of EARTH again.

'Ianthe, dearest, see! how dim that ray!
How lovely 'tis to look so far away!
She seem'd not thus upon that autumn eve
I left her gorgeous halls – nor mourn'd to leave.
That eve – that eve – I should remember well –
The sun-ray dropp'd, in Lemnos, with a spell
On th' Arabesque carving of a gilded hall
Wherein I sate, and on the draperied wall –
And on my eye-lids – O the heavy light!
How drowsily it weigh'd them into night!
On flowers, before, and mist, and love they ran
With Persian Saadi in his Gulistan:
But O that light! – I slumber'd – Death, the while,
Stole o'er my senses in that lovely isle
So softly that no single silken hair
Awoke that slept – or knew that he was there.

The last spot of Earth's orb I trod upon
Was a proud temple call'd the Parthenon –
More beauty clung around her column'd wall
Than ev'n thy glowing bosom beats withal,
And when old Time my wing did disenthral
Thence sprang I – as the eagle from his tower,
And years I left behind me in an hour.
What time upon her airy bounds I hung
One half the garden of her globe was flung
Unrolling as a chart unto my view –
Tenantless cities of the desert too!
Ianthe, beauty crowded on me then,
And half I wish'd to be again of men.'

'My Angelo! and why of them to be?
A brighter dwelling-place is there for thee –
And greener fields than in yon world above,
And woman's loveliness – and passionate love.'

'But, list, Ianthe! when the air so soft
Fail'd, as my pennon'd spirit leapt aloft,
Perhaps my brain grew dizzy – but the world
I left so late was into chaos hurl'd –
Sprang from her station, on the winds apart,
And roll'd, a flame, the fiery Heaven athwart.
Methought, my sweet one, then I ceased to soar
And fell – not swiftly as I rose before,
But with a downward, tremulous motion thro'
Light, brazen rays, this golden star unto!
Nor long the measure of my falling hours,
For nearest of all stars was thine to ours –
Dread star! that came, amid a night of mirth,
A red Dædalion on the timid Earth.

'We came – and to thy Earth – but not to us
Be given our lady's bidding to discuss:
We came, my love; around, above, below,
Gay fire-fly of the night we come and go,
Nor ask a reason save the angel-nod
She grants to us, as granted by her God –
But, Angelo, than thine grey Time unfurl'd
Never his fairy wing o'er fairier world!
Dim was its little disk, and angel eyes
Alone could see the phantom in the skies,
When first Al Aaraaf knew her course to be
Headlong thitherward o'er the starry sea –
But when its glory swell'd upon the sky,
As glowing Beauty's bust beneath man's eye,
We paus'd before the heritage of men,
And thy star trembled – as doth Beauty then!'

Thus, in discourse, the lovers whiled away
The night that waned and waned and brought no day.
They fell: for Heaven to them no hope imparts
Who hear not for the beating of their hearts.

ROMANCE

Romance, who loves to nod and sing,
With drowsy head and folded wing,
Among the green leaves as they shake
Far down within some shadowy lake,
To me a painted paroquet
Hath been – a most familiar bird –
Taught me my alphabet to say –
To lisp my very earliest word
While in the wild wood I did lie,
A child – with a most knowing eye.

Of late, eternal Condor years
So shake the very Heaven on high
With tumult as they thunder by,
I have no time for idle cares
Through gazing on the unquiet sky.
And when an hour with calmer wings
Its down upon my spirit flings –
That little time with lyre and rhyme
To while away – forbidden things!
My heart would feel to be a crime
Unless it trembled with the strings.

TO —

The bowers whereat, in dreams, I see
  The wantonest singing birds,
Are lips – and all thy melody
  Of lip-begotten words –

Thine eyes, in Heaven of heart enshrined
  Then desolately fall,
O God! on my funereal mind
  Like starlight on a pall –

Thy heart – *thy* heart! – I wake and sigh,
  And sleep to dream till day
Of the truth that gold can never buy –
  Of the baubles that it may.

TO THE RIVER —

Fair river! in thy bright, clear flow
Of crystal, wandering water,
Thou art an emblem of the glow
Of beauty – the unhidden heart –
The playful maziness of art
In old Alberto's daughter;

But when within thy wave she looks –
Which glistens then, and trembles –
Why, then, the prettiest of brooks
Her worshipper resembles;
For in his heart, as in thy stream,
Her image deeply lies –
His heart which trembles at the beam
Of her soul-searching eyes.

TO —

I heed not that my earthly lot
Hath little of Earth in it,
That years of love have been forgot
In the hatred of a minute:
I mourn not that the desolate
Are happier, sweet, than I,
But that you sorrow for my fate
Who am a passer-by.

FAIRY-LAND

Dim vales – and shadowy floods –
And cloudy-looking woods,
Whose forms we can't discover
For the tears that drip all over.
Huge moons there wax and wane –
Again – again – again –
Every moment of the night –
Forever changing places –
And they put out the star-light
With the breath from their pale faces.
About twelve by the moon-dial
One more filmy than the rest
(A kind which, upon trial,
They have found to be the best)
Comes down – still down – and down
With its centre on the crown
Of a mountain's eminence,
While its wide circumference
In easy drapery falls
Over hamlets, over halls,
Wherever they may be –
O'er the strange woods – o'er the sea –
Over spirits on the wing –
Over every drowsy thing –
And buries them up quite
In a labyrinth of light –
And then, how deep! – O, deep!
Is the passion of their sleep.
In the morning they arise,
And their moony covering
Is soaring in the skies,
With the tempests as they toss,
Like — almost any thing –
Or a yellow Albatross.
They use that moon no more
For the same end as before –

Videlicet a tent –
Which I think extravagant:
Its atomies, however,
Into a shower dissever,
Of which those butterflies,
Of Earth, who seek the skies,
And so come down again
(Never-contented things!)
Have brought a specimen
Upon their quivering wings.

TO HELEN

Helen, thy beauty is to me
  Like those Nicéan barks of yore,
That gently, o'er a perfumed sea,
  The weary, way-worn wanderer bore
  To his own native shore.

On desperate seas long wont to roam,
  Thy hyacinth hair, thy classic face,
Thy Naiad airs have brought me home
  To the glory that was Greece.
  And the grandeur that was Rome.

Lo! in yon brilliant window-niche
  How statue-like I see thee stand,
The agate lamp within thy hand!
  Ah, Psyche, from the regions which
  Are Holy-Land!

ISRAFEL

In Heaven a spirit doth dwell
 'Whose heart-strings are a lute;'
None sing so wildly well
As the angel Israfel,
And the giddy stars (so legends tell)
Ceasing their hymns, attend the spell
 Of his voice, all mute.

Tottering above
 In her highest noon,
 The enamoured moon
Blushes with love,
 While, to listen, the red levin
 (with the rapid Pleiads, even,
 Which were seven)
 Pauses in Heaven.

And they say (the starry choir
 And the other listening things)
That Israfeli's fire
Is owing to that lyre
 By which he sits and sings –
The trembling living wire
Of those unusual strings.

But the skies that angel trod,
 Where deep thoughts are a duty –
Where Love's a grown-up God –
 Where the Houri glances are
Imbued with all the beauty
 Which we worship in a star.

Therefore, thou art not wrong,
 Israfeli, who despisest
An unimpassioned song;
To thee the laurels belong,
 Best bard, because the wisest!
Merrily live, and long!

The ecstasies above
  With thy burning measures suit –
Thy grief, thy joy, thy hate, thy love,
  With the fervour of thy lute –
  Well may the stars be mute!

Yes, Heaven is thine; but this
  Is a world of sweets and sours;
  Our flowers are merely – flowers,
And the shadow of thy perfect bliss
  Is the sunshine of ours.

If I could dwell
Where Israfel
  Hath dwelt, and he where I,
He might not sing so wildly well
  A mortal melody,
While a bolder note than this might swell
  From my lyre within the sky.

THE CITY IN THE SEA

Lo! Death has reared himself a throne
In a strange city lying alone
Far down within the dim West,
Where the good and the bad and the worst and the best
Have gone to their eternal rest.
There shrines and palaces and towers
(Time-eaten towers that tremble not!)
Resemble nothing that is ours.
Around, by lifting winds forgot,
Resignedly beneath the sky
The melancholy waters lie.

No rays from the holy heaven come down
On the long night-time of that town;
But light from out the lurid sea
Streams up the turrets silently –
Gleams up the pinnacles far and free –
Up domes – up spires – up kingly halls –
Up fanes – up Babylon-like walls –
Up shadowy long-forgotten bowers
Of sculptured ivy and stone flowers –
Up many and many a marvellous shrine
Whose wreathéd friezes intertwine
The viol, the violet, and the vine.

Resignedly beneath the sky
The melancholy waters lie.
So blend the turrets and shadows there
That all seem pendulous in air,
While from a proud tower in the town
Death looks gigantically down.

There open fanes and gaping graves
Yawn level with the luminous waves
But not the riches there that lie
In each idol's diamond eye –
Not the gaily-jewelled dead
Tempt the waters from their bed;

For no ripples curl, alas!
Along that wilderness of glass –
No swellings tell that winds may be
Upon some far-off happier sea –
No heavings hint that winds have been
On seas less hideously serene.

But lo, a stir is in the air!
The wave – there is a movement there!
As if the towers had thrust aside,
In slightly sinking, the dull tide –
As if their tops had feebly given
A void within the filmy Heaven.
The waves have now a redder glow –
The hours are breathing faint and low –
And when, amid no earthly moans,
Down, down that town shall settle hence,
Hell, rising from a thousand thrones,
Shall do it reverence.

THE SLEEPER

At midnight, in the month of June,
I stand beneath the mystic moon.
An opiate vapour, dewy, dim,
Exhales from out her golden rim,
And, softly dripping, drop by drop,
Upon the quiet mountain top,
Steals drowsily and musically
Into the universal valley.
The rosemary nods upon the grave;
The lily lolls upon the wave;
Wrapping the fog about its breast,
The ruin moulders into rest;
Looking like Lethë, see! the lake
A conscious slumber seems to take,
And would not, for the world, awake.
All Beauty sleeps! – and lo! where lies
Irenë, with her Destinies!

Oh, lady bright! can it be right –
This window open to the night?
The wanton airs, from the tree-top,
Laughingly through the lattice drop –
The bodiless airs, a wizard rout,
Flit through thy chamber in and out,
And wave the curtain canopy
So fitfully – so fearfully –
Above the closed and fringéd lid
'Neath which thy slumb'ring soul lies hid,
That o'er the floor and down the wall,
Like ghosts the shadows rise and fall!
Oh, lady dear, hast thou no fear?
Why and what art thou dreaming here?
Sure thou art come o'er far-off seas,
A wonder to these garden trees!
Strange is thy pallor! strange thy dress!
Strange, above all, thy length of tress,
And this all solemn silentness!

The lady sleeps! Oh, may her sleep,
Which is enduring, so be deep!
Heaven have her in its sacred keep!
This chamber changed for one more holy,
This bed for one more melancholy,
I pray to God that she may lie
Forever with unopened eye,
While the pale sheeted ghosts go by!

My love, she sleeps! Oh, may her sleep,
As it is lasting, so be deep!
Soft may the worms about her creep!
Far in the forest, dim and old,
For her may some tall vault unfold –
Some vault that oft hath flung its black
And wingéd panels fluttering back,
Triumphant, o'er the crested palls,
Of her grand family funerals –
Some sepulchre, remote, alone,
Against whose portal she hath thrown,
In childhood, many an idle stone –
Some tomb from out whose sounding door
She ne'er shall force an echo more,
Thrilling to think, poor child of sin!
It was the dead who groaned within.

LENORE

Ah, broken is the golden bowl! the spirit flown forever
Let the bell toll! – a saintly soul floats on the Stygian river;
And, Guy De Vere, hast *thou* no tear? – weep now or never more!
See! on yon drear and rigid bier low lies thy love, Lenore!
Come! let the burial rite be read – the funeral song be sung! –
An anthem for the queenliest dead that ever died so young –
A dirge for her the doubly dead in that she died so young.

'Wretches! ye loved her for her wealth and hated her for her pride,
And when she fell in feeble health, ye blessed her – that she died!
How *shall* the ritual, then, be read? – the requiem how be sung
By you – by yours, the evil eye, – by yours, the slanderous tongue
That did to death the innocence that died, and died so young?'

Peccavimus; but rave not thus! and let a Sabbath song
Go up to God so solemnly the dead may feel no wrong!
The sweet Lenore hath 'gone before,' with Hope, that flew beside,
Leaving thee wild for the dear child that should have been thy bride –
For her, the fair and *debonair*, that now so lowly lies,
The life upon her yellow hair but not within her eyes –
The life still there, upon her hair – the death upon her eyes.

'Avaunt! – avaunt! from fiends below, the indignant ghost is riven –
From Hell unto a high estate far up within the Heaven –
From grief and groan, to a golden throne, beside the King of Heaven.'
Let no bell toll then! – lest her soul, amid its hallowed mirth,
Should catch the note as it doth float up from the damnéd Earth! –
And I! – to-night my heart is light! No dirge will I upraise,
But waft the angel on her flight with a Pæan of old days!

THE VALLEY OF UNREST

Once it smiled a silent dell
Where the people did not dwell;
They had gone unto the wars,
Trusting to the mild-eyed stars,
Nightly, from their azure towers,
To keep watch above the flowers,
In the midst of which all day
The red sun-light lazily lay.
Now each visitor shall confess
The sad valley's restlessness.
Nothing there is motionless –
Nothing save the airs that brood
Over the magic solitude.
Ah, by no wind are stirred those trees
That palpitate like the chill seas
Around the misty Hebrides!
Ah, by no wind those clouds are driven
That rustle through the unquiet Heaven
Uneasily, from morn till even,
Over the violets there that lie
In myriad types of the human eye –
Over the lilies three that wave
And weep above a nameless grave!
They wave: – from out their fragrant tops
Eternal dews come down in drops.
They weep: – from off their delicate stems
Perennial tears descend in gems.

THE COLISEUM

Type of the antique Rome! Rich reliquary
Of lofty contemplation left to Time
By buried centuries of pomp and power!
At length – at length – after so many days
Of weary pilgrimage and burning thirst,
(Thirst for the springs of lore that in thee lie,)
I kneel, an altered and an humble man,
Amid thy shadows, and so drink within
My very soul thy grandeur, gloom, and glory!

Vastness! and Age! and Memories of Eld!
Silence! and Desolation! and dim Night!
I feel ye now – I feel ye in your strength –
O spells more sure than e'er Judæan king
Taught in the gardens of Gethsemane!
O charms more potent than the rapt Chaldee
Ever drew down from out the quiet stars!

Here, where a hero fell, a column falls!
Here, where the mimic eagle glared in gold,
A midnight vigil holds the swarthy bat!
Here, where the dames of Rome their gilded hair
Waved to the wind, now wave the reed and thistle!
Here, where on golden throne the monarch lolled,
Glides, spectre-like, unto his marble home,
Lit by the wan light of the hornéd moon,
The swift and silent lizard of the stones!

But stay! these walls – these ivy-clad arcades –
These mouldering plinths – these sad and blackened shafts –
These vague entablatures – this crumbling frieze –
These shattered cornices – this wreck – this ruin –
These stones – alas! these grey stones – are they all –
All of the famed, and the colossal left
By the corrosive Hours to Fate and me?

'Not all' – the Echoes answer me – 'not all!
Prophetic sounds and loud, arise forever
From us, and from all Ruin, unto the wise,

As melody from Memnon to the Sun.
We rule the hearts of mightiest men – we rule
With a despotic sway all giant minds.
We are not impotent – we pallid stones.
Not all our power is gone – not all our fame –
Not all the magic of our high renown –
Not all the wonder that encircles us –
Not all the mysteries that in us lie –
Not all the memories that hang upon
And cling around about us as a garment,
Clothing us in a robe of more than glory.'

TO ONE IN PARADISE

Thou wast all that to me, love,
For which my soul did pine –
A green isle in the sea, love,
A fountain and a shrine,
All wreathed with fairy fruits and flowers,
And all the flowers were mine.

Ah, dream too bright to last!
Ah, starry Hope! that didst arise
But to be overcast!
A voice from out the Future cries,
'On! on!' – but o'er the Past
(Dim gulf!) my spirit hovering lies
Mute, motionless, aghast!

For, alas! alas! with me
The light of Life is o'er!
'No more – no more – no more –'
(Such language holds the solemn sea
To the sands upon the shore)
Shall bloom the thunder-blasted tree,
Or the stricken eagle soar!

And all my days are trances,
And all my nightly dreams
Are where thy grey eye glances,
And where thy footstep gleams –
In what ethereal dances,
By what eternal streams.

HYMN

At morn – at noon – at twilight dim –
Maria! thou hast heard my hymn!
In joy and wo – in good and ill –
Mother of God, be with me still!
When the Hours flew brightly by,
And not a cloud obscured the sky,
My soul, lest it should truant be,
Thy grace did guide to thine and thee;
Now, when storms of Fate o'ercast
Darkly my Present and my Past,
Let my Future radiant shine
With sweet hopes of thee and thine!

TO F—

Beloved! amid the earnest woes
  That crowd around my earthly path –
(Drear path, alas! where grows
Not even one lonely rose) –
  My soul at least a solace hath
In dreams of thee, and therein knows
An Eden of bland repose.

And thus thy memory is to me
  Like some enchanted far-off isle
In some tumultuous sea –
Some ocean throbbing far and free
  With storms – but where meanwhile
Serenest skies continually
  Just o'er that one bright island smile.

TO F—S S. O—D

Thou wouldst be loved? – then let thy heart
  From its present pathway part not!
Being everything which now thou art,
  Be nothing which thou art not.
So with the world thy gentle ways,
  Thy grace, thy more than beauty,
Shall be an endless theme of praise,
  And love – a simple duty.

SCENES FROM *POLITIAN*

AN UNPUBLISHED DRAMA

I

Rome. – A Hall in a Palace. ALESSANDRA *and* CASTIGLIONE.

ALESSANDRA. Thou art sad, Castiglione.
CASTIGLIONE. Sad! not I.
Oh, I'm the happiest, happiest man in Rome!
A few days more, thou knowest, my Alessandra,
Will make thee mine. Oh, I am very happy!
ALESS. Methinks thou hast a singular way of showing
Thy happiness! – what ails thee, cousin of mine?
Why didst thou sigh so deeply?
CAS. Did I sigh?
I was not conscious of it. It is a fashion,
A silly – a most silly fashion I have
When I am *very* happy. Did I sigh? (*sighing*)
ALESS. Thou didst. Thou art not well. Thou hast indulged
Too much of late, and I am vexed to see it.
Late hours and wine, Castiglione, – these
Will ruin thee! thou art already altered –
Thy looks are haggard – nothing so wears away
The constitution as late hours and wine.
CAS. (*musing*) Nothing, fair cousin, nothing – not even deep sorrow –
Wears it away like evil hours and wine.
I will amend.
ALESS. Do it! I would have thee drop
Thy riotous company, too – fellows low born –
Ill suit the like with old Di Broglio's heir
And Alessandra's husband.
CAS. I will drop them.
ALESS. Thou wilt – thou must. Attend thou also more
To thy dress and equipage – they are over plain
For thy lofty rank and fashion – much depends
Upon appearances.

CAS. I'll see to it.
ALESS. Then see to it! – pay more attention, sir,
To a becoming carriage – much thou wantest
In dignity.
CAS. Much, much, oh much I want
In proper dignity
ALESS. (*haughtily*) Thou mockest me, sir!
CAS. (*abstractedly*) Sweet, gentle Lalage!
ALESS. Heard I aright?
I speak to him – he speaks of Lalage!
Sir Count! (*places her hand on his shoulder*) what art thou dreaming? he's not well!
What ails thee, sir?
CAS. (*starting*) Cousin! fair cousin! – madam!
I crave thy pardon – indeed I am not well –
Your hand from off my shoulder, if you please.
This air is most oppressive! – Madam – the Duke!

Enter DI BROGLIO

DI BROGLIO. My son, I've news for thee! – hey? – what's the matter? (*observing Alessandra*)
I' the pouts? Kiss her, Castiglione! kiss her,
You dog! and make it up, I say, this minute!
I've news for you both. Politian is expected
Hourly in Rome – Politian, Earl of Leicester!
We'll have him at the wedding. 'Tis his first visit
To the imperial city.
ALESS. What! Politian
Of Britain, Earl of Leicester?
DI BROG. The same, my love.
We'll have him at the wedding. A man quite young
In years, but grey in fame. I have not seen him,
But Rumour speaks of him as of a prodigy
Pre-eminent in arts and arms, and wealth,
And high descent. We'll have him at the wedding.
ALESS. I have heard much of this Politian.
Gay, volatile and giddy – is he not?
And little given to thinking.
DI BROG. Far from it, love.
No branch, they say, of all philosophy
So deep abstruse he has not mastered it.

Learned as few are learned.
ALESS. 'Tis very strange!
I have known men have seen Politian
And sought his company. They speak of him
As of one who entered madly into life,
Drinking the cup of pleasure to the dregs.
CAS. Ridiculous! Now *I* have seen Politian
And know him well – nor learned nor mirthful he.
He is a dreamer and a man shut out
From common passions.
DI BROG. Children, we disagree.
Let us go forth and taste the fragrant air
Of the garden. Did I dream, or did I hear
Politian was a *melancholy* man? (*Exeunt*)

II

A Lady's apartment, with a window open and looking into a garden. LALAGE, *in deep mourning, reading at a table on which lie some books and a hand mirror. In the background* JACINTA (*a servant maid*) *leans carelessly upon a chair.*

LAL. Jacinta! is it thou?
JAC. (*pertly*) Yes, Ma'am, I'm here.
LAL. I did not know, Jacinta, you were in waiting.
Sit down! – let not my presence trouble you –
Sit down! – for I am humble, most humble.
JAC. (*aside*) 'Tis time.

JACINTA *seats herself in a side-long manner upon the chair, resting her elbows upon the back, and regarding her mistress with a contemptuous look.* LALAGE *continues to read.*

LAL. 'It in another climate, so he said,
Bore a bright golden flower, but not i' this soil!'

(*pauses – turns over some leaves, and resumes*)

'No lingering winters there, nor snow, nor shower –
But Ocean ever to refresh mankind
Breathes the shrill spirit of the western wind.'
Oh, beautiful! – most beautiful! – how like
To what my fevered soul doth dream of Heaven!

O happy land! (*pauses*) She died! – the maiden died!
O still more happy maiden who couldst die!
Jacinta!

JACINTA *returns no answer, and* LALAGE *presently resumes.*

Again! – a similar tale
Told of a beauteous dame beyond the sea!
Thus speaketh one Ferdinand in the words of the play –
'She died full young' – one Bossola answers him –
'I think not so – her infelicity
Seemed to have years too many' – Ah luckless lady!
Jacinta! (*still no answer*)
Here's a far sterner story
But like – oh, very like in its despair –
Of that Egyptian queen, winning so easily
A thousand hearts – losing at length her own.
She died. Thus endeth the history – and her maids
Lean over her and weep – two gentle maids
With gentle names – Eiros and Charmion?
Rainbow and Dove! – Jacinta!

JAC. (*pettishly*) Madam, what *is* it?

LAL. Wilt thou, my good Jacinta, be so kind
As go down in the library and bring me
The Holy Evangelists.

JAC. Pshaw! (*Exit*)

LAL. If there be balm
For the wounded spirit in Gilead it is there!
Dew in the night time of my bitter trouble
Will there be found – 'dew sweeter far than that
Which hangs like chains of pearl on Hermon Hill.'

Re-enter JACINTA, *and throws a volume on the table*

There, ma'am, 's the book. Indeed she is very troublesome. (*aside*)

LAL. (*astonished*) What didst thou say, Jacinta? Have I done aught
To grieve thee or to vex thee? – I am sorry.
For thou hast served me long and ever been
Trust-worthy and respectful. (*resumes her reading*)

JAC. I can't believe
She has any more jewels – no – no – she gave me all. (*aside*)

LAL. What didst thou say, Jacinta? Now I bethink me

Thou hast not spoken lately of thy wedding.
How fares good Ugo? – and when is it to be?
Can I do aught? – is there no farther aid
Thou needest, Jacinta?

JAC. Is there no *farther* aid!
That's meant for me. (*aside*) I'm sure, Madam, you need not
Be always throwing those jewels in my teeth.

LAL. Jewels! Jacinta, – now indeed, Jacinta,
I thought not of the jewels.

JAC. Oh! perhaps not!
But then I might have sworn it. After all,
There's Ugo says the ring is only paste,
For he's sure the Count Castiglione never
Would have given a real diamond to such as you;
And at the best I'm certain, Madam, you cannot
Have use for jewels *now*. But I might have sworn it. (*Exit*)

LALAGE *bursts into tears and leans her head upon the table – after a short pause raises it.*

LAL. Poor Lalage! – and is it come to this?
Thy servant maid! – but courage! – 'tis but a viper
Whom thou hast cherished to sting thee to the soul!

(*taking up the mirror*)

Ha! here at least's a friend – too much a friend
In earlier days – a friend will not deceive thee.
Fair mirror and true! now tell me (for thou canst)
A tale – a pretty tale – and heed thou not
Though it be rife with woe. It answers me.
It speaks of sunken eyes, and wasted cheeks,
And Beauty long deceased – remembers me
Of Joy departed – Hope, the Seraph Hope,
Inurned and entombed! – now, in a tone
Low, sad, and solemn, but most audible,
Whispers of early grave untimely yawning
For ruined maid. Fair mirror and true! – thou liest not!
Thou hast no end to gain – no heart to break –
Castiglione lied who said he loved –
Thou true – he false! – false! – false!

While she speaks, a MONK *enters her apartment, and approaches unobserved.*

MONK. Refuge thou hast,
Sweet daughter! in Heaven. Think of eternal things!
Give up thy soul to penitence, and pray!
LAL. (*arising hurriedly*) I *cannot* pray! – My soul is at war with God!
The frightful sounds of merriment below
Disturb my senses – go! I cannot pray –
The sweet airs from the garden worry me!
Thy presence grieves me – go! – thy priestly raiment
Fills me with dread – thy ebony crucifix
With horror and awe!
MONK. Think of thy precious soul!
LAL. Think of my early days! – think of my father
And mother in Heaven! think of our quiet home,
And the rivulet that ran before the door!
Think of my little sisters – think of them!
And think of me! – think of my trusting love
And confidence – his vows – my ruin – think – think
Of my unspeakable misery! – begone!
Yet stay! yet stay! – what was it thou saidst of prayer
And penitence? Didst thou not speak of faith
And vows before the throne?
MONK. I did.
LAL. 'Tis well.
There *is* a vow were fitting should be made –
A sacred vow, imperative, and urgent,
A solemn vow!
MONK. Daughter, this zeal is well!
LAL. Father, this zeal is anything but well!
Hast thou a crucifix fit for this thing?
A crucifix whereon to register
This sacred vow? (*He hands her his own.*)
Not that – Oh! no! – no! – no! (*shuddering*)
Not that! Not that! – I tell thee, holy man
Thy raiments and thy ebony cross affright me!
Stand back! I have a crucifix myself, –
I have a crucifix! Methinks 'twere fitting
The deed – the vow – the symbol of the deed –

And the deed's register should tally, father!

(*draws a cross-handled dagger and raises it on high*)

Behold the cross wherewith a vow like mine
Is written in Heaven!
MONK. Thy words are madness, daughter,
And speak a purpose unholy – thy lips are livid –
Thine eyes are wild – tempt not the wrath divine!
Pause ere too late! – oh be not – be not rash!
Swear not the oath – oh swear it not.
LAL. 'Tis sworn!

III

An apartment in a palace. POLITIAN *and* BALDAZZAR.

BALDAZZAR. — Arouse thee now, Politian!
Thou must not – nay indeed, indeed, thou shalt not
Give way unto these humours. Be thyself!
Shake off the idle fancies that beset thee,
And live, for now thou diest!
POLITIAN. Not so, Baldazzar!
Surely I live.
BAL. Politian, it doth grieve me
To see thee thus.
POL. Baldazzar, it doth grieve me
To give thee cause for grief, my honoured friend.
Command me, sir! what wouldst thou have me do?
At thy behest I will shake off that nature
Which from my forefathers I did inherit,
Which with my mother's milk I did imbibe,
And be no more Politian, but some other.
Command me, sir!
BAL. To the field then – to the field –
To the senate or the field.
POL. Alas! alas!
There is an imp would follow me even there!
There is an imp *hath* followed me even there!
There is — what voice was that?
BAL. I heard it not.
I heard not any voice except thine own,

And the echo of thine own.

POL. Then I but dreamed.

BAL. Give not thy soul to dreams: the camp – the court
Befit thee – Fame awaits thee – Glory calls –
And her the trumpet-tongued thou wilt not hear
In hearkening to imaginary sounds
And phantom voices.

POL. It *is* a phantom voice!
Didst thou not hear it *then*?

BAL. I heard it not.

POL. Thou heardst it not! — Baldazzar, speak no more
To me, Politian, of thy camps and courts.
Oh! I am sick, sick, sick, even unto death,
Of the hollow and high-sounding vanities
Of the populous Earth! Bear with me yet awhile!
We have been boys together – school-fellows –
And now are friends – yet shall not be so long –
For in the eternal city thou shalt do me
A kind and gentle office, and a Power –
A Power august, benignant and supreme –
Shall then absolve thee of all farther duties
Unto thy friend.

BAL. Thou speakest a fearful riddle
I *will* not understand.

POL. Yet now as Fate
Approaches, and the Hours are breathing low,
The sands of Time are changed to golden grains,
And dazzle me, Baldazzar. Alas! alas!
I *cannot* die, having within my heart
So keen a relish for the beautiful
As hath been kindled within it. Methinks the air
Is balmier now than it was wont to be –
Rich melodies are floating in the winds –
A rarer loveliness bedecks the earth –
And with a holier lustre the quiet moon
Sitteth in Heaven. – Hist! hist! thou canst not say
Thou hearest not *now*, Baldazzar?

BAL. Indeed I hear not.

POL. Not hear it! – listen now – listen! – the faintest sound
And yet the sweetest that ear ever heard!
A lady's voice! – and sorrow in the tone!

Baldazzar, it oppresses me like a spell!
Again! – again! – how solemnly it falls
Into my heart of hearts! that eloquent voice
Surely I never heard – yet it were well
Had I *but* heard it with its thrilling tones
In earlier days!

BAL. I myself hear it now.
Be still! – the voice, if I mistake not greatly,
Proceeds from yonder lattice – which you may see
Very plainly through the window – it belongs,
Does it not? unto this palace of the Duke.
The singer is undoubtedly beneath
The roof of his Excellency – and perhaps
Is even that Alessandra of whom he spoke
As the betrothed of Castiglione,
His son and heir.

POL. Be still! – it comes again!

VOICE (*very faintly*) 'And is thy heart so strong
As for to leave me thus
Who hath loved thee so long
In wealth and wo among?
And is thy heart so strong
As for to leave me thus?
Say nay – say nay!'

BAL. The song is English, and I oft have heard it
In merry England – never so plaintively –
Hist! hist! it comes again!

VOICE (*more loudly*) 'Is it so strong
As for to leave me thus
Who hath loved thee so long
In wealth and wo among?
And is thy heart so strong
As for to leave me thus?
Say nay – say nay!'

BAL. 'Tis hushed and all is still!

POL. All *is not* still.

BAL. Let us go down.

POL. Go down, Baldazzar, go!

BAL. The hour is growing late – the Duke awaits us, –
Thy presence is expected in the hall
Below. What ails thee, Earl Politian?

VOICE (*distinctly*) 'Who hath loved thee so long,
In wealth and wo among,
And is thy heart so strong?
Say nay – say nay!'

BAL. Let us descend! – 'tis time. Politian, give
These fancies to the wind. Remember, pray,
Your bearing lately savoured much of rudeness
Unto the Duke. Arouse thee! and remember!

POL. Remember? I do. Lead on! I *do* remember. (*going*)
Let us descend. Believe me I would give,
Freely would give the broad lands of my earldom
To look upon the face hidden by yon lattice –
'To gaze upon that veiled face, and hear
Once more that silent tongue.'

BAL. Let me beg you, sir.
Descend with me – the Duke may be offended.
Let us go down, I pray you.

VOICE (*loudly*) *Say nay! – say nay!*

POL. (*aside*) 'Tis strange – 'tis very strange – methought the voice
Chimed in with my desires and bade me stay!

(*approaching the window*)

Sweet voice! I heed thee, and will surely stay.
Now be this Fancy, by Heaven, or be it Fate,
Still will I not descend. Baldazzar, make
Apology unto the Duke for me;
I go not down to-night.

BAL. Your lordship's pleasure
Shall be attended to. Good night, Politian.

POL. Good night, my friend, good night.

IV

The gardens of a palace – Moonlight. LALAGE *and* POLITIAN.

LALAGE. And dost thou speak of love.
To *me*, Politian? – dost thou speak of love
To Lalage? – ah wo – ah wo is me!
This mockery is most cruel – most cruel indeed!

POLITIAN. Weep not! oh, sob not thus! – thy bitter tears
Will madden me. Oh mourn not, Lalage –

Be comforted! I know – I know it all,
And *still* I speak of love. Look at me, brightest,
And beautiful Lalage! – turn here thine eyes!
Thou askest me if I could speak of love,
Knowing what I know, and seeing what I have seen.
Thou askest me that – and thus I answer thee –
Thus on my bended knee I answer thee. (*kneeling*)
Sweet Lalage, *I love thee – love thee – love thee*;
Thro' good and ill – thro' weal and wo I *love thee*.
Not mother, with her first born on her knee,
Thrills with intenser love than I for thee.
Not on God's altar, in any time or clime,
Burned there a holier fire than burneth now
Within my spirit for *thee*. And do I love? (*arising*)
Even for thy woes I love thee – even for thy woes –
Thy beauty and thy woes.

LAL. Alas, proud Earl,
Thou dost forget thyself, remembering me!
How, in thy father's halls, among the maidens
Pure and reproachless of thy princely line,
Could the dishonoured Lalage abide?
Thy wife, and with a tainted memory –
My seared and blighted name, how would it tally
With the ancestral honours of thy house,
And with thy glory?

POL. Speak not to me of glory!
I hate – I loathe the name; I do abhor
The unsatisfactory and ideal thing.
Art thou not Lalage and I Politian?
Do I not love – art thou not beautiful –
What need we more? Ha! glory! – now speak not of it:
By all I hold most sacred and most solemn –
By all my wishes now – my fears heareafter –
By all I scorn on earth and hope in heaven –
There is no deed I would more glory in,
Than in thy cause to scoff at this same glory
And trample it under foot. What matters it –
What matters it, my fairest, and my best,
That we go down unhonoured and forgotten
Into the dust – so we descend together.
Descend together – and then – and then perchance —

LAL. Why dost thou pause, Politian?
POL. And then perchance
Arise together, Lalage, and roam
The starry and quiet dwellings of the blest,
And still —
LAL. Why dost thou pause, Politian?
POL. And still *together – together*.
LAL. Now Earl of Leicester!
Thou *lovest* me, and in my heart of hearts
I feel thou lovest me truly.
POL. Oh, Lalage! (*throwing himself upon his knee*)
And lovest thou *me*?
LAL. Hist! hush! within the gloom
Of yonder trees methought a figure past –
A spectral figure, solemn, and slow, and noiseless –
Like the grim shadow Conscience, solemn and noiseless.

(*walks across and returns*)

I was mistaken – 'twas but a giant bough
Stirred by the autumn wind. Politian!
POL. My Lalage – my love! why art thou moved?
Why dost thou turn so pale? Not Conscience' self,
Far less a shadow which thou likenest to it,
Should shake the firm spirit thus. But the night wind
Is chilly – and these melancholy boughs
Throw over all things a gloom.
LAL. Politian!
Thou speakest to me of love. Knowest thou the land
With which all tongues are busy – a land new found –
Miraculously found by one of Genoa –
A thousand leagues within the golden west?
A fairy land of flowers, and fruit, and sunshine,
And crystal lakes, and over-arching forests,
And mountains, around whose towering summits the winds
Of Heaven untrammelled flow – which air to breathe
Is Happiness now, and will be Freedom hereafter
In days that are to come?
POL. O, wilt thou – wilt thou
Fly to that Paradise – my Lalage, wilt thou
Fly thither with me? There Care shall be forgotten
And Sorrow shall be no more, and Eros be all.

And life shall then be mine, for I will live
For thee, and in thine eyes – and thou shalt be
No more a mourner – but the radiant Joys
Shall wait upon thee, and the angel Hope
Attend thee ever; and I will kneel to thee
And worship thee, and call thee my beloved,
My own, my beautiful, my love, my wife,
My all – oh, wilt thou – wilt thou, Lalage,
Fly thither with me?

LAL. A deed is to be done –
Castiglione lives!

POL. And he shall die! (*Exit*)

LAL. (*after a pause*) – And – he – shall – die! — alas!
Castiglione die? Who spoke the words?
Where am I? – what was it he said? – Politian!
Thou *art* not gone – thou art not *gone*, Politian!
I *feel* thou art not gone – yet dare not look,
Lest I behold thee not; thou *couldst* not go
With those words upon thy lips – O, speak to me!
And let me hear thy voice – one word – one word,
To say thou art not gone, – one little sentence,
To say how thou dost scorn – how thou dost hate
My womanly weakness. Ha! ha! thou *art* not gone –
O speak to me! I *knew* thou wouldst not go!
I knew thou wouldst not, couldst not, *durst* not go.
Villain, thou *art* not gone – thou mockest me!
And thus I clutch thee – thus! — He is gone, he is gone –
Gone – gone. Where am I? — 'tis well – 'tis very well!
So that the blade be keen – the blow be sure,
'Tis well, 'tis *very* well – alas! alas! (*Exit*)

V

The suburbs. POLITIAN *alone.*

POLITIAN: This weakness grows upon me. I am faint,
And much I fear me ill – it will not do
To die ere I have lived! Stay – stay thy hand,
O Azrael, yet awhile! – Prince of the Powers
Of Darkness and the Tomb, O pity me!
O pity me! let me not perish now,

In the budding of my Paradisal Hope!
Give me to live yet – yet a little while:
'Tis I who pray for life – I who so late
Demanded but to die! – what sayeth the Count?

Enter BALDAZZAR

BALDAZZAR: That knowing no cause of quarrel or of feud
Between the Earl Politian and himself,
He doth decline your cartel.
POL. *What* didst thou say?
What answer was it you brought me, good Baldazzar?
With what excessive fragrance the zephyr comes
Laden from yonder bowers! – a fairer day,
Or one more worthy Italy, methinks
No mortal eyes have seen! – *what* said the Count?
BAL. That he, Castiglione, not being aware
Of any feud existing, or any cause
Of quarrel between your lordship and himself
Cannot accept the challenge.
POL. It is most true –
All this is very true. When saw you, sir,
When saw you now, Baldazzar, in the frigid
Ungenial Britain which we left so lately,
A heaven so calm as this – so utterly free
From the evil taint of clouds? – and he did *say*?
BAL. No more, my lord, than I have told you, sir:
The Count Castiglione will not fight,
Having no cause for quarrel.
POL. Now this is true –
All very true. Thou art my friend, Baldazzar,
And I have not forgotten it – thou'lt do me
A piece of service; wilt thou go back and say
Unto this man, that I, the Earl of Leicester,
Hold him a villain? – thus much, I prythee, say
Unto the Count – it is exceeding just
He should have cause for quarrel.
BAL. My lord! – my friend! —
POL. (*aside* 'Tis he – he comes himself! (*aloud*) thou reasonest well.
I know what thou wouldst say – not send the message –
Well! – I will think of it – I will not send it.
Now prythee, leave me – hither doth come a person

With whom affairs of a most private nature
I would adjust.

BAL. I go – to-morrow we meet.
Do we not? – at the Vatican.

POL. At the Vatican. *Exit* BAL.

Enter CASTIGLIONE

CAS. The Earl of Leicester here!

POL. I *am* the Earl of Leicester, and thou seest,
Dost thou not? that I am here.

CAS. My lord, some strange,
Some singular mistake – misunderstanding –
Hath without doubt arisen: thou hast been urged
Thereby, in heat of anger, to address
Some words most unaccountable, in writing,
To me, Castiglione; the bearer being
Baldazzar, Duke of Surrey. I am aware
Of nothing which might warrant thee in this thing,
Having given thee no offence. Ha! – am I right?
'Twas a mistake? – undoubtedly – we all
Do err at times.

POL. Draw, villain, and prate no more!

CAS. Ha! – draw? – and villain? have at thee then at once, —
Proud Earl! (*draws*)

POL. (*drawing*) Thus to the expiatory tomb,
Untimely sepulchre, I do devote thee
In the name of Lalage!

CAS. (*letting fall his sword and recoiling to the extremity of the stage*)
Of Lalage!
Hold off – thy sacred hand! – avaunt I say!
Avaunt – I will not fight thee – indeed I dare not.

POL. Thou wilt not fight with me didst say, Sir Count?
Shall I be baffled thus? – now this is well;
Didst say thou *darest* not? Ha!

CAS. I dare not – dare not –
Hold off thy hand – with that beloved name
So fresh upon thy lips I will not fight thee –
I cannot – dare not.

POL. Now by my halidom

I do believe thee! – coward, I do believe thee!
CAS. Ha! – coward! – this may not be!

(*clutches his sword and staggers towards* POLITIAN, *but his purpose is changed before reaching him, and he falls upon his knee at the feet of the Earl*)

Alas! my lord,
It is – it is – most true. In such a cause
I am the veriest coward. O pity me!
POL. (*greatly softened*) Alas! – I do – indeed I pity thee.
CAS. And Lalage ——
POL. *Scoundrel! – arise and die!*
CAS. It needeth not be – thus – thus – O let me die
Thus on my bended knee. It were most fitting
That in this deep humiliation I perish.
For in the fight I will not raise a hand
Against thee, Earl of Leicester. Strike thou home –
(*baring his bosom*)
Here is no let or hindrance to thy weapon –
Strike home. I *will not* fight thee.
POL. Now's Death and Hell!
Am I not – am I not sorely – grievously tempted
To take thee at thy word? But mark me, sir:
Think not to fly me thus. Do thou prepare
For public insult in the streets – before
The eyes of the citizens. I'll follow thee –
Like an avenging spirit I'll follow thee
Even unto death. Before those whom thou lovest –
Before all Rome I'll taunt thee, villain, – I'll taunt thee,
Dost hear? with *cowardice* – thou *wilt not* fight me?
Thou liest! thou *shalt*! *Exit*
CAS. Now this indeed is just!
Most righteous, and most just, avenging Heaven!

BRIDAL BALLAD

TO —

The ring is on my hand,
  And the wreath is on my brow;
Satins and jewels grand
Are all at my command,
  And I am happy now.

And my lord he loves me well;
  But, when first he breathed his vow,
I felt my bosom swell –
For the words rang as a knell,
And the voice seemed *his* who fell
In the battle down the dell,
  And who is happy now.

But he spoke to re-assure me,
  And he kissed my pallid brow,
While a reverie came o'er me,
And to the churchyard bore me,
And I sighed to him before me,
(Thinking him dead D'Elormie),
  'Oh, I am happy now!'

And thus the words were spoken;
  And this the plighted vow;
And, though my faith be broken,
And, though my heart be broken,
Here is a ring as token
  That I am happy now!

Would God I could awaken!
  For I dream I know not how,
And my soul is sorely shaken
Lest an evil step be taken, –
Lest the dead who is forsaken
  May not be happy now.

SONNET TO ZANTE

Fair isle, that from the fairest of all flowers,
  Thy gentlest of all gentle names dost take!
How many memories of what radiant hours
  At sight of thee and thine at once awake!
How many scenes of what departed bliss!
  How many thoughts of what entombéd hopes!
How many visions of a maiden that is
  No more – no more upon thy verdant slopes!
No more! alas, that magical sad sound
  Transforming all! Thy charms shall please *no more* –
Thy memory *no more!* Accurséd ground
  Henceforth I hold thy flower-enamelled shore,
O hyacinthine isle! O purple Zante!
  'Isola d'oro! Fior di Levante!'

THE HAUNTED PALACE

In the greenest of our valleys
   By good angels tenanted,
Once a fair and stately palace –
   Radiant palace – reared its head.
In the monarch Thought's dominion –
   It stood there!
Never seraph spread a pinion
   Over fabric half so fair!

Banners yellow, glorious, golden,
   On its roof did float and flow,
(This – all this – was in the olden
   Time long ago,)
And every gentle air that dallied,
   In that sweet day,
Along the ramparts plumed and pallid,
   A wingéd odour went away.

Wanderers in that happy valley,
   Through two luminous windows, saw
Spirits moving musically,
   To a lute's well-tunéd law,
Round about a throne where, sitting,
   (Porphyrogene!)
In state his glory well befitting,
   The ruler of the realm was seen.

And all with pearl and ruby glowing
   Was the fair palace door,
Through which came flowing, flowing, flowing
   And sparkling evermore,
A troop of Echoes, whose sweet duty
   Was but to sing,
In voices of surpassing beauty,
   The wit and wisdom of their king.

But evil things, in robes of sorrow,
   Assailed the monarch's high estate.

(Ah, let us mourn! – for never morrow
  Shall dawn upon him desolate!)
And round about his home the glory
  That blushed and bloomed,
Is but a dim-remembered story
  Of the old time entombed.

And travellers, now, within that valley,
  Through the red-litten windows see
Vast forms, that move fantastically
  To a discordant melody,
While, like a ghastly rapid river,
  Through the pale door
A hideous throng rush out forever
  And laugh – but smile no more.

SONNET – SILENCE

There are some qualities – some incorporate things,
  That have a double life, which thus is made
A type of that twin entity which springs
  From matter and light, evinced in solid and shade.
There is a two-fold *Silence* – sea and shore –
  Body and soul. One dwells in lonely places,
  Newly with grass o'ergrown; some solemn graces,
Some human memories and tearful lore,
Render him terrorless: his name's 'No More.'
He is the corporate Silence: dread him not!
  No power hath he of evil in himself;
But should some urgent fate (untimely lot!)
  Bring thee to meet his shadow (nameless elf,
That haunteth the lone regions where hath trod
No foot of man,) commend thyself to God!

THE CONQUEROR WORM

Lo! 'tis a gala night
  Within the lonesome latter years!
An angel throng, bewinged, bedight
  In veils, and drowned in tears,
Sit in a theatre, to see
  A play of hopes and fears,
While the orchestra breathes fitfully
  The music of the spheres.

Mimes, in the form of God on high,
  Mutter and mumble low,
And hither and thither fly –
  Mere puppets they, who come and go
At bidding of vast formless things
  That shift the scenery to and fro,
Flapping from out their Condor wings
  Invisible Wo!

That motley drama – oh, be sure
  It shall not be forgot!
With its Phantom chased for evermore.
  By a crowd that seize it not,
Through a circle that ever returneth in
  To the self-same spot,
And much of Madness, and more of Sin,
  And Horror the soul of the plot.

But see, amid the mimic rout
  A crawling shape intrude!
A blood-red thing that writhes from out
  The scenic solitude!
It writhes! – it writhes! – with mortal pangs
  The mimes become its food,
And seraphs sob at vermin fangs
  In human gore imbued.

Out – out are the lights – out all!
  And, over each quivering form,
The curtain, a funeral pall,

Comes down with the rush of a storm,
While the angels, all pallid and wan,
Uprising, unveiling, affirm
That the play is the tragedy, 'Man,'
And its hero the Conqueror Worm.

DREAM-LAND

By a route obscure and lonely,
Haunted by ill angels only,
Where an Eidolon, named NIGHT,
On a black throne reigns upright,
I have reached these lands but newly
  From an ultimate dim Thule –
From a wild weird clime that lieth, sublime,
    Out of SPACE – out of TIME.

Bottomless vales and boundless floods,
And chasms, and caves and Titan woods,
With forms that no man can discover
For the tears that drip all over;
Mountains toppling evermore
Into seas without a shore;
Seas that restlessly aspire,
Surging, unto skies of fire;
Lakes that endlessly outspread
Their lone waters – lone and dead, –
Their still waters – still and chilly
With the snows of the lolling lily.

By the lakes that thus outspread
Their lone waters, lone and dead, –
Their sad waters, sad and chilly
With the snows of the lolling lily, –
By the mountains – near the river
Murmuring lowly, murmuring ever, –
By the grey woods, – by the swamp
Where the toad and the newt encamp, –
By the dismal tarns and pools
    Where dwell the Ghouls, –
By each spot the most unholy –
In each nook most melancholy, –
There the traveller meets, aghast,
Sheeted Memories of the Past –
Shrouded forms that start and sigh
As they pass the wanderer by –

White-robed forms of friends long given,
In agony, to the Earth – and Heaven.

For the heart whose woes are legion
'Tis a peaceful, soothing region –
For the spirit that walks in shadow
'Tis – oh 'tis an Eldorado!
But the traveller, travelling through it,
May not – dare not openly view it;
Never its mysteries are exposed
To the weak human eye unclosed;
So wills its King, who hath forbid
The uplifting of the fringéd lid;
And thus the sad Soul that here passes
Beholds it but through darkened glasses.

By a route obscure and lonely,
Haunted by ill angels only,
Where an Eidolon, named NIGHT,
On a black throne reigns upright,
I have wandered home but newly
From this ultimate dim Thule.

THE RAVEN

Once upon a midnight dreary, while I pondered, weak and weary,
Over many a quaint and curious volume of forgotten lore –
While I nodded, nearly napping, suddenly there came a tapping,
As of some one gently rapping, rapping at my chamber door.
''Tis some visiter,' I muttered, 'tapping at my chamber door –
Only this and nothing more.'

Ah, distinctly I remember it was in the bleak December;
And each separate dying ember wrought its ghost upon the floor.
Eagerly I wished the morrow; – vainly I had sought to borrow
From my books surcease of sorrow – sorrow for the lost Lenore –
For the rare and radiant maiden whom the angels name Lenore –
Nameless *here* for evermore.

And the silken, sad, uncertain rustling of each purple curtain
Thrilled me – filled me with fantastic terrors never felt before;
So that now, to still the beating of my heart, I stood repeating
''Tis some visiter entreating entrance at my chamber door –
Some late visiter entreating entrance at my chamber door; –
This it is and nothing more.'

Presently my soul grew stronger; hesitating then no longer,
'Sir,' said I, 'or Madam, truly your forgiveness I implore;
But the fact is I was napping, and so gently you came rapping,
And so faintly you came tapping, tapping at my chamber door,
That I scarce was sure I heard you' – here I opened wide the door; —
Darkness there and nothing more.

Deep into that darkness peering, long I stood there wondering, fearing,
Doubting, dreaming dreams no mortal ever dared to dream before;
But the silence was unbroken, and the stillness gave no token,
And the only word there spoken was the whispered word, 'Lenore!'
This I whispered, and an echo murmured back the word 'Lenore!'
Merely this and nothing more.

Back into the chamber turning, all my soul within me burning,
Soon again I heard a tapping somewhat louder than before
'Surely,' said I, 'surely that is something at my window lattice;

Let me see, then, what thereat is, and this mystery explore –
Let my heart be still a moment and this mystery explore; –
'Tis the wind and nothing more!'

Open here I flung the shutter, when, with many a flirt and flutter
In there stepped a stately Raven of the saintly days of yore.
Not the least obeisance made he; not a minute stopped or stayed he;
But, with mien of lord or lady, perched above my chamber door –
Perched upon a bust of Pallas just above my chamber door –
Perched, and sat, and nothing more.

Then this ebony bird beguiling my sad fancy into smiling,
By the grave and stern decorum of the countenance it wore,
'Though thy crest be shorn and shaven, thou,' I said, 'art sure no craven,
Ghastly grim and ancient Raven wandering from the Nightly shore –
Tell me what thy lordly name is on the Night's Plutonian shore!'
Quoth the Raven, 'Nevermore.'

Much I marvelled this ungainly fowl to hear discourse so plainly,
Though its answer little meaning – little relevancy bore;
For we cannot help agreeing that no living human being
Ever yet was blessed with seeing bird above his chamber door –
Bird or beast upon the sculptured bust above his chamber door,
With such name as 'Nevermore.'

But the Raven, sitting lonely on the placid bust, spoke only
That one word, as if his soul in that one word he did outpour.
Nothing farther then he uttered – not a feather then he fluttered –
Till I scarcely more than muttered 'Other friends have flown before –
On the morrow *he* will leave me, as my hopes have flown before.'
Then the bird said 'Nevermore.'

Startled at the stillness broken by reply so aptly spoken,
'Doubtless,' said I, 'what it utters is its only stock and store
Caught from some unhappy master whom unmerciful Disaster
Followed fast and followed faster till his songs one burden bore –
Till the dirges of his Hope that melancholy burden bore
'Of "Never – nevermore."'

But the Raven still beguiling all my fancy into smiling,
Straight I wheeled a cushioned seat in front of bird, and bust and door;

Then, upon the velvet sinking, I betook myself to linking
Fancy unto fancy, thinking what this ominous bird of yore –
What this grim, ungainly, ghastly, gaunt, and ominous bird of yore
Meant in croaking 'Nevermore.'

This I sat engaged in guessing, but no syllable expressing
To the fowl whose fiery eyes now burned into my bosom's core;
This and more I sat divining, with my head at ease reclining
On the cushion's velvet lining that the lamp-light gloated o'er,
But whose velvet violet lining with the lamp-light gloating o'er,
She shall press, ah, nevermore!

Then, methought, the air grew denser, perfumed from an unseen censer
Swung by Seraphim whose foot-falls tinkled on the tufted floor.
'Wretch,' I cried, 'thy God hath lent thee – by these angels he hath sent thee
Respite – respite and nepenthe from thy memories of Lenore;
Quaff, oh quaff this kind nepenthe and forget this lost Lenore!'
Quoth the Raven 'Nevermore.'

'Prophet!' said I, 'thing of evil! prophet still, if bird or devil! –
Whether Tempter sent, or whether tempest tossed thee here ashore,
Desolate yet all undaunted, on this desert land enchanted –
On this home by Horror haunted – tell me truly, I implore –
Is there – *is* there balm in Gilead? – tell me – tell me, I implore!'
Quoth the Raven 'Nevermore.'

'Prophet!' said I, 'thing of evil! – prophet still, if bird or devil!
By that Heaven that bends above us – by that God we both adore –
Tell this soul with sorrow laden if, within the distant Aidenn,
It shall clasp a sainted maiden whom the angels name Lenore –
Clasp a rare and radiant maiden whom the angels name Lenore.'
Quoth the Raven 'Nevermore.'

'Be that word our sign of parting, bird or fiend!' I shrieked, upstarting –
'Get thee back into the tempest and the Night's Plutonian shore!
Leave no black plume as a token of that lie thy soul hath spoken!
Leave my loneliness unbroken! – quit the bust above my door!
Take thy beak from out my heart, and take thy form from off my door!'
Quoth the Raven 'Nevermore.'

And the Raven, never flitting, still is sitting, *still* is sitting
On the pallid bust of Pallas just above my chamber door;
And his eyes have all the seeming of a demon's that is dreaming,
And the lamp-light o'er him streaming throws his shadow on the floor;
And my soul from out that shadow that lies floating on the floor
Shall be lifted – nevermore!

EULALIE – A SONG

I dwelt alone
In a world of moan,
And my soul was a stagnant tide,
Till the fair and gentle Eulalie became my blushing bride –
Till the yellow-haired young Eulalie became my smiling bride.

Ah, less – less bright
The stars of the night
Than the eyes of the radiant girl!
And never a flake
That the vapour can make
With the moon-tints of purple and pearl,
Can vie with the modest Eulalie's most unregarded curl –
Can compare with the bright-eyed Eulalie's most humble and careless curl.

Now Doubt – now Pain
Come never again,
For her soul gives me sigh for sigh,
And all day long
Shines, bright and strong,
Astarté within the sky,
While ever to her dear Eulalie upturns her matron eye –
While ever to her young Eulalie upturns her violet eye.

A VALENTINE

TO — — —

For her this rhyme is penned, whose luminous eyes,
  Brightly expressive as the twins of Leda,
Shall find her own sweet name, that, nestling lies
  Upon the page, enwrapped from every reader,
Search narrowly the lines! – they hold a treasure
  Divine – a talisman – an amulet
That must be worn *at heart*. Search well the measure –
  The words – the syllables! Do not forget
The trivialest point, or you may lose your labour!
  And yet there is in this no Gordian knot
Which one might not undo without a sabre,
  If one could merely comprehend the plot.
Enwritten upon the leaf where now are peering
  Eyes scintillating soul, there lie *perdus*
Three eloquent words oft uttered in the hearing
  Of poets, by poets – as the name is a poet's, too,
Its letters, although naturally lying
  Like the knight Pinto – Mendez Ferdinando –
Still form a synonym for Truth. – Cease trying!
  You will not read the riddle, though you do the best you *can* do.

TO M. L. S—

Of all who hail thy presence as the morning –
Of all to whom thine absence is the night –
The blotting utterly from out high heaven
The sacred sun – of all who, weeping, bless thee
Hourly for hope – for life – ah, above all,
For the resurrection of deep-buried faith
In truth, in virtue, in humanity –
Of all who, on despair's unhallowed bed
Lying down to die, have suddenly arisen
At thy soft-murmured words, 'Let there be light!'
At the soft-murmured words that were fulfilled
In the seraphic glancing of thine eyes –
Of all who owe thee most, whose gratitude
Nearest resembles worship, – oh, remember
The truest, the most fervently devoted,
And think that these weak lines are written by him –
By him, who, as he pens them, thrills to think
His spirit is communing with an angel's.

ULALUME

The skies they were ashen and sober;
    The leaves they were crispéd and sere –
    The leaves they were withering and sere;
It was night in the lonesome October
    Of my most immemorial year;
It was hard by the dim lake of Auber,
    In the misty mid region of Weir –
It was down by the dank tarn of Auber,
    In the ghoul-haunted woodland of Weir.

Here once, through an alley Titanic,
    Of cypress, I roamed with my Soul –
    Of cypress, with Psyche, my Soul.
These were days when my heart was volcanic
    As the scoriac rivers that roll –
    As the lavas that restlessly roll
Their sulphurous currents down Yaanek
    In the ultimate climes of the pole –
That groan as they roll down Mount Yaanek
    In the realms of the Boreal Pole.

Our talk had been serious and sober,
    But our thoughts they were palsied and sere –
    Our memories were treacherous and sere –
For we knew not the month was October,
    And we marked not the night of the year –
    (Ah, night of all nights in the year!)
We noted not the dim lake of Auber –
    (Though once we had journeyed down here) –
Remembered not the dank tarn of Auber,
    Nor the ghoul-haunted woodland of Weir.

And now, as the night was senescent
    And star-dials pointed to morn –
    As the star-dials hinted of morn –
At the end of our path a liquescent
    And nebulous lustre was born,

Out of which a miraculous crescent
    Arose with a duplicate horn –
Astarté's bediamonded crescent
    Distinct with its duplicate horn.

And I said – 'She is warmer than Dian:
    She rolls through an ether of sighs –
    She revels in a region of sighs:
She has seen that the tears are not dry on
    These cheeks, where the worm never dies
And has come past the stars of the Lion
    To point us the path to the skies –
    To the Lethean peace of the skies –
Come up, in despite of the Lion,
    To shine on us with her bright eyes –
Come up through the lair of the Lion,
    With love in her luminous eyes.'

But Psyche, uplifting her finger,
    Said – 'Sadly this star I mistrust –
    Her pallor I strangely mistrust: –
Oh, hasten! – oh, let us not linger!
    Oh, fly! – let us fly! – for we must.'
In terror she spoke, letting sink her
    Wings until they trailed in the dust –
In agony sobbed, letting sink her
    Plumes till they trailed in the dust –
    Till they sorrowfully trailed in the dust.

I replied – 'This is nothing but dreaming:
    Let us on by this tremulous light!
    Let us bathe in this crystalline light!
Its Sibyllic splendour is beaming
    With Hope and in Beauty to-night: –
    See! – it flickers up the sky through the night!
Ah, we safely may trust to its gleaming,
    And be sure it will lead us aright –
We safely may trust to a gleaming
    That cannot but guide us aright,
    Since it flickers up to Heaven through the night.'

Thus I pacified Psyche and kissed her,
    And tempted her out of her gloom –

And conquered her scruples and gloom;
And we passed to the end of the vista,
But were stopped by the door of a tomb –
By the door of a legended tomb;
And I said – 'What is written, sweet sister,
On the door of this legended tomb?'
She replied – 'Ulalume – Ulalume –
'Tis the vault of thy lost Ulalume!'

Then my heart it grew ashen and sobér
As the leaves that were crispéd and sere –
As the leaves that were withering and sere,
And I cried – 'It was surely October
On *this* very night of last year
That I journeyed – I journeyed down here –
That I brought a dread burden down here –
On this night of all nights in the year,
Ah, what demon has tempted me here?
Well I know, now, this dim lake of Auber –
This misty mid region of Weir –
Well I know, now, this dank tarn of Auber,
This ghoul-haunted woodland of Weir.'

AN ENIGMA

'Seldom we find,' says Solomon Don Dunce,
'Half an idea in the profoundest sonnet.
Through all the flimsy things we see at once
As easily as through a Naples bonnet –
Trash of all trash! – how *can* a lady don it?
Yet heavier far than your Petrarchan stuff –
Owl-downy nonsense that the faintest puff
Twirls into trunk-paper the while you con it.'
And, veritably, Sol is right enough.
The general tuckermanities are arrant
Bubbles – ephemeral and *so* transparent –
But *this* is, now, – you may depend upon it –
Stable, opaque, immortal – all by dint
Of the dear names that lie concealed within 't.

TO — —

Not long ago, the writer of these lines,
In the mad pride of intellectuality,
Maintained 'the power of words' -- denied that ever
A thought arose within the human brain
Beyond the utterance of the human tongue:
And now, as if in mockery of that boast,
Two words – two foreign soft dissyllables –
Italian tones, made only to be murmured
By angels dreaming in the moonlit 'dew
That hangs like chains of pearl on Hermon hill,' –
Have stirred from out the abysses of his heart,
Unthought-like thoughts that are the souls of thought,
Richer, far wilder, far diviner visions
Than even the seraph harper, Israfel,
(Who has 'the sweetest voice of all God's creatures,')
Could hope to utter. And I! my spells are broken.
The pen falls powerless from my shivering hand.
With thy dear name as text, though bidden by thee,
I cannot write – I cannot speak or think –
Alas, I cannot feel; for 'tis not feeling,
This standing motionless upon the golden
Threshold of the wide-open gate of dreams,
Gazing, entranced, adown the gorgeous vista,
And thrilling as I see, upon the right,
Upon the left, and all the way along,
Amid empurpled vapours, far away
To where the prospect terminates – *thee only*.

THE BELLS

I

Hear the sledges with the bells –
Silver bells!
What a world of merriment their melody foretells!
How they tinkle, tinkle, tinkle,
In the icy air of night!
While the stars that oversprinkle
All the heavens, seem to twinkle
With a crystalline delight;
Keeping time, time, time,
In a sort of Runic rhyme,
To the tintinnabulation that so musically wells
From the bells, bells, bells, bells,
Bells, bells, bells –
From the jingling and the tinkling of the bells.

II

Hear the mellow wedding bells –
Golden bells!
What a world of happiness their harmony foretells!
Through the balmy air of night
How they ring out their delight! –
From the molten-golden notes,
And all in tune,
What a liquid ditty floats
To the turtle-dove that listens, while she gloats
On the moon!
Oh, from out the sounding cells,
What a gush of euphony voluminously wells!
How it swells!
How it dwells
On the Future! – how it tells
Of the rapture that impels
To the swinging and the ringing
Of the bells, bells, bells –

Of the bells, bells, bells, bells,
Bells, bells, bells –
To the rhyming and the chiming of the bells!

III

Hear the loud alarum bells –
Brazen bells!
What a tale of terror, now, their turbulency tells!
In the startled ear of night
How they scream out their affright!
Too much horrified to speak,
They can only shriek, shriek,
Out of tune,
In a clamorous appealing to the mercy of the fire,
In a mad expostulation with the deaf and frantic fire,
Leaping higher, higher, higher,
With a desperate desire,
And a resolute endeavour
Now – now to sit, or never,
By the side of the pale-faced moon.
Oh, the bells, bells, bells!
What a tale their terror tells
Of Despair!
How they clang, and clash, and roar!
What a horror they outpour
On the bosom of the palpitating air!
Yet the ear, it fully knows,
By the twanging,
And the clanging,
How the danger ebbs and flows;
Yet the ear distinctly tells,
In the jangling,
And the wrangling,
How the danger sinks and swells,
By the sinking or the swelling in the anger of the bells –
Of the bells –
Of the bells, bells, bells,
Bells, bells, bells –
In the clamour and the clangor of the bells!

IV

Hear the tolling of the bells –
Iron bells!
What a world of solemn thought their monody compels!
In the silence of the night,
How we shiver with affright
At the melancholy menace of their tone!
For every sound that floats
From the rust within their throats
Is a groan.
And the people – ah, the people –
They that dwell up in the steeple,
All alone,
And who, tolling, tolling, tolling,
In that muffled monotone,
Feel a glory in so rolling
On the human heart a stone –
They are neither man nor woman –
They are neither brute nor human –
They are Ghouls: –
And their king it is who tolls: –
And he rolls, rolls, rolls, rolls
A pæan from the bells!
And his merry bosom swells
With the pæan of the bells!
And he dances, and he yells;
Keeping time, time, time,
In a sort of Runic rhyme,
To the pæan of the bells: –
Of the bells:
Keeping time, time, time,
In a sort of Runic rhyme,
To the throbbing of the bells –
Of the bells, bells, bells –
To the sobbing of the bells: –
Keeping time, time, time,
As he knells, knells, knells,
In a happy Runic rhyme,
To the rolling of the bells –

Of the bells, bells, bells: –
To the tolling of the bells –
Of the bells, bells, bells, bells,
Bells, bells, bells –
To the moaning and the groaning of the bells.

TO HELEN

I saw thee once – once only – years ago:
I must not say *how* many – but *not* many.
It was a July midnight; and from out
A full-orbed moon, that, like thine own soul, soaring,
Sought a precipitate pathway up through heaven,
There fell a silvery-silken veil of light,
With quietude and sultriness and slumber,
Upon the upturn'd faces of a thousand
Roses that grew in an enchanted garden,
Where no wind dared to stir, unless on tiptoe –
Fell on the upturn'd faces of these roses
That gave out, in return for the love-light,
Their odorous souls in an ecstatic death –
Fell on the upturn'd face of these roses
That smiled and died in this parterre, enchanted
By thee, and by the poetry of thy presence.

Clad all in white, upon a violet bank
I saw thee half reclining; while the moon
Fell on the upturn'd faces of the roses,
And on thine own, upturn'd – alas, in sorrow!

Was it not Fate, that, on this July midnight –
Was it not Fate, (whose name is also Sorrow,)
That bade me pause before that garden-gate,
To breathe the incense of those slumbering roses:
No footstep stirred: the hated world all slept,
Save only thee and me. (Oh, heaven! – oh, God!
How my heart beats in coupling those two words!)
Save only thee and me. I paused – I looked –
And in an instant all things disappeared.
(Ah, bear in mind this garden was enchanted!)
The pearly lustre of the moon went out:
The mossy banks and the meandering paths,
The happy flowers and the repining trees,
Were seen no more: the very roses' odours
Died in the arms of the adoring airs.
All – all expired save thee – save less than thou:

Save only the divine light in thine eyes –
Save but the soul in thine uplifted eyes.
I saw but them – they were the world to me.
I saw but them – saw only them for hours –
Saw only them until the moon went down.
What wild heart-histories seemed to lie enwritten
Upon those crystalline, celestial spheres!
How dark a wo! yet how sublime a hope!
How silently serene a sea of pride!
How daring an ambition! yet how deep –
How fathomless a capacity for love

But now, at length, dear Dian sank from sight,
Into a western couch of thunder-cloud;
And thou, a ghost, amid the entombing trees
Didst glide away. *Only thine eyes remained.*
They *would not* go – they never yet have gone.
Lighting my lonely pathway home that night,
They have not left me (as my hopes have) since.
They follow me – they lead me through the years
They are my ministers – yet I their slave.
Their office is to illumine and enkindle –
My duty, *to be saved* by their bright light,
And purified in their electric fire,
And sanctified in their elysian fire.
They fill my soul with Beauty (which is Hope,)
And are far up in Heaven – the stars I kneel to
In the sad, silent watches of my night;
While even in the meridian glare of day
I see them still – two sweetly scintillant
Venuses, unextinguished by the sun!

ELDORADO

Gaily bedight,
A gallant knight,
In sunshine and in shadow,
Had journeyed long,
Singing a song,
In search of Eldorado.

But he grew old –
This knight so bold –
And o'er his heart a shadow
Fell as he found
No spot of ground
That looked like Eldorado.

And, as his strength
Failed him at length,
He met a pilgrim shadow –
'Shadow,' said he,
'Where can it be –
This land of Eldorado?'

'Over the Mountains
Of the Moon,
Down the Valley of the Shadow,
Ride, boldly ride,'
The shade replied, –
'If you seek for Eldorado.'

FOR ANNIE

Thank Heaven! the crisis –
  The danger is past,
And the lingering illness
  Is over at last –
And the fever called 'Living'
  Is conquered at last.

Sadly, I know
  I am shorn of my strength,
And no muscle I move
  As I lie at full length –
But no matter! – I feel
  I am better at length.

And I rest so composedly
  Now, in my bed,
That any beholder
  Might fancy me dead –
Might start at beholding me,
  Thinking me dead.

The moaning and groaning,
  The sighing and sobbing,
Are quieted now,
  With that horrible throbbing
At heart: – ah that horrible,
  Horrible throbbing!

The sickness – the nausea –
  The pitiless pain –
Have ceased with the fever
  That maddened my brain –
With the fever called 'Living'
  That burned in my brain.

And oh! of all tortures
  That torture the worst
Has abated – the terrible
  Torture of thirst

For the napthaline river
  Of Passion accurst: –
I have drank of a water
  That quenches all thirst: –

Of a water that flows,
  With a lullaby sound,
From a spring but a very few
  Feet under ground –
From a cavern not very far
  Down under ground.

And ah! let it never
  Be foolishly said
That my room it is gloomy
  And narrow my bed;
For man never slept
  In a different bed –
And, to sleep, you must slumber
  In just such a bed.

My tantalized spirit
  Here blandly reposes,
Forgetting, or never
  Regretting, its roses –
Its old agitations
  Of myrtles and roses:

For now, while so quietly
  Lying, it fancies
A holier odour
  About it, of pansies –
A rosemary odour,
  Commingled with pansies –
With rue and the beautiful
  Puritan pansies

And so it lies happily,
  Bathing in many
A dream of the truth
  And the beauty of Annie –
Drowned in a bath
  Of the tresses of Annie.

She tenderly kissed me,
  She fondly caressed,
And then I fell gently
  To sleep on her breast –
Deeply to sleep
  From the heaven of her breast.

When the light was extinguished,
  She covered me warm,
And she prayed to the angels
  To keep me from harm –
To the queen of the angels
  To shield me from harm.

And I lie so composedly,
  Now, in my bed,
(Knowing her love)
  That you fancy me dead –
And I rest so contentedly,
  Now, in my bed,
(With her love at my breast)
  That you fancy me dead –
That you shudder to look at me,
  Thinking me dead: –

But my heart it is brighter
  Than all of the many
Stars of the sky,
  For it sparkles with Annie –
It glows with the light
  Of the love of my Annie –
With the thought of the light
  Of the eyes of my Annie.

TO MY MOTHER

Because I feel that, in the Heavens above,
  The angels, whispering to one another,
Can find, among their burning terms of love,
  None so devotional as that of 'Mother,'
Therefore by that dear name I long have called you –
  You who are more than mother unto me,
And fill my heart of hearts, where Death installed you,
  In setting my Virginia's spirit free.
My mother – my own mother, who died early,
  Was but the mother of myself; but you
Are mother to the one I loved so dearly,
  And thus are dearer than the mother I knew
By that infinity with which my wife
  Was dearer to my soul than its soul-life.

ANNABEL LEE

It was many and many a year ago,
    In a kingdom by the sea
That a maiden there lived whom you may know
    By the name of ANNABEL LEE;
And this maiden she lived with no other thought
    Than to love and be loved by me.

I was a child and *she* was a child,
    In this kingdom by the sea,
But we loved with a love that was more than love –
    I and my ANNABEL LEE –
With a love that the wingéd seraphs of heaven
    Coveted her and me.

And this was the reason that, long ago,
    In this kingdom by the sea,
A wind blew out of a cloud, chilling
    My beautiful ANNABEL LEE;
So that her highborn kinsmen came
    And bore her away from me,
To shut her up in a sepulchre
    In this kingdom by the sea.

The angels, not half so happy in heaven,
    Went envying her and me –
Yes! – that was the reason (as all men know,
    In this kingdom by the sea)
That the wind came out of the cloud by night,
    Chilling and killing my ANNABEL LEE.

But our love it was stronger by far than the love
    Of those who were older than we –
    Of many far wiser than we –
And neither the angels in heaven above,
    Nor the demons down under the sea,
Can ever dissever my soul from the soul
    Of the beautiful ANNABEL LEE:

For the moon never beams, without bringing me dreams
Of the beautiful ANNABEL LEE;
And the stars never rise, but I feel the bright eyes
Of the beautiful ANNABEL LEE;
And so, all the night-tide, I lie down by the side
Of my darling – my darling – my life and my bride,
In her sepulchre there by the sea –
In her tomb by the sounding sea.

SELECTED ESSAYS

LETTER TO MR — —

Dear B— West Point — 1831

. . . . .

Believing only a portion of my former volume to be worthy a second edition – that small portion I thought it as well to include in the present book as to republish by itself. I have, therefore, herein combined Al Aaraaf and Tamberlane with other Poems hitherto unprinted. Nor have I hesitated to insert from the 'Minor Poems,' now omitted, whole lines, and even passages, to the end that being placed in a fairer light, and the trash shaken from them in which they were imbedded, they may have some chance of being seen by posterity.

. . . . .

It has been said, that a good critique on a poem may be written by one who is no poet himself. This, according to *your* idea and *mine* of poetry, I feel to be false – the less poetical the critic, the less just the critique, and the converse. On this account, and because there are but few B—s in the world, I would be as much ashamed of the world's good opinion as proud of your own. Another than yourself might here observe 'Shakspeare is in possession of the world's good opinion, and yet Shakspeare is the greatest of poets. It appears then that the world judge correctly, why should you be ashamed of their favorable judgment?' The difficulty lies in the interpretation of the word 'judgment' or 'opinion.' The opinion is the world's, truly, but it may be called theirs as a man would call a book his, having bought it; he did not write the book, but it is his; they did not originate the opinion, but it is theirs. A fool, for example, thinks Shakspeare a great poet – yet the fool has never read Shakspeare. But the fool's neighbor, who is a step higher on the Andes of the mind, whose head (that is to say his more exalted thought) is too far above the fool to be seen or understood, but whose feet (by which I mean his every-day actions) are sufficiently near to be discerned, and by means of which that superiority is ascertained, which *but* for them would never have been discovered – this neighbor asserts that Shakspeare is a great poet – the fool believes him, and it is henceforward his *opinion*. This neighbor's own opinion has, in like manner, been adopted from one above *him*, and so, ascendingly, to a few gifted individuals, who kneel around the summit, beholding, face to face, the master spirit who stands upon the pinnacle.

. . . . .

You are aware of the great barrier in the path of an American writer. He is read, if at all, in preference to the combined and established wit of the world. I say established; for it is with literature as with law or empire – an established name is an estate in tenure, or a throne in possession. Besides, one might suppose that books, like their authors, improve by travel – their having crossed the sea is, with us, so great a distinction. Our antiquaries abandon time for distance; our very fops glance from the binding to the bottom of the title-page, where the mystic characters which spell London, Paris, or Genoa, are precisely so many letters of recommendation.

. . . . .

I mentioned just now a vulgar error as regards criticism. I think the notion that no poet can form a correct estimate of his own writings is another. I remarked before, that in proportion to the poetical talent, would be the justice of a critique upon poetry. Therefore, a bad poet would, I grant, make a false critique and his self-love would infallibly bias his little judgment in his favor; but a poet, who is indeed a poet, could not, I think, fail of making a just critique. Whatever should be deducted on the score of self-love, might be replaced on account of his intimate acquaintance with the subject; in short, we have more instances of false criticism than of just, where one's own writings are the test, simply because we have more bad poets than good. There are of course many objections to what I say: Milton is a great example of the contrary; but his opinion with respect to the Paradise Regained, is by no means fairly ascertained. By what trivial circumstances men are often led to assert what they do not really believe! Perhaps an inadvertent world has descended to posterity. But, in fact, the Paradise Regained is little, if at all, inferior to the Paradise Lost, and is only supposed so to be because men do not like epics, whatever they may say to the contrary, and reading those of Milton in their natural order, are too much wearied with the first to derive any pleasure from the second.

I dare say Milton preferred Comus to either – if so – justly.

As I am speaking of poetry, it will not be amiss to touch slightly upon the most singular heresy in its modern history – the heresy of what is called very foolishly, the Lake School. Some years ago I might have been induced, by an occasion like the present, to attempt a formal refutation of their doctrine; at present it would be a work of supererogation. The wise must bow to the wisdom of such men as Coleridge and Southey, but being wise, have laughed at poetical theories so prosaically exemplified.

Aristotle, with singular assurance, has declared poetry the most philosophical of all writing – but it required a Wordsworth to pronounce it the most metaphysical. He seems to think that the end of poetry is, or should be, instruction – yet it is a truism that the end of our existence is happiness; if so, the end of every separate part of our existence – every thing connected with our existence should be still happiness. Therefore the end of instruction should be happiness; and happiness is another name for pleasure; – therefore the end of instruction should be pleasure; yet we see the above mentioned opinion implies precisely the reverse.

To proceed: ceteris paribus, he who pleases, is of more importance to his fellow men than he who instructs, since utility is happiness, and pleasure is the end already obtained which instruction is merely the means of obtaining.

I see no reason, then, why our metaphysical poets should plume themselves so much on the utility of their works, unless indeed they refer to instruction with eternity in view; in which case, sincere respect for their piety would not allow me to express my contempt for their judgment; contempt which it would be difficult to conceal, since their writings are professedly to be understood by the few, and it is the many who stand in need of salvation. In such case I should no doubt be tempted to think of the evil in Melmoth, who labors indefatigably through three octavo volumes, to accomplish the destruction of one or two souls, while any common devil would have demolished one or two thousand.

. . . . .

Against the subtleties which would make poetry a study – not a passion – it becomes the metaphysician to reason – but the poet to protest. Yet Wordsworth and Coleridge are men in years; the one imbued in contemplation from his childhood, the other a giant in intellect and learning. The diffidence, then, with which I venture to dispute their authority would be overwhelming, did I not feel, from the bottom of my heart, that learning has little to do with the imagination – intellect with the passions – or age with poetry.

Trifles, like straws, upon the surface flow,
He who would search for pearls must dive below,

are lines which have done much mischief. As regards the greater truths, men oftener err by seeking them at the bottom than at the top; the depth lies in the huge abysses where wisdom is sought – not in the palpable palaces where she is found. The ancients were not always right in hiding the goddess in a well: witness the light which Bacon has thrown upon philosophy; witness the principles of our divine faith – that moral mechanism by which the simplicity of a child may overbalance the wisdom of a man.

Poetry, above all things, is a beautiful painting whose tints, to minute inspection, are confusion worse confounded, but start boldly out to the cursory glance of the connoisseur.

We see an instance of Coleridge's liability to err in his *Biographia Literaria* – professedly his literary life and opinions, but, in fact, a treatise *de omni scibili et quibusdam aliis*. He goes wrong by reason of his very profundity, and of his error we have a natural type in the contemplation of a star. He who regards it directly and intensely sees, it is true, the star, but it is the star without a ray – while he who surveys it less inquisitively is conscious of all for which the star is useful to us below – its brilliancy and its beauty.

. . . . .

As to Wordsworth, I have no faith in him: That he had, in youth, the feelings of a poet, I believe – for there are glimpses of extreme delicacy in his writings – (and delicacy is the poet's own kingdom – his *El Dorado*) – but they have the appearance of a better day recollected; and glimpses, at best, are little evidence of present poetic fire – we know that a few straggling flowers spring up daily in the crevices of the Avalanche.

He was to blame in wearing away his youth in contemplation with the end of poeticizing in his manhood. With the increase of his judgment the light which should make it apparent has faded away. His judgment consequently is too correct. This may not be understood, but the Old Goths of Germany would have understood it, who used to debate matters of importance to their State twice, once when drunk, and once when sober – sober that they might not be deficient in formality – drunk lest they should be destitute of vigor.

The long wordy discussions by which he tries to reason us into admiration of his poetry, speak very little in his favor: they are full of such assertions as this – (I have opened one of his volumes at random) 'Of genius the only proof is the act of doing well what is worthy to be done, and what was never done before' – indeed! then it follows that in doing what is *un*worthy to be done, or what *has* been done before, no genius can be evinced: yet the picking of pockets is an unworthy act, pockets have been picked time immemorial, and Barrington, the pick-pocket, in point of genius, would have thought hard of a comparison with William Wordsworth, the poet.

Again – in estimating the merit of certain poems, whether they be Ossian's or McPherson's, can surely be of little consequence, yet, in order to prove their worthlessness, Mr W. has expended many pages in the controversy. *Tantœne animis?* Can great minds descend to such absurdity? But worse still: that he may bear down every argument in favor of these poems, he triumphantly drags forward a passage in his abomination of which he expects the reader to sympathize. It is the beginning of the epic poem *'Temora.'* 'The blue waves of Ullin roll in light; the green hills are covered with day; trees shake their dusky heads in the breeze.' And this – this gorgeous, yet simple imagery – where all is alive and panting with immortality – than which earth has nothing more grand, nor paradise more beautiful – this – William Wordsworth, the author of Peter Bell, has *selected* to dignify with his imperial contempt. We shall see what better he, in his own person, has to offer. Imprimis:

And now she's at the pony's head,
And now she's at the pony's tail,
On that side now, and now on this,
And almost stifled her with bliss –
A few sad tears does Betty shed,
She pats the pony where or when
She knows not: happy Betty Foy!
O Johnny! never mind the Doctor!

Secondly:

The dew was falling fast, the – stars began to blink,
I heard a voice, it said – drink, pretty creature, drink;
And looking o'er the hedge, be – fore me I espied
A snow-white mountain lamb with a – maiden at its side.
No other sheep were near, the lamb was all alone.
And by a slender cord was – tether'd to a stone.

Now we have no doubt this is all true; we *will* believe it, indeed we will, Mr W. Is it sympathy for the sheep you wish to excite? I love a sheep from the bottom of my heart.

. . . . .

But there *are* occasions, dear B—, there are occasions when even Wordsworth is reasonable. Even Stamboul, it is said, shall have an end, and the most unlucky blunders must come to a conclusion. Here is an extract from his preface.

'Those who have been accustomed to the phraseology of modern writers, if they persist in reading this book to a conclusion (*impossible!*) will, no doubt, have to struggle with feelings of awkwardness; (ha! ha! ha!) they will look round for poetry (ha! ha! ha! ha!) and will be induced to inquire by what species of courtesy these attempts have been permitted to assume that title.' Ha! ha! ha! ha!

Yet let not Mr W. despair; he has given immortality to a wagon, and the bee Sophocles has eternalized a sore toe, and dignified a tragedy with a chorus of turkeys.

. . . . .

Of Coleridge I cannot speak but with reverence. His towering intellect! his gigantic power! To use an author quoted by himself, 'Jai trouve souvent que la plupart des sectes ont raison dans une bonne partie de ce quelles avancent, mais non pas en ce quelles nient,' and, to employ his own language, he has imprisoned his own conceptions by the barrier he has erected against those of others. It is lamentable to think that such a mind should be buried in metaphysics, and, like the Nyctanthes, waste its perfume upon the night alone. In reading that man's poetry I tremble, like one who stands upon a volcano, conscious, from the very darkness bursting from the crater, of the fire and the light that are weltering below.

. . . . .

What is Poetry? Poetry! that Proteus-like idea, with as many appellations as the nine-titled Corcyra! Give me, I demanded of a scholar some time ago, give me a definition of poetry? 'Tres volontiers,' – and he proceeded to his library, brought me a Dr Johnson, and overwhelmed me with a definition. Shade of the immortal Shakspeare! I imagined to myself the scowl of your spiritual eye upon the profanity of that scurrilous Ursa Major. Think of poetry, dear B—, think of poetry, and then think of – Dr Samuel

Johnson! Think of all that is airy and fairy-like, and then of all that is hideous and unwieldy; think of his huge bulk, the Elephant! and then – and then think of the Tempest – the Midsummer Night's Dream – Prospero – Oberon – and Titania!

. . . . .

A poem, in my opinion, is opposed to a work of science by having, for its *immediate* object, pleasure, not truth; to romance, by having for its object an *indefinite* instead of a *definite* pleasure, being a poem only so far as this object is attained: romance presenting perceptible images with definite, poetry with *in*definite sensations, to which end music is an *essential*, since the comprehension of sweet sound is our most indefinite conception. Music, when combined with a pleasurable idea, is poetry; music without the idea is simply music; the idea without the music is prose from its very definitiveness.

What was meant by the invective against him who had no music in his soul?

. . . . .

To sum up this long rigmarole, I have, dear B—, what you no doubt perceive, for the metaphysical poets, *as* poets, the most sovereign contempt. That they have followers proves nothing –

> No Indian prince has to his palace
> More followers than a thief to the gallows.

THE PHILOSOPHY OF COMPOSITION

Charles Dickens, in a note now lying before me, alluding to an examination I once made of the mechanism of *Barnaby Rudge*, says – 'By the way, are you aware that Godwin wrote his *Caleb Williams* backwards? He first involved his hero in a web of difficulties, forming the second volume and then, for the first, cast about him for some mode of accounting for what had been done.'

I cannot think this the *precise* mode of procedure on the part of Godwin – and indeed what he himself acknowledges, is not altogether in accordance with Mr Dickens' idea – but the author of *Caleb Williams* was too good an artist not to perceive the advantage derivable from at least a somewhat similar process. Nothing is more clear than that every plot, worth the name, must be elaborated to its *dénouement* before anything be attempted with the pen. It is only with the *dénouement* constantly in view that we can give a plot its indispensable air of consequence, or causation, by making the incidents, and especially the tone at all points, tend to the development of the intention.

There is a radical error, I think, in the usual mode of constructing a story. Either history affords a thesis – or one is suggested by an incident of the day – or, at best, the author sets himself to work in the combination of striking events to form merely the basis of his narrative – designing, generally, to fill in with description, dialogue, or autorial comment, whatever crevices of fact, or action, may, from page to page, render themselves apparent.

I prefer commencing with the consideration of an *effect*. Keeping originality *always* in view – for he is false to himself who ventures to dispense with so obvious and so easily attainable a source of interest – I say to myself, in the first place, 'Of the innumerable effects, or impressions, of which the heart, the intellect, or (more generally) the soul is susceptible, what one shall I, on the present occasion, select?' Having chosen a novel, first, and secondly a vivid effect, I consider whether it can be best wrought by incident or tone – whether by ordinary incidents and peculiar tone, or the converse, or by peculiarity both of incident and tone – afterward looking about me (or rather within) for such combinations of event, or tone, as shall best aid me in the construction of the effect.

I have often thought how interesting a magazine paper might be written by any author who would – that is to say, who could – detail, step by step, the processes by which any one of his compositions attained its ultimate point of completion. Why such a paper has never been given to the world, I am much at a loss to say – but, perhaps, the autorial vanity has had more to do with the omission than any one other cause. Most writers – poets in especial – prefer having it understood that they compose by a species of fine frenzy – an ecstatic intuition – and would positively shudder at letting the public take a peep behind the scenes, at the elaborate and vacillating crudities of thought – at the true purposes seized only at the last moment – at the innumerable glimpses of idea that arrived not at the maturity of full view – at the fully matured fancies discarded in despair as unmanageable – at the cautious selections and rejections – at the painful erasures and interpolations – in a word, at the wheels and pinions – the tackle for scene-shifting – the step-ladders and demon-traps – the cock's feathers, the red paint and the black patches, which, in ninety-nine cases out of the hundred, constitute the properties of the literary *histrio*.

I am aware, on the other hand, that the case is by no means common, in which an author is at all in condition to retrace the steps by which his conclusions have been attained. In general, suggestions, having arisen pell-mell, are pursued and forgotten in a similar manner.

For my own part, I have neither sympathy with the repugnance alluded to, nor, at any time, the least difficulty in recalling to mind the progressive steps of any of my compositions; and, since the interest of an analysis or reconstruction, such as I have considered a *desideratum*, is quite independent of any real or fancied interest in the thing analysed, it will not be regarded as a breach of decorum on my part to show the *modus operandi* by which some one of my own works was put together. I select *The Raven* as most generally known. It is my design to render it manifest that no one point in its composition is referable either to accident or intuition – that the work proceeded, step by step, to its completion with the precision and rigid consequence of a mathematical problem.

Let us dismiss, as irrelevant to the poem, *per se*, the circumstance – or say the necessity – which, in the first place, gave rise to the intention of composing *a* poem that should suit at once the popular and the critical taste.

We commence, then, with this intention.

The initial consideration was that of extent. If any literary work is too long to be read at one sitting, we must be content to dispense with the immensely important effect derivable from unity of impression – for, if two sittings be required, the affairs of the world interfere, and everything like totality is at once destroyed. But since, *ceteris paribus*, no poet can afford to dispense with *anything* that may advance his design, it but remains to be seen whether there is, in extent, any advantage to counterbalance the loss of unity which attends it. Here I say no, at once. What we term a long poem is, in fact, merely a succession of brief ones – that is to say, of brief poetical effects. It is needless to demonstrate that a poem is such, only inasmuch as it intensely excites, by elevating, the soul; and all intense excitements are, through a psychal necessity, brief. For this reason, at least one half of the *Paradise Lost* is essentially prose – a succession of poetical excitements interspersed, *inevitably*, with corresponding depressions – the whole being deprived, through the extremeness of its length, of the vastly important artistic element, totality, or unity, of effect.

It appears evident, then, that there is a distinct limit, as regards length, to all works of literary art – the limit of a single sitting – and that, although in certain classes of prose composition, such as *Robinson Crusoe*, (demanding no unity,) this limit may be advantageously overpassed, it can never properly be overpassed in a poem. Within this limit, the extent of a poem may be made to bear mathematical relation to its merit – in other words, to the excitement or elevation – again, in other words, to the degree of the true poetical effect which it is capable of inducing; for it is clear that the brevity must be in direct ratio of the intensity of the intended effect: – this, with one proviso – that a certain degree of duration is absolutely requisite for the production of any effect at all.

Holding in view these considerations, as well as that degree of excitement which I deemed not above the popular, while not below the critical, taste, I reached at once what I conceived the proper *length* for my intended poem – a length of about one hundred lines. It is, in fact, a hundred and eight.

My next thought concerned the choice of an impression, or effect, to be conveyed: and here I may as well observe that, throughout the construction, I kept steadily in view the design of rendering the work *universally* appreciable. I should be carried too far out of my immediate topic were I to demonstrate a point upon which I have repeatedly insisted, and which, with the poetical, stands not in the slightest need of demonstration – the point, I mean, that Beauty is the sole legitimate province of the poem. A few words, however, in elucidation of my real meaning, which some of my friends have evinced a disposition to misrepresent. That pleasure which is at once the most intense, the most elevating, and the most pure, is, I believe, found in the contemplation of the beautiful. When, indeed, men speak of Beauty, they mean, precisely, not a quality, as is supposed, but an effect – they refer, in short, just to that intense and pure elevation of *soul* – *not* of intellect, or of heart – upon which I have commented, and which is experienced in consequence of contemplating 'the beautiful.' Now I designate Beauty as the province of the poem, merely because it is an obvious rule of Art that effects should be made to spring from direct causes – that objects should be attained through means best adapted for their attainment – no one as yet having been weak enough to deny that the peculiar elevation alluded to, is *most readily* attained in the poem. Now the object Truth, or the satisfaction of the intellect, and the object Passion, or the excitement of the heart, are, although attainable, to a certain extent, in poetry, far more readily attainable in prose. Truth, in fact, demands a precision, and Passion a *homeliness* (the truly passionate will comprehend me) which are absolutely antagonistic to that Beauty which, I maintain, is the excitement, or pleasurable elevation, of the soul. It by no means follows from anything here said, that passion, or even truth, may not be introduced, and even profitably introduced, into a poem – for they may serve in elucidation, or aid the general effect, as do discords in music, by contrast – but the true artist will always contrive, first, to tone them into proper subservience to the predominant aim, and, secondly, to enveil them, as far as possible, in that Beauty which is the atmosphere and the essence of the poem.

Regarding, then, Beauty as my province, my next question referred to the *tone* of its highest manifestation – and all experience has shown that this tone is one of *sadness*. Beauty of whatever kind, in its supreme development, invariably excites the sensitive soul to tears. Melancholy is thus the most legitimate of all the poetical tones.

The length, the province, and the tone, being thus determined, I betook myself to ordinary induction, with the view of obtaining some artistic piquancy which might serve me as a key-note in the construction of the poem – some pivot upon which the whole structure might turn. In carefully thinking over all the usual artistic effects – or more properly *points*, in the theatrical sense – I did not fail to perceive immediately that no one had been so universally employed as that of the *refrain*. The universality of its employment sufficed to assure me of its intrinsic value, and spared me the necessity of submitting it to analysis. I considered it, however, with regard to its susceptibility of improvement, and soon saw it to be in a primitive condition. As commonly used, the *refrain*, or burden, not only is limited to lyric verse, but depends for its impression upon the force of monotone – both in sound and thought. The pleasure is deduced solely from the sense of identity – of repetition. I resolved to diversify, and so heighten, the effect, by adhering, in general, to the monotone of sound, while I continually varied that of thought: that is to say, I determined to produce continuously novel effects, by the variation *of the application* of the *refrain* – the *refrain* itself remaining, for the most part, unvaried.

These points being settled, I next bethought me of the *nature* of my *refrain*. Since its application was to be repeatedly varied, it was clear that the *refrain* itself must be brief, for there would have been an insurmountable difficulty in frequent variations of application in any sentence of length. In proportion of the brevity of the sentence, would, of course, be the facility of the variation. This led me at once to a single word as the best *refrain*.

The question now arose as to the *character* of the word. Having made up my mind to a *refrain*, the division of the poem into stanzas was, of course, a corollary: the *refrain* forming the close to each stanza. That such a close, to have force, must be sonorous and susceptible of protracted emphasis, admitted no doubt: and these considerations inevitably led me to the long *o* as the most sonorous vowel, in connection with *r* as the most producible consonant.

The sound of the *refrain* being thus determined, it became necessary to select a word embodying this sound, and at the same time in the fullest possible keeping with that melancholy which I had predetermined as the tone of the poem. In such a search it would have been absolutely impossible to overlook the word 'Nevermore.' In fact, it was the very first which presented itself.

The next *desideratum* was a pretext for the continuous use of the one word 'nevermore.' In observing the difficulty which I at once found in inventing a sufficiently plausible reason for its continuous repetition, I did not fail to perceive that this difficulty arose solely from the pre-assumption that the word was to be so continuously or monotonously spoken by *a human* being – I did not fail to perceive, in short, that the difficulty lay in the reconciliation of this monotony with the exercise of reason on the part of the creature repeating the word. Here, then, immediately arose the idea of a *non*-reasoning creature capable of speech; and, very naturally, a parrot, in the first instance, suggested itself, but was superseded forthwith by a Raven, as equally capable of speech, and infinitely more in keeping with the intended *tone*.

I had now gone so far as the conception of a Raven – the bird of ill omen – monotonously repeating the one word, 'Nevermore,' at the conclusion of each stanza, in a poem of melancholy tone, and in length about one hundred lines. Now, never losing sight of the object *supremeness*, or perfection, at all points, I asked myself – 'Of all melancholy topics, what, according to the *universal* understanding of mankind, is the *most* melancholy?' Death – was the obvious reply. 'And when,' I said, 'is this most melancholy of topics most poetical?' From what I have already explained at some length, the answer, here also, is obvious – 'When it most closely allies itself to *Beauty*: the death, then, of a beautiful woman is, unquestionably, the most poetical topic in the world – and equally is it beyond doubt that the lips best suited for such topic are those of a bereaved lover.'

I had now to combine the two ideas, of a lover lamenting his deceased mistress and a Raven continuously repeating the word 'Nevermore.' – I had to combine these, bearing in mind my design of varying, at every turn, the *application* of the word repeated; but the only intelligible mode of such combination is that of imagining the Raven employing the word in answer to the queries of the lover. And here it was that I saw at once the opportunity afforded for the effect on which I had been depending – that is to say, the effect of the *variation of application*. I saw that I could make the first query propounded by the lover – the first query to which the Raven should reply 'Nevermore' – that I could make this first query a commonplace one – the second less so – the third still less, and so on – until at length the lover, startled from his original *nonchalance* by the melancholy character of the word itself – by its frequent repetition – and by a consideration of the ominous reputation of the fowl that uttered it – is at length excited to superstition, and wildly propounds queries of a far different character – queries whose solution he has passionately at heart – propounds them half in superstition and half in that species of despair which delights in self-torture – propounds them not altogether because he believes in the prophetic or demoniac character of the bird (which, reason assures him, is merely repeating a lesson learned by rote) but because he experiences a frenzied pleasure in so modelling his questions as to receive from the *expected* 'Nevermore' the most delicious because the most intolerable of sorrow. Perceiving the opportunity thus afforded me – or, more strictly, thus forced upon me in the progress of the construction – I first established in mind the climax, or concluding query – that query to which 'Nevermore' should be in the last place an answer – that query in reply to which this word 'Nevermore' should involve the utmost conceivable amount of sorrow and despair.

Here then the poem may be said to have its beginning – at the end, where all works of art should begin – for it was here, at this point of my preconsiderations, that I first put pen to paper, in the composition of the stanza:

> 'Prophet,' said I, 'thing of evil! prophet still if bird or devil!
> By that heaven that bends above us – by that God we both adore,
> Tell this soul with sorrow laden, if within the distant Aidenn,
> I shall clasp a sainted maiden whom the angels name Lenore –
> Clasp a rare and radiant maiden whom the angels name Lenore.'
> Quoth the raven 'Nevermore.'

I composed this stanza, at this point, first that, by establishing the climax, I might the better vary and graduate, as regards seriousness and importance, the preceding queries of the lover – and, secondly, that I might definitely settle the rhythm, the metre, and the length and general arrangement of the stanza – as well as graduate the stanzas which were to precede, so that none of them might surpass this in rhythmical effect. Had I been able, in the subsequent composition, to construct more vigorous stanzas, I should, without scruple, have purposely enfeebled them, so as not to interfere with the climacteric effect.

And here I may as well say a few words of the versification. My first object (as usual) was originality. The extent to which this has been neglected, in versification, is one of the most unaccountable things in the world. Admitting that there is little possibility of variety in mere *rhythm*, it is still clear that the possible varieties of metre and stanza are absolutely infinite – and yet, *for centuries, no man, in verse, has ever done, or ever seemed to think of doing, an original thing*. The fact is, that originality (unless in minds of very unusual force) is by no means a matter, as some suppose, of impulse or intuition. In general, to be found, it must be elaborately sought, and although a positive merit of the highest class, demands in its attainment less of invention than negation.

Of course, I pretend to no originality in either the rhythm or metre of the *Raven*. The former is trochaic – the latter is octameter acatalectic, alternating with heptameter catalectic repeated in the *refrain* of the fifth verse, and terminating with tetrameter catalectic. Less pedantically – the feet employed throughout (trochees) consist of a long syllable followed by a short: the first line of the stanza consists of eight of these feet – the second of seven and a half (in effect two-thirds) – the third of eight – the fourth of seven and a half – the fifth the same – the sixth three and a half. Now, each of these lines, taken individually, has been employed before, and what originality the *Raven* has, is in their *combination into stanza*; nothing even remotely approaching this combination has ever been attempted. The effect of this originality of combination is aided by other unusual, and some altogether novel effects, arising from an extension of the application of the principles of rhyme and alliteration.

The next point to be considered was the mode of bringing together the lover and the Raven – and the first branch of this consideration was the *locale*. For this the most natural suggestion might seem to be a forest, or the fields – but it has always appeared to me that a close *circumscription of space* is absolutely necessary to the effect of insulated incident: – it has the force of a frame to a picture. It has an indisputable moral power in keeping concentrated the attention, and, of course, must not be confounded with mere unity of place.

I determined, then, to place the lover in his chamber – in a chamber rendered sacred to him by memories of her who had frequented it. The room is represented as richly furnished – this in mere pursuance of the ideas I have already explained on the subject of Beauty, as the sole true poetical thesis.

The *locale* being thus determined, I had now to introdue the bird – and the thought of introducing him through the window was inevitable. The idea of making the lover suppose, in the first instance, that the flapping of the wings of the bird against the shutter, is a 'tapping' at the door, originated in a wish to increase, by prolonging, the reader's curiosity, and in a desire to admit the incidental effect arising from the lover's throwing open the door, finding all dark, and thence adopting the half-fancy that it was the spirit of his mistress that knocked.

I made the night tempestuous, first, to account for the Raven's seeking admission, and secondly, for the effect of contrast with the (physical) serenity within the chamber.

I made the bird alight on the bust of Pallas, also for the effect of contrast between the marble and the plumage – it being understood that the bust was absolutely *suggested* by the bird – the bust of *Pallas* being chosen, first, as most in keeping with the scholarship of the lover, and, secondly, for the sonorousness of the word, Pallas, itself.

About the middle of the poem, also, I have availed myself of the force of contrast, with a view of deepening the ultimate impression. For example, an air of the fantastic – approaching as nearly to the ludicrous as was admissible – is given to the Raven's entrance. He comes in 'with many a flirt and flutter.'

Not the *least obeisance made he* – not a moment stopped or stayed he,
But with mien of lord or lady, perched above my chamber door.

In the two stanzas which follow, the design is more obviously carried out: –

Then this ebony bird beguiling my sad fancy into smiling
By the *grave and stern decorum of the countenance it wore*,'
'Though thy *crest be shorn and shaven* thou,' I said, 'art sure no craven
Ghastly grim and ancient Raven wandering from the nightly shore –
Tell me what thy lordly name is on the Night's Plutonian shore?'
Quoth the Raven 'Nevermore.'

Much I marvelled *this ungainly fowl* to hear discourse so plainly,
Though its answer little meaning – little relevancy bore;
For we cannot help agreeing that no living human being
Ever yet was blessed with seeing bird above his chamber door –
Bird or beast upon the sculptured bust above his chamber door,
With such name as 'Nevermore.'

The effect of the *dénouement* being thus provided for, I immediately drop the fantastic for a tone of the most profound seriousness: – this tone commencing in the stanza directly following the one last quoted, with the line,

But the Raven, sitting lonely on that placid bust spoke only, etc.

From this epoch the lover no longer jests – no longer sees anything even of the fantastic in the Raven's demeanour. He speaks of him as a 'grim, ungainly, ghastly, gaunt, and ominous bird of yore,' and feels the 'fiery eyes' burning into his 'bosom's core.' This revolution of thought, or fancy, on the lover's part, is intended to induce a similar one on the part of the reader – to bring the mind into a proper frame for the *dénouement* – which is now brought about as rapidly and as *directly* as possible.

With the *dénouement* proper – with the Raven's reply, 'Nevermore,' to the lover's final demand if he shall meet his mistress in another world – the poem, in its obvious phase, that of a simple narrative, may be said to have its completion. So far, everything is within the limits of the accountable – of the real. A raven, having learned by rote the single word 'Nevermore,' and having escaped from the custody of its owner, is driven at midnight, through the violence of a storm, to seek admission at a window from which a light still gleams – the chamber-window of a student, occupied half in poring over a volume, half in dreaming of a beloved mistress deceased. The casement being thrown open at the fluttering of the bird's wings, the bird itself perches on the most convenient seat out of the immediate reach of the student, who, amused by the incident and the oddity of the visitor's demeanour, demands of it, in jest and without looking for a reply, its name. The raven addressed, answers with its customary word, 'Nevermore' – a word which finds immediate echo in the melancholy heart of the student, who, giving utterance aloud to certain thoughts suggested by the occasion, is again startled by the fowl's repetition of 'Nevermore.' The student now guesses the state of the case, but is impelled as I have before explained, by the human thirst for self-torture, and in part by superstition, to propound such queries to the bird as will bring him, the lover, the most of the luxury of sorrow, through the anticipated answer 'Nevermore.' With the indulgence, to the extreme, of this self-torture, the narration, in what I have termed its first or obvious phase, has a natural termination, and so far there has been no overstepping of the limits of the real.

But in subjects so handled, however skilfully, or with however vivid an array of incident, there is always a certain hardness or nakedness, which repels the artistical eye. Two things are invariably required – first, some amount of complexity, or more properly, adaptation; and, secondly, some amount of suggestiveness – some under-current, however indefinite, of meaning. It is this latter, in especial, which imparts to a work of art so much of that *richness* (to borrow from colloquy a forcible term) which we are too fond of confounding with *the ideal*. It is the *excess* of the suggested meaning – it is the rendering this the upper instead of the under current of the theme – which turns into prose (and that of the very flattest kind) the so-called poetry of the so-called transcendentalists.

Holding these opinions, I added the two concluding stanzas of the poem – their suggestiveness being thus made to pervade all the narrative which has preceded them. The under-current of meaning is rendered first apparent in the lines –

'Take thy beak from out *my heart*, and take thy form from off my door!'
Quoth the Raven 'Nevermore!'

It will be observed that the words, 'from out my heart,' involve the first metaphorical expression in the poem. They, with the answer, 'Nevermore,' dispose the mind to seek a moral in all that has been previously narrated. The reader begins now to regard the Raven as emblematical – but it is not until the very last line of the very last stanza that the intention of making him emblematical of *Mournful and Never-ending Remembrance* is permitted distinctly to be seen:

And the Raven, never flitting, still is sitting, still is sitting,
On the pallid bust of Pallas just above my chamber door;
And his eyes have all the seeming of a demon's that is dreaming,
And the lamplight o'er him streaming throws his shadow on the floor;
And my soul *from out that shadow* that lies floating on the floor
Shall be lifted – nevermore.

THE RATIONALE OF VERSE

The word 'Verse' is here used not in its strict or primitive sense, but as the term most convenient for expressing generally and without pedantry all that is involved in the consideration of rhythm, rhyme, metre, and versification.

There is, perhaps, no topic in polite literature which has been more pertinaciously discussed, and there is certainly not one about which so much inaccuracy, confusion, misconception, misrepresentation, mystification, and downright ignorance on all sides, can be fairly said to exist. Were the topic really difficult, or did it lie, even, in the cloud-land of metaphysics, where the doubt-vapours may be made to assume any and every shape at the will or at the fancy of the gazer, we should have less reason to wonder at all this contradiction and perplexity; but in fact the subject is exceedingly simple; one-tenth of it, possibly, may be called ethical; nine-tenths, however, appertain to the mathematics; and the whole is included within the limits of the commonest common sense.

'But, if this is the case, how,' it will be asked, 'can so much misunderstanding have arisen? Is it conceivable that a thousand profound scholars, investigating so very simple a matter for centuries, have not been able to place it in the fullest light, at least, of which it is susceptible'? These queries I confess, are not easily answered: – at all events a satisfactory reply to them might cost more trouble than would, if properly considered, the whole *vexata quæstio* to which they have reference. Nevertheless, there is little difficulty or danger in suggesting that the 'thousand profound scholars' *may* have failed, first, because they were scholars, secondly, because they were profound, and thirdly, because they were a thousand – the impotency of the scholarship and profundity having been thus multiplied a thousand fold. I am serious in these suggestions; for, first again, there is something in 'scholarship' which seduces us into blind worship of Bacon's Idol of the Theatre – into irrational deference to antiquity; secondly, the proper 'profundity' is rarely profound – it is the nature of Truth in general, as of some ores in particular, to be richest when most superficial; thirdly, the clearest subject may be overclouded by mere superabundance of talk. In chemistry, the best way of separating two bodies is to add a third; in speculation, fact often agrees with fact and argument with argument, until an additional well-meaning fact or argument sets every thing by the ears. In one case out of a hundred a point is excessively discussed because it is obscure; in the ninety-nine remaining it is obscure because excessively discussed. When a topic is thus circumstanced, the readiest mode of investigating it is to forget that any previous investigation has been attempted.

But, in fact, while much has been written on the Greek and Latin rhythms, and even on the Hebrew, little effort has been made at examining that of any of the modern tongues. As regards the English, comparatively nothing has been done. It may be said, indeed, that we are without a treatise on our own verse. In our ordinary grammars and in our works on rhetoric or prosody in general, may be found occasional chapters, it is true, which have the heading, 'Versification,' but these are, in all instances, exceedingly meagre. They pretend to no analysis; they propose nothing like system; they make no attempt at even rule; everything depends upon 'authority.' They are confined, in fact, to mere exemplification of the supposed varieties of English feet and English lines; – although in no work with which I am acquainted are these feet correctly given or these lines detailed in anything like their full extent. Yet what has been mentioned is all – if we except the occasional introduction of some pedagogue-ism, such as this, borrowed from the Greek Prosodies: 'When a syllable is wanting, the verse is said to be catalectic; when the measure is exact, the line is acatalectic; when there is a redundant syllable it forms hypermeter.' Now whether a line be termed catalectic or acatalectic is, perhaps, a point of no vital importance; – it is even possible that the student may be able to decide promptly, when the *a* should be employed and when omitted, yet be incognizant, at the same time, of *all* that is worth knowing in regard to the structure of verse.

A leading defect in each of our treatises, (if treatises they can be called,) is the confining the subject to mere *Versification*, while *Verse* in general, with the understanding given to the term in the heading of this paper, is the real question at issue. Nor am I aware of even one of our Grammars which so much as properly defines the word versification itself. 'Versification,' says a work now before me, of which the accuracy is far more than usual – the *English Grammar* of Goold Brown – 'Versification is the art of arranging words into lines of correspondent length, so as to produce harmony by the regular alternation of syllables differing in quantity.' The commencement of this definition might apply, indeed, to the *art* of versification, but not versification itself. Versification is not the art of arranging, etc., but the actual arranging – a distinction too obvious to need comment. The error here is identical with one which has been too long permitted to disgrace the initial page of every one of our school grammars. I allude to the definitions of English Grammar itself. 'English Grammar,' it is said, 'is the art of speaking and writing the English language correctly.' This phraseology, or something essentially similar, is employed, I believe, by Bacon, Miller, Fisk, Greenleaf, Ingersoll, Kirkland, Cooper, Flint, Pue, Comly and many others. These gentlemen, it is presumed, adopted it without examination from Murray, who derived it from Lily, (whose work was '*quam solam Regia Majestas in omnibus scholis docendam præcipit*,') and who appropriated it without acknowledgment, but with some unimportant modification, from the Latin Grammar of Leonicenus. It may be shown, however, that this definition, so complacently received, is not, and cannot be, a proper definition of English Grammar. A definition is that which so describes its object as to distinguish it from all others: – it is no definition of any one thing if its terms are applicable to any one other. But if it be asked – 'What is the design – the end – the aim of English Grammar?' our obvious answer is, 'The art of speaking and writing the English language correctly: – that is to say, we must use the precise words employed as the definition of English Grammar itself. But the object to be obtained by any means is, assuredly, not the means. English Grammar and the end contemplated by English Grammar, are two matters sufficiently distinct; nor can the one be more reasonably regarded as the other than a fishing-hook as a fish. The definition, therefore, which is applicable in the latter instance, *cannot*, in the former, be true. Grammar in general is the analysis of language; English Grammar of the English.

But to return to Versification as defined in our extract above. 'It is the art,' says the extract, 'of arranging words into lines *of correspondent length*.' Not so: – a correspondence in the length of lines is by no means essential. Pindaric odes are, surely, instances of versification, yet these compositions are noted for extreme diversity in the length of their lines.

The arrangement is moreover said to be for the purpose of producing '*harmony* by the regular alternation,' etc. But *harmony* is not the sole aim – not even the principal one. In the construction of verse, *melody* should never be left out of view; yet this is a point which all our Prosodies have most unaccountably forborne to touch.

Reasoned rules on this topic should form a portion of all systems of rhythm.

'So as to produce harmony,' says the definition, '*by the regular alternation*,' etc. A *regular* alternation, as described, forms no part of any principle of versification. The arrangement of spondees and dactyls, for example, in the Greek hexameter, is an arrangement which may be termed *at random*. At least it is arbitrary. Without interference with the line as a whole, a dactyl may be substituted for a spondee, or the converse, at any point other than the ultimate and penultimate feet, of which the former is always a spondee, the latter nearly always a dactyl. Here, it is clear, we have no '*regular* alternation of syllables differing in quantity.'

'So as to produce harmony,' proceeds the definition, 'by the regular alternation of *syllables differing in quantity*,' – in other words by the alternation of long and short syllables; for in rhythm all syllables are necessarily either short or long. But not only do I deny the necessity of any *regularity* in the succession of feet and, by consequence, of syllables, but dispute the essentiality of any *alternation*, regular or irregular, of syllables long and short. Our author, observe, is now engaged in a definition of versification in general, not of English versification in particular. But the Greek and Latin metres abound in the spondee and pyrrhic – the former consisting of two long syllables; the latter of two short; and there are innumerable instances of the immediate succession of many spondees and many pyrrhics.

Here is a passage from Silius Italicus:

> Fallis te mensas inter quod credis inermem
> Tot bellis quæsitā viro, tot cædibus armat
> Majestas eterna ducem: si admoveris ora
> Cannas et Trebium ante oculos Trasymenaque busta,
> Et Pauli stare ingentem miraberis umbram.

Making the elisions demanded by the classic Prosodies, we should scan these Hexameters thus:

> Fāllīs | tē mēn | sās īn | tēr qūod | crēdĭs ĭn | ērmēm |
> Tōt bēl | līs qūæ | sītă vĭ | rō tōt | cædĭbŭs | ārmāt |
> Mājēs | tās ē | tērnă dŭ | cēm s'ād | mōvĕrĭs | ōrā |
> Cānnās | ēt Trĕbĭ' | ānt'ŏcŭ | lōs Trăsy | mēnăqŭe | būstā
> ēt Pāu | lī stā | r'ingēn | tēm mī | rābĕrĭs | ūmbrām |

It will be seen that, in the first and last of these lines, we have only two short syllables in thirteen, with an uninterrupted succession of no less than *nine* long syllables. But how are we to reconcile all this with a definition of versification which describes it as 'the art of arranging words into lines of correspondent length so as to produce harmony by the *regular alternation of syllables differing in quantity*?'

It may be urged, however, that our prosodist's *intention* was to speak of the English metres alone, and that, by omitting all mention of the spondee and pyrrhic, he has virtually avowed their exclusion from our rhythms. A grammarian is never excusable on the ground of good intentions. We demand from him, if from any one, rigorous precision of style. But grant the design. Let us admit that our author, following the example of all authors on English Prosody, has, in defining versification at large, intended a definition merely of the English. All these prosodists, we will say, reject the spondee and pyrrhic. Still all admit the iambus, which consists of a short syllable followed by a long; the trochee, which is the converse of the iambus; the dactyl, formed of one long syllable followed by two short; and the anapæst – two short succeeded by a long. The spondee is improperly rejected, as I shall presently show. The pyrrhic is rightfully dismissed. Its existence in either ancient or modern rhythm is purely chimerical, and the insisting on so perplexing a nonentity as a foot of *two short* syllables, affords, perhaps, the best evidence of the gross irrationality and subservience to authority which characterize our Prosody. In the meantime the acknowledged dactyl and anapæst are enough to sustain my proposition about the 'alternation,' etc., without reference to feet which are assumed to exist in the Greek and Latin metres alone: for an anapæst and a dactyl may meet in the same line; when of course we shall have an uninterrupted succession of four short syllables. The meeting of these two feet, to be sure, is an accident not contemplated in the definition now discussed; for this definition, in demanding a 'regular alternation of syllables differing in quantity,' insists on a regular succession of similar *feet*. But here is an example:

Sīng tŏ mĕ | Isăbēlle.

This is the opening line of a little ballad now before me, which proceeds in the same rhythm – a peculiarly beautiful one. More than all this: – English lines are often well composed, entirely, of a regular succession of syllables *all of the same quantity*: – the first lines, for instance, of the following quatrain by Arthur C. Coxe:

March! march! march!
  Making sounds as they tread,
Ho! ho! how they step,
  Going down to the dead!

The line italicized is formed of three cæsuras. The cæsura, of which I have much to say hereafter, is rejected by the English Prosodies and grossly misrepresented in the classic. It is a perfect foot – the most important in all verse – and consists of a single *long* syllable; *but the length of this syllable varies.*

It has thus been made evident that there is *not one* point of the definition in question which does not involve an error. And for anything more satisfactory or more intelligible we shall look in vain to any published treatise on the topic.

So general and so total a failure can be referred only to radical misconception. In fact the English Prosodists have blindly followed the pedants. These latter, like *les moutons de Panurge*, have been occupied in incessant tumbling into ditches, for the excellent reason that their leaders have so tumbled before. The Iliad, being taken as a starting point, was made to stand instead of Nature and common sense. Upon this poem, in place of facts and deduction from fact, or from natural law, were built systems of feet, metres, rhythms, rules, – rules that contradict each other every five minutes, and for nearly all of which there may be found twice as many exceptions as examples. If any one has a fancy to be thoroughly confounded – to see how far the infatuation of what is termed 'classical scholarship' can lead a bookworm in the manufacture of darkness out of sunshine, let him turn over, for a few moments, any of the German Greek Prosodies. The only thing clearly made out in them is a very magnificent contempt for Liebnitz's principle of 'a sufficient reason.'

To divert attention from the real matter in hand by any further reference to these works, is unnecessary, and would be weak. I cannot call to mind, at this moment, one essential particular of information that is to be gleaned from them; and I will drop them here with merely this one observation: that, employing from among the numerous '*ancient*' feet the spondee, the trochee, the iambus, the anapæst, the dactyl, and the cæsura alone, I will engage to scan *correctly* any of the Horatian rhythms, or any true rhythm that human ingenuity can conceive. And this excess of chimerical feet is, perhaps, the very least of the scholastic supererogations. *Ex uno disce omnia.* The fact is that *Quantity* is a point in whose investigation the lumber of mere learning may be dispensed with, if ever in any. Its appreciation is universal. It appertains to no region, nor race, nor æra in especial. To melody and to harmony the Greeks hearkened with ears precisely similar to those which we employ for similar purposes at present; and

I should not be condemned for heresy in asserting that a pendulum at Athens would have vibrated much after the same fashion as does a pendulum in the city of Penn.

Verse originates in the human enjoyment of equality, fitness. To this enjoyment, also, all the moods of verse – rhythm, metre, stanza, rhyme, alliteration, the *refrain*, and other analogous effects – are to be referred. As there are some readers who habitually confound rhythm and metre, it may be as well here to say that the former concerns the *character* of feet (that is, the arrangements of syllables) while the latter has to do with the *number* of these feet. Thus by 'a dactylic *rhythm*' we express a sequence of dactyls. By 'a dactylic hexa*meter*' we imply a line or measure consisting of six of these dactyls.

To return to *equality*. Its idea embraces those of similarity, proportion, identity, repetition, and adaptation or fitness. It might not be very difficult to go even behind the idea of equality, and show both how and why it is that the human nature takes pleasure in it, but such an investigation would, for any purpose now in view, be supererogatory. It is sufficient that the *fact* is undeniable – the fact that man derives enjoyment from his perception of equality. Let us examine a crystal. We are at once interested by the equality between the sides and between the angles of one of its faces: the equality of the sides pleases us; that of the angles doubles the pleasure. On bringing to view a second face in all respects similar to the first, this pleasure seems to be squared; on bringing to view a third it appears to be cubed, and so on. I have no doubt, indeed, that the delight experienced, if measurable, would be found to have exact mathematical relations such as I suggest; that is to say, as far as a certain point, beyond which there would be a decrease in similar relations.

The perception of pleasure in the equality of *sounds* is the principle of *Music*. Unpractised ears can appreciate only simple equalities, such as are found in ballad airs. While comparing one simple sound with another they are too much occupied to be capable of comparing the equality subsisting between these two simple sounds, taken conjointly, and two other similar simple sounds taken conjointly. Practised ears, on the other hand, appreciate both equalities at the same instant – although it is absurd to suppose that both are *heard* at the same instant. One is heard and appreciated from itself: the other is heard by the memory; and the instant glides into and is confounded with the secondary, appreciation. Highly cultivated musical taste in this manner enjoys not only these double equalities, all appreciated at once, but takes pleasurable cognizance, through memory, of equalities the members of which occur at intervals so great that the uncultivated taste loses them altogether. That this latter can properly estimate or decide on the merits of what is called scientific music, is of course impossible. But scientific music has no claim to intrinsic excellence – it is fit for scientific ears alone. In its excess it is the triumph of the *physique* over the *morale* of music. The sentiment is overwhelmed by the sense. On the whole, the advocates of the simpler melody and harmony have infinitely the best of the argument; although there has been very little of real argument on the subject.

In *verse*, which cannot be better designated than as inferior or less capable Music, there is, happily, little chance for complexity. Its rigidly simple character not even Science – not even Pedantry can greatly pervert.

The rudiment of verse may, possibly, be found in the *spondee*. The very germ of a thought seeking satisfaction in equality of sound, would result in the construction of words of two syllables, equally accented. In corroboration of this idea we find that spondees most abound in the most ancient tongues. The second step we can easily suppose to be the comparison, that is to say, the collocation, of two spondees – of two words composed each of a spondee. The third step would be the juxtaposition of three of these words. By this time the perception of monotone would induce further consideration: and thus arises what Leigh Hunt so flounders in discussing under the title of 'The *Principle* of Variety in Uniformity.' Of course there is no principle in the case – nor in maintaining it. The 'Uniformity' is the principle: – the 'Variety' is but the principle's natural safeguard from self-destruction by excess of self. 'Uniformity,' besides, is the very worst word that could have been chosen for the expression of the *general* idea at which it aims.

The perception of monotone having given rise to an attempt at its relief, the first thought in this new direction would be that of collating two or more words formed each of two syllables differently accented (that is to say, short and long) but having the same order in each word: – in other terms, of collating two or more iambuses, or two or more trochees. And here let me pause to assert that more pitiable nonsense has been written on the topic of *long* and *short* syllables than on any other subject under the sun. In general, a syllable is long or short, just as it is difficult or easy of enunciation. The *natural* long syllables are those encumbered – the *natural* short syllables are those *un*encumbered, with consonants; all the rest is mere artificiality and jargon. The Latin Prosodies have a rule that 'a vowel before two consonants is long.' This rule is deduced from 'authority' – that is, from the observation that vowels so circumstanced, in the ancient poems, are always in syllables long by the laws of scansion. The philosophy of the rule is untouched, and lies simply in the physical difficulty of giving voice to such syllables – of performing the lingual evolutions necessary for their utterance. Of course, it is not the *vowel* that is long, (although the rule says so) but the syllable of which the vowel is a part. It will be seen that the length of a syllable, depending on the facility or difficulty of its enunciation, must have great variation in various syllables; but for the purposes of verse we suppose a long syllable equal to two short ones: – and the natural deviation from this relativeness we correct in perusal. The more closely our long syllables approach this relation with our short ones, the better, *ceteris paribus*, will be our verse; but if the relation does not exist of itself, we force it by emphasis, which can, of course, make any syllable as long as desired; – or, by an effort we can pronounce with unnatural brevity a syllable that is naturally too long. *Accented* syllables are of course always long – but, where *un*encumbered with consonants, must be classed among the *unnaturally* long. Mere custom has declared that we shall accent them – that is to say, dwell upon them; but no inevitable lingual difficulty forces us to do so. In fine, every long syllable must of its own accord occupy in its utterance, or must be *made* to occupy, precisely the time demanded for two short ones. The only exception to this rule is found in the cæsura – of which more anon.

The success of the experiment with the trochees or iambuses (the one would have suggested the other) must have led to a trial of dactyls or anapæsts – natural dactyls or anapæsts – dactylic or anapæstic *words*. And now some degree of complexity has been attained. There is an appreciation, first, of the equality between the several dactyls, or anapæsts, and, secondly, of that between the long syllable and the two short conjointly. But here it may be said, that step after step would have been taken, in continuation of this routine, until all the feet of the Greek Prosodies became exhausted. Not so: – these remaining feet have no existence except in the brains of the scholiasts. It is needless to imagine men inventing these things, and folly to explain how and why they invented them, until it shall first show that they are actually invented. All other 'feet' than those which I have specified, are, if not impossible at first view, merely combinations of the specified; and, although this assertion is rigidly true, I will, to avoid misunderstanding, put it in a somewhat different shape. I will say, then, that at present I am aware of no *rhythm* – nor do I believe that any one can be constructed – which, in its last analysis, will not be found to consist altogether of the feet I have mentioned, either existing in their individual and obvious condition, or interwoven with each other in accordance with simple natural laws which I will endeavour to point out hereafter.

We have now gone so far as to suppose men constructing indefinite sequences of spondaic, iambic, trochaic, dactylic, or anapæstic words. In *extending* these sequences, they would be again arrested by the sense of monotone. A succession of spondees would *immediately* have displeased; one of iambuses or of trochees, on account of the variety included within the foot itself, would have taken longer to displease; one of dactyls or anapæsts, still longer; but even the last, if extended very far, must have become wearisome. The idea, first, of curtailing, and secondly, of defining the length of, a sequence, would thus at once have arisen. Here then is the *line*, or verse proper.[1] The principle of equality being constantly at the bottom of the whole process, lines would naturally be made, in the first instance, equal in the number of their feet; in the second instance, there would be variation in the mere number; one line would be twice as long as another; then one would be some less obvious multiple of another; then still less obvious proportions would be adopted: – nevertheless there would be *proportion*, that is to say, a phase of equality, still.

Lines being once introduced, the necessity of distinctly defining these lines *to the ear*, (as yet written verse does not exist,) would lead to a scrutiny of their capabilities *at their terminations*: – and now would spring up the idea of equality in sound between the final syllables – in other words, of *rhyme*. First, it would be used only in the iambic, anapæstic, and spondaic rhythms, (granting that the latter had not been thrown aside, long since, on account of its tameness;) because in these rhythms, the concluding syllable being long, could best sustain the necessary protraction of the voice. No great while could elapse, however, before the effect, found pleasant

[1] Verse, from the Latin *vertere*, to turn, is so called on account of the turning or re-commencement of the series of feet. Thus a verse, strictly speaking, is a line. In this sense, however, I have preferred using the latter word alone; employing the former in the general acceptation given it in the heading of this paper.

as well as useful, would be applied to the two remaining rhythms. But as the chief force of rhyme must lie in the accented syllable, the attempt to create rhyme at all in these two remaining rhythms, the trochaic and dactylic, would necessarily result in double and triple rhymes, such as *beauty* with *duty* (trochaic,) and *beautiful* with *dutiful* (dactylic).

It must be observed, that in suggesting these processes, I assign them no date; nor do I even insist upon their order. Rhyme is supposed to be of modern origin, and were this proved, my positions remain untouched. I may say, however, in passing, that several instances of rhyme occur in the *Clouds* of Aristophanes, and that the Roman poets occasionally employ it. There is an effective species of ancient rhyming which has never descended to the moderns: that in which the ultimate and penultimate syllables rhyme with each other. For example:

Parturiunt montes et nascitur ridicu*lus mus*.

And again:

Litoreis ingens inventa sub ilici*bus sus*.

The terminations of Hebrew verse, (as far as understood,) show no signs of rhyme; but what thinking person can doubt that it did actually exist? That men have so obstinately and blindly insisted, *in general*, even up to the present day, in confining rhyme to the *ends* of lines, when its effect is even better applicable elsewhere, intimates, in my opinion, the sense of some *necessity* in the connexion of the end with the rhyme – hints that the origin of rhyme lay in a necessity which connected it with the end – shows that neither mere accident nor mere fancy gave rise to the connexion – points, in a word, at the very necessity which I have suggested, (that of some mode of defining lines *to the ear*,) as the true origin of rhyme. Admit this, and we throw the origin far back in the night of Time – beyond the origin of written verse.

But, to resume. The amount of complexity I have now supposed to be attained is very considerable. Various systems of equalization are appreciated at once (or nearly so) in their respective values and in the value of each system with reference to all the others. As our present *ultimatum* of complexity, we have arrived at triple-rhymed, natural-dactylic lines, existing proportionally as well as equally with regard to other triple-rhymed, natural-dactylic lines. For example:

> Virginal Lilian, rigidly, humblily dutiful;
> Saintlily, lowlily,
> Thrillingly, holily
> Beautiful!

Here we appreciate, first, the absolute equality between the long syllable of each dactyl and the two short conjointly; secondly, the absolute equality between each dactyl and any other dactyl – in other words, among all the dactyls; thirdly, the absolute equality between the two middle lines; fourthly, the absolute equality between the first line and the three others taken conjointly; fifthly, the absolute equality between the last two syllables of the respective words 'dutiful' and 'beautiful'; sixthly, the absolute equality between the two last syllables of the respective words 'lowlily' and 'holily'; seventhly, the proximate equality between the first syllable of 'dutiful' and the first syllable of 'beautiful'; eighthly, the proximate equality between the first syllable of 'lowlily' and that of 'holily'; ninthly, the proportional equality (that of five to one,) between the first line and each of its members, the dactyls; tenthly, the proportional equality (that of two to one,) between each of the middle lines and its members, the dactyls; eleventhly, the proportional equality between the first line and each of the two middle – that of five to two; twelfthly, the proportional equality between the first line and the last – that of five to one; thirteenthly, the proportional equality between each of the middle lines and the last – that of two to one; lastly, the proportional equality, as concerns number, between all the lines, taken collectively and any individual line – that of four to one.

The consideration of this last equality would give birth immediately to the idea of *stanza*[1] – that is to say, the insulation of lines into equal or obviously proportional masses. In its primitive (which was also its best) form, the stanza would most probably have had absolute unity. In other words, the removal of any one of its lines would have rendered it imperfect; as in the case above, where, if the last line, for example, be taken away, there is left no rhyme to the 'dutiful' of the first. Modern stanza is excessively loose – and where so, ineffective, as a matter of course.

[1] A stanza is often vulgarly, and with gross impropriety called a *verse*.

Now, although in the deliberate written statement which I have here given of these various systems of equalities, there seems to be an affinity of complexity – so much that it is hard to conceive the mind taking cognizance of them all in the brief period occupied by the perusal or recital of the stanza – yet the difficulty is in fact apparent only when we will it to become so. Anyone fond of mental experiment may satisfy himself, by trial, that, in listening to the lines, he does actually (although with a seeming unconsciousness, on account of the rapid evolutions of sensation,) recognize and instantaneously appreciate (more or less intensely as his ear is cultivated,) each and all of the equalizations detailed. The pleasure received, or receivable, has very much such progressive increase, and in very nearly such mathematical relations, as those which I have suggested in the case of the crystal.

It will be observed that I speak of merely a proximate equality between the first syllable of 'dutiful' and that of 'beautiful'; and it may be asked why we cannot imagine the earliest rhymes to have had absolute instead of proximate equality of sound. But absolute equality would have involved the use of identical words; and it is the duplicate sameness or monotony – that of sense as well as that of sound – which would have caused these rhymes to be rejected in the very first instance.

The narrowness of the limits within which verse composed of natural feet alone, must necessarily have been confined, would have led, after a *very* brief interval, to the trial and immediate adoption of artificial feet – that is to say, of feet *not* constituted each of a single word, but two or even three words; or of parts of words. These feet would be intermingled with natural ones. For example:

ă brēath | căn māke | thĕm ās | ă breāth | hăs māde.

This is an iambic line in which each iambus is formed of two words. Again:

Thĕ ūn | ĭmā | gĭnā | blĕ mīght | ŏf Jōve.

This is an iambic line in which the first foot is formed of a word and a part of a word; the second and third, of parts taken from the body or interior of a word; the fourth, of a part and a whole; the fifth, of two complete words. There are no *natural* feet in either line. Again:

Cān ĭt bĕ | fānciĕd thăt | Dēĭty | ēvĕr vĭn | dīctĭvely
Māde ĭn hĭs | īmăge ă | mānnĭkĭn | mĕrely tŏ | māddĕn ĭt?

These are two dactylic lines in which we find natural feet, ('Deity,' 'mannikin';) feet composed of two words ('fancied that,' 'image a,' 'merely to,' 'madden it';) feet composed of three words ('can it be,' 'made in his';) a foot composed of a part of a word ('dictively';) and a foot composed of a word and a part of a word ('ever vin').

And now, in our supposititious progress, we have gone so far as to exhaust all the *essentialities* of verse. What follows may, strictly speaking, be regarded as embellishment merely – but even in this embellishment, the rudimental sense of *equality* would have been the never-ceasing impulse. It would, for example, be simply in seeking further administration to this sense that men would come, in time, to think of the *refrain*, or burden, where, at the closes of the several stanzas of a poem, one word or phrase is *repeated*; and of alliteration, in whose simplest form a consonant is *repeated* in the commencements of various words. This effect would be extended so as to embrace repetitions both of vowels and of consonants, in the bodies as well as in the beginnings of words; and, at a later period, would be made to infringe on the province of rhyme, by the introduction of general similarity of sound between whole feet occurring in the body of a line: – all of which modifications I have exemplified in the line above,

Made in his i*m*age a *mannikin m*erely to *madden it*.

Further cultivation would improve also the *refrain* by relieving its monotone in slightly varying the phrase at each repetition, or, (as I have attempted to do in *The Raven*,) in retaining the phrase and varying its application – although this latter point is not strictly a rhythmical effect *alone*. Finally, poets when fairly wearied with following precedent – following it the more closely the less they perceived it in company with Reason – would adventure so far as to indulge in positive rhyme at other points than the ends of lines. First, they would put it in the middle of the line; then at some point where the multiple would be less obvious; then, alarmed at their own audacity, they would undo all their work by cutting these lines in two. And here is the fruitful source of the infinity of 'short metre,' by which modern poetry, if not distinguished, is at least disgraced. It would require a high degree, indeed, both of cultivation and of courage, on the part of any versifier, to enable him to place his rhymes – and let them remain – at unquestionably their best position, that of unusual and *unanticipated* intervals.

On account of the stupidity of some people, or, (if talent be a more respectable word,) on account of their talent for misconception – I think it necessary to add here, first, that I believe the 'processes' above detailed to be nearly if not accurately those which *did* occur in the gradual creation of what we now call verse; secondly, that, although I so believe, I yet urge neither the assumed fact nor my belief in it, as a part of the true propositions of this paper; thirdly, that in regard to the aim of this paper, it is of no consequence whether these processes did occur either in the order I have assigned them, or at all; my design being simply, in presenting a general type of what such processes *might* have been and *must* have resembled, to help *them*, the 'some people,' to an easy understanding of what I have further to say on the topic of Verse.

There is one point which, in my summary of the processes, I have purposely forborne to touch; because this point, being the most important of all, on account of the immensity of error usually involved in its consideration, would have led me into a series of detail inconsistent with the object of a summary.

Every reader of verse must have observed how seldom it happens that even any one line proceeds uniformly with a succession, such as I have supposed, of absolutely equal feet; that is to say, with a succession of iambuses only, or of trochees only, or of dactyls only, or of anapæsts only, or of spondees only. Even in the most musical lines we find the succession interrupted. The iambic pentameters of Pope, for example, will be found, on examination, frequently varied by trochees in the beginning, or by (what seem to be) anapæsts in the body, of the line.

> ŏh thōu | whătē | vĕr tī | tlĕ | plēase | thĭne eār |
> Dĕan Drā | piĕr Bīck | ĕrstāff | ŏr Gūl | ĭvēr |
> Whēthĕr | thŏu choōse | Cĕrvān | tĕs' sē | rĭoŭs āir |
> ŏr laūgh | ănd shāke | ĭn Rāb | ĕlaĭs' eā | sy chaīr. |

Were any one weak enough to refer to the Prosodies for the solution of the difficulty here, he would find it *solved* as usual by a *rule*, stating the fact, (or what it, the rule, supposes to be the fact,) but without the slightest attempt at the *rationale*. 'By a *synæresis* of the two short syllables,' say the books, 'an anapæst may sometimes be employed for an iambus, or a dactyl for a trochee . . . In the beginning of a line a trochee is often used for an iambus.'

Blending is the plain English for *synæresis* – but there should be *no* blending; neither is an anapæst *ever* employed for an iambus, or a dactyl for a trochee. These feet differ in time; and *no* feet so differing can ever be legitimately used in the same line. An anapæst is equal to four short syllables – an iambus only to three. Dactyls and trochees hold the same relation. The principle of *equality*, in verse, admits, it is true, of variation at certain points, for the relief of monotone, as I have already shown, but the point of *time* is that point which, being the rudimental one, must never be tampered with at all.

To explain: – In further efforts for the relief of monotone than those to which I have alluded in the summary, men soon came to see that there was no absolute necessity for adhering to the precise number of syllables, provided the time required for the whole foot was preserved inviolate. They saw, for instance, that in such a line as

ŏr lāugh | ănd shāke | ĭn Rāb | ĕlaĭs' ēa | sy chāir,

the equalization of the three syllables *elais ea* with the two syllables composing any of the other feet, could be readily effected by pronouncing the two syllables *elais* in double quick time. By pronouncing each of the syllables *e* and *lais* twice as rapidly as the syllable *sy*, or the syllable *in*, or any other short syllable, they could bring the two of them, taken together, to the length, that is to say to the time, of any one short syllable. This consideration enabled them to effect the agreeable variation of three syllables in place of the uniform two. And variation was the object – variation to the ear. What sense is there, then, in supposing this object rendered null by the *blending* of the two syllables so as to render them, in absolute effect, one? Of course, there must be *no* blending. Each syllable must be pronounced as distinctly as possible, (or the variation is lost,) but with twice the rapidity in which the ordinary short syllable is enunciated. That the syllables *elais ea* do not compose an *anapæst* is evident, and the signs (˘˘‐) of their accentuation are erroneous. The foot might be written thus (⌢⌢‐) the inverted crescents expressing double quick time; and might be called a bastard iambus.

Here is a trochaic line:

Sēe thĕ dēlĭcăte | fōotĕd | rēin-deĕr. |

The prosodies – that is to say the most considerate of them – would here decide that '*delicate*' is a dactyl used in place of a trochee, and would refer to what they call their 'rule,' for justification. Others, varying the stupidity, would insist upon a Procrustean adjustment thus (del'cate) – an adjustment recommended to all such words as *silvery*, *murmuring*, etc., which, it is said, should be not only pronounced, but written *silv'ry*, *murm'ring*, and so on, whenever they find themselves in trochaic predicament. I have only to say that 'delicate,' when circumstanced as above, is neither a dactyl nor a dactyl's equivalent; that I would suggest for it this (ᵕ̭ᵕ̭ᵕ̱) accentuation; that I think it as well to call it a bastard trochee; and that all words, at all events, should be written and pronounced *in full*, and as nearly as possible as nature intended them.

About eleven years ago, there appeared in *The American Monthly Magazine*, (then edited, I believe, by Mess. Hoffman and Benjamin,) a review of Mr Willis' Poems; the critic putting forth his strength, or his weakness, in an endeavour to show that the poet was either absurdly affected, or grossly ignorant of the laws of verse; the accusation being based altogether on the fact that Mr W. made occasional use of this very word 'delicate,' and other similar words, in 'the Heroic measure which every one knew consisted of feet of two syllables.' Mr W. has often, for example, such lines as

> That binds him to a woman's *delicate* love –
> In the gay sunshine, *reverent* in the storm –
> With its *invisible* fingers my loose hair.

Here, of course, the feet *licate love*, *verent in*, and *sible fin*, are bastard iambuses; are *not* anapæsts; and are *not* improperly used. Their employment, on the contrary, by Mr Willis, is but one of the innumerable instances he has given of keen sensibility in all those matters of taste which may be classed under the general head of *fanciful embellishment*.

It is also about eleven years ago, if I am not mistaken, since Mr Horne, (of England,) the author of *Orion*, one of the noblest epics in any language, thought it necessary to preface his *Chaucer Modernized* by a very long and evidently a very elaborate essay, of which the greater portion was occupied in a discussion of the seemingly anomalous foot of which we have been speaking. Mr Horne upholds Chaucer in its frequent use; maintains his superiority, *on account* of his so frequently using it, over all English versifiers; and, indignantly repelling the common idea of those who make verse on their fingers – that the superfluous syllable is a roughness and an error – very chivalrously makes battle for it as 'a grace.' That a grace it *is*, there can be no doubt; and what I complain of is, that the author of the most happily versified long poem in existence, should have been under the necessity of discussing this grace merely *as* a grace, through forty or fifty vague pages, solely because of his inability to show *how* and *why* it is a grace – by which showing the question would have been settled in an instant.

About the trochee used for an iambus, as we see in the beginning of the line,

Whēthĕr thou choose Cervantes' serious air,

there is little that need be said. It brings me to the general proposition that, in all rhythms, the prevalent or distinctive feet may be varied at will, and nearly at random, by the *occasional* introduction of equivalent feet – that is to say, feet the sum of whose syllabic times is equal to the sum of the syllabic times of the distinctive feet. Thus the trochee, *whēthĕr*, is equal, in the sum of the times of its syllables, to the iambus, *thŏu choōse*, in the sum of the times of *its* syllables; each foot being, in time, equal to three short syllables. Good versifiers who happen to be, also, good poets, contrive to relieve the monotone of a series of feet, by the use of equivalent feet only at rare intervals, and at such points of their subject as seem in accordance with the *startling* character of the variation. Nothing of this care is seen in the line quoted above – although Pope has some fine instances of the duplicate effect. Where vehemence is to be strongly expressed, I am not sure that we should be wrong in venturing on *two consecutive* equivalent feet – although I cannot say that I have ever known the adventure made, except in the following passage, which occurs in *Al Aaraaf*, a boyish poem, written by myself when a boy. I am referring to the sudden and rapid advent of a star.

Dim was its little disk, and angel eyes
Alone could see the phantom in the skies,
Whĕn first thĕ phāntŏm's cōursĕ wăs fōund tŏ bē
*Hēadlŏng hīthĕr*ward o'er the starry sea.

In the 'general proposition' above, I speak of the *occasional* introduction of equivalent feet. It sometimes happens that unskilful versifiers, without knowing what they do, or why they do it, introduce so many 'variations' as to exceed in number the 'distinctive' feet; when the ear becomes at once balked by the *bouleversement* of the rhythm. Too many trochees, for example, inserted in an iambic rhythm, would convert the latter to a trochaic. I may note here, that, in all cases, the rhythm designed should be commenced and continued, *without* variation, until the ear has had full time to comprehend what *is* the rhythm. In violation of a rule so obviously founded in common sense, many even of our best poets do not scruple to begin an iambic rhythm with a trochee, or the converse; or a dactylic with an anapæst, or the converse; and so on.

A somewhat less objectionable error, although still a decided one, is that of commencing a rhythm, not with a different equivalent foot, but with a 'bastard' foot of the rhythm intended. For example:

Māny ă | thoūght wĭll | cōme tŏ | mēmŏry.

Here *many a* is what I have explained to be a bastard trochee, and to be understood should be accented with inverted crescents. It is objectionable solely on account of its position as the *opening* foot of a trochaic rhythm. *Memory*, similarly accented, is also a bastard trochee, but *un*objectionable, although by no means demanded.

The further illustration of this point will enable me to take an important step.

One of our finest poets, Mr Christopher Pease Cranch, begins a very beautiful poem thus:

> Many are the thoughts that come to me
>   In my lonely musing;
> And they drift so strange and swift
>   There's no time for choosing
> Which to follow; for to leave
>   Any, seems a losing.

'A losing' to Mr Cranch, of course – but this *en passant*. It will be seen here that the intention is trochaic; – although we do *not* see this intention by the opening foot, as we should do – or even by the opening line. Reading the whole stanza, however, we perceive the trochaic rhythm as the general design, and so, after some reflection, we divide the first line thus:

Many are the | thōughts thăt | cōme tŏ | mē. |

Thus scanned, the line will seem musical. It *is* highly so. And it is because there is no end to instances of just such lines of apparently incomprehensible music, that Coleridge thought proper to invent his nonsensical *system* of what he calls 'scanning by accents' – as if 'scanning by accents' were anything more than a phrase. Whenever *Christabel* is really *not rough*, it can be as readily scanned by the true *laws* (not the supposititious *rules*) of verse, as can the simplest pentameter of Pope; and where it *is* rough (*passim*) these same laws will enable any one of common sense to show *why* it is rough and to point out, instantaneously, the remedy for the roughness.

A reads and re-reads a certain line, and pronounces it false in rhythm – unmusical. *B*, however, reads it to *A*, and *A* is at once struck with the perfection of the rhythm, and wonders at his dullness in not 'catching' it before. Henceforward he admits the line to be musical. *B*, triumphant, asserts that, to be sure, the line is musical – for it is the work of Coleridge – and that it is *A* who is *not*; the fault being in *A*'s false reading. Now here *A* is right and *B* wrong. *That* rhythm is erroneous, (at some point or other more or less obvious,) which *any* ordinary reader *can*, without design, read improperly. It is the business of the poet so to construct his line that the intention *must* be caught *at once*. Even when these men have precisely the same understanding of a sentence, they differ, and often widely, in their modes of enunciating it. Anyone who has taken the trouble to examine the topic of emphasis, (by which I here mean not *accent* of particular syllables, but the dwelling on entire words,) must have seen that men emphasize in the most singularly arbitrary manner. There are certain large classes of people, for example, who persist in emphasizing their monosyllables. Little uniformity of emphasis prevails; because the thing itself – the idea, emphasis – is referable to no natural – at least, to no well comprehended and therefore uniform law. Beyond a very narrow and vague limit, the whole matter is conventionality. And if we differ in emphasis even when we agree in comprehension, how much more so in the former when in the latter too! Apart, however, from the consideration of natural disagreement, is it not clear that, by tripping here and mouthing there, any sequence of words may be twisted into any species of rhythm? But are we thence to deduce that all sequences of words are rhythmical in a rational understanding of the term? – for this is the deduction, precisely to which the *reductio ad absurdum* will, in the end, bring all the propositions of Coleridge. Out of a hundred readers of *Christabel*, fifty will be able to make nothing of its rhythm, while forty-nine of the remaining fifty will, with some ado, fancy they comprehend it, after the fourth or fifth perusal. The one out of the whole hundred who shall both comprehend and admire it at first sight – must be an unaccountably clever person – and I am by far too modest to assume, for a moment, that that very clever person is myself.

In illustration of what is here advanced I cannot do better than quote a poem:

> Pease porridge hot – pease porridge cold –
> Pease porridge in the pot – nine days old.

Now those of my readers who have never *heard* this poem pronounced according to the nursery conventionality, will find its rhythm as obscure as an explanatory note; while those who *have* heard it, will divide it thus, declare it musical, and wonder how there can be any doubt about it.

Pease | porridge | hot | pease | porridge | cold |
Pease | porridge | in the | pot | nine | days | old. |

The chief thing in the way of this species of rhythm, is the necessity which it imposes upon the poet of travelling in constant company with his compositions, so as to be ready at a moment's notice to avail himself of a well understood poetical licence – that of reading aloud one's own doggerel.

In Mr Cranch's line,

Many are the | thoughts that | come to | me, |

the general error of which I speak is, of course, very partially exemplified, and the purpose for which, chiefly, I cite it, lies yet further on in our topic.

The two divisions (*thoughts that*) and (*come to*) are ordinary trochees. Of the last division (*me*) we will talk hereafter. The first division (many are the) would be thus accented by the Greek Prosodies (māny ăre thĕ) and would be called by them αστρολογος. The Latin books would style the foot *Pæon Primus*, and both Greek and Latin would swear that it was composed of a trochee and what they term a pyrrhic – that is to say, a foot of two *short* syllables – a thing that *cannot be*, as I shall presently show.

But now, there is an obvious difficulty. The *astrologos*, according to the Prosodies' own showing, is equal to *five* short syllables, and the trochee to *three* – yet, in the line quoted, these two feet are equal. They occupy *precisely* the same time. In fact, the whole music of the line depends upon their being *made* to occupy the same time. The Prosodies, then, have demonstrated what all mathematicians have stupidly failed in demonstrating – that three and five are one and the same thing.

After what I have already said, however, about the bastard trochee and the bastard iambus, no one can have any trouble in understanding that *many are the* is of similar character. It is merely a bolder variation than usual from the routine of trochees, and introduces to the bastard trochee one additional syllable. But this syllable is not *short*. That is, it is not short in the sense of '*short*' as applied to the final syllable of the ordinary trochee, where the word means merely *the half of long.*

In this case, (that of the additional syllable) 'short,' if used at all, must be used in the sense of *the sixth of long.* And all the three final syllables can be called *short* only with the same understanding of the term. The three together are equal only to the one short syllable (whose place they supply) of the ordinary trochee. It follows that there is no sense in thus (˘) accenting these syllables. We must devise for them some new character which shall denote the sixth of long. Let it be (☾) – the crescent placed with the curve to the left. The whole foot (māny are thĕ) might be called a *quick trochee.*

We come now to the final division (*me*) of Mr Cranch's line. It is clear that this foot, short as it appears, is fully equal in time to each of the preceding. It is in fact the cæsura – the foot which, in the beginning of this paper, I called the most important in all verse. Its chief office is that of pause or termination; and here – at the end of a line – its use is easy, because there is no danger of misapprehending its value. We pause on it, by a seeming necessity, just so long as it has taken us to pronounce the preceding feet, whether iambusses, trochees, dactyls, or anapæsts. It is thus a *variable foot*, and, with some care, may be well introduced into the body of a line, as in a little poem of great beauty by Mrs Welby:

I have | a lit | tle step | s͠on | of on |ly three | years old. |

Here we dwell on the cæsura, *son*, just as long as it requires us to pronounce either of the preceding or succeeding iambusses. Its value, therefore, in this line, is that of three short syllables. In the following dactylic line its value is that of four short syllables.

Pale as a | lily was | Emily | G͠ray.

I have accented the cæsura with a (͠) by way of expressing this variability of value.

I observed, just now, that there could be no such foot as one of two short syllables. What we start from in the very beginning of all idea on the topic of verse, is quantity, *length.* Thus when we enunciate an independent syllable it is long, as a matter of course. If we enunciate two, dwelling on both equally, we express equality in the enumeration, or length, and have a right to call them two long syllables. If we dwell on one more than the other, we have also a right to call one short, because it is short in relation to the other. But if we dwell on both equally and with a tripping voice, saying to ourselves here are two short syllables, the query might well be asked of us – 'in relation to what are they short?' Shortness is but the negation of length. To say, then, that two syllables, placed independently of any other syllable, are short, is merely to say that they have no positive length, or enunciation – in other words that they are no syllables – that they do not exist at all. And if, persisting, we add anything about their equality, we are merely floundering in the idea of an identical equation, where x being equal to x, nothing is shown to be equal to zero. In a word, we can form no conception of a pyrrhic as of an independent foot. It is a mere chimera bred in the mad fancy of a pedant.

From what I have said about the equalization of the several feet of a *line*, it must not be deduced that any *necessity* for equality in time exists between the rhythm of *several* lines. A poem, or even a stanza, may begin with iambusses, in the first line, and proceed with anapæsts in the second, or even with the less accordant dactyls, as in the opening of quite a pretty specimen of verse by Miss Mary A. S. Aldrich:

The wa | ter li | ly sleeps | in pride | ‿‿‿

Dōwn ĭn thĕ | dēpths ŏf thĕ | āzūre | lake. |

Here *azure* is a spondee, equivalent to a dactyl; *lake* a cæsura.

I shall now best proceed in quoting the initial lines of Byron's *Bride of Abydos*:

Know ye the land where the cypress and myrtle
  Are emblems of deeds that are done in their clime –
Where the rage of the vulture, the love of the turtle
  Now melt into softness, now madden to crime?
Know ye the land of the cedar and vine,
Where the flowers ever blossom, the beams ever shine,
And the light wings of Zephyr, oppressed with perfume,
Wax faint o'er the gardens of Gul in their bloom?
Where the citron and olive are fairest of fruit
And the voice of the nightingale never is mute –
Where the virgins are soft as the roses they twine,
And all save the spirit of man is divine?
'Tis the land of the East – 'tis the clime of the Sun –
Can he smile on such deeds as his children have done?
Oh, wild as the accents of lovers' farewell
Are the hearts that they bear and the tales that they tell.

Now the flow of these lines, (as times go,) is very sweet and musical. They have been often admired and justly – as times go – that is to say, it is a rare thing to find better versification of its kind. And where verse is pleasant to the ear, it is silly to find fault with it because it refuses to be scanned. Yet I have heard men, professing to be scholars, who made no scruple that they were musical in spite of *all law*. Other gentlemen, *not* scholars, abused 'all law' for the same reason: – and it occurred neither to the one party nor to the other that the law about which they were disputing might possibly be no law at all – an ass of a law in the skin of a lion.

The Grammars said something about dactylic lines, and it was easily seen that *these* lines were at least meant for dactylic. The first one was, therefore, thus divided:

Knōw yĕ thĕ | lānd whĕre thĕ | cyprĕss ănd | myrtlĕ. |

The concluding foot was a mystery; but the Prosodies said something about the dactylic 'measure' calling now and then for a double rhyme; and the court of inquiry were content to rest in the double rhyme, without exactly perceiving what a double rhyme had to do with the question of an irregular foot. Quitting the first line, the second was thus scanned:

Arē ĕmblĕms | ōf deēds thăt | āre dŏne ĭn | thēir clīme. |

It was immediately seen, however, that *this* would not do: – it was at war with the whole emphasis of the reading. It could not be supposed that Byron, or anyone in his senses, intended to place stress upon such monosyllables as 'are,' 'of,' and 'their,' nor could 'their clime,' collated with 'to crime,' in the corresponding line below, be fairly twisted into anything like a 'double rhyme,' so as to bring everything within the category of the Grammars. But further these Grammars spoke not. The inquirers, therefore, in spite of their sense of harmony in the lines, when considered without reference to scansion, fell back upon the idea that the 'Are' was a blunder – an excess for which the poet should be sent to Coventry – and, striking it out, they scanned the remainder of the line as follows:

– ēmblĕms ŏf | deēds thăt ăre | dōne ĭn thĕir | clīme. |

This answered pretty well; but the Grammars admitted no such foot as a foot of one syllable; and besides the rhythm was dactylic. In despair, the books are well searched, however, and at last the investigators are gratified by a full solution of the riddle in the profound 'Observation' quoted in the beginning of this article: – 'When a syllable is wanting, the verse is said to be catalectic; when the measure is exact, the line is acatalectic; when there is a redundant syllable it forms hypermeter.' This is enough. The anomalous line is pronounced to be catalectic at the head and to form hypermeter at the tail: – and so on, and so on; it being soon discovered that nearly all the remaining lines are in a similar predicament, and that what flows so smoothly to the ear, although so roughly to the eye, is, after all, a mere jumble of catalecticism, acatalecticism, and hypermeter – not to say worse.

Now, had this court of inquiry been in possession of even the shadow of the *philosophy* of Verse, they would have had no trouble in reconciling this oil and water of the eye and ear, by merely scanning the passage without reference to lines, and, continuously, thus:

> Know ye the | land where the | cypress and | myrtle Are | emblems of | deeds that are | done in their | clime Where the | rage of the | vulture the | love of the | turtle Now | melt into | softness now | madden to | *crime* | Know ye the | land of the | cedar and | vine Where the | flowers ever | blossom the | beams ever | shine Where the | light wings of | Zephyr op | pressed by per | *fume Wax* | faint o'er the | gardens of | Gul in their | bloom Where the | citron and | olive are | fairest of | fruit And the | voice of the | nightingale | never is | mute Where the | virgins are | soft as the | roses they | *twine And* | all save the | spirit of | man is di | vine 'Tis the | land of the | East 'tis the | clime of the | Sun Can he | smile on such | deeds as his | children have | *done Oh* | wild as the | accents of | lovers' fare | well Are the | hearts that they | bear and the | tales that they | *tell.*

Here 'crime' and 'tell' (italicized) are cæsuras, each having the value of a dactyl, four short syllables; while 'fume Wax,' 'twine and,' and 'done Oh,' are spondees which, of course, being composed of two long syllables, are also equal to four short, and are the dactyl's natural equivalent. The nicety of Byron's ear has led him into a succession of feet which, with two trivial exceptions as regards melody, are absolutely accurate – a very rare occurrence this in dactylic or anapæstic rhythms. The exceptions are found in the spondee '*twine And*,' and the dactyl, '*smile on such*.' Both feet are false in point of melody. In '*twine And*,' to make out the rhythm, we must force '*And*' into a length which it will not naturally bear. We are called on to sacrifice either the proper length of the syllable as demanded by its position as a member of a spondee, or the customary accentuation of the word in conversation. There is no hesitation, and should be none. We at once give up the sound for the sense; and the rhythm is imperfect. In this instance it is *very* slightly so; – not one person in ten thousand could, by ear, detect the inaccuracy. But the *perfection* of verse, as regards melody, consists in its *never* demanding any such sacrifice as is here demanded. The rhythmical must agree, *thoroughly*, with the reading, flow. This perfection has in no instance been attained – but is unquestionably attainable. '*Smile on such*,' the dactyl, is incorrect, because '*such*,' from the character of the two consonants *ch*, cannot *easily* be enunciated in the ordinary time of a short syllable, which its position declares that it is. Almost every reader will be able to appreciate the slight difficulty here; and yet the error is by no means so important as that of the '*And*' in the spondee. By dexterity we *may* pronounce '*such*' in the true time; but the attempt to remedy the rhythmical deficiency of the *And* by drawing it out, merely aggravates the offence against natural enunciation, by directing attention to the offence.

My main object, however, in quoting these lines, is to show that, in spite of the Prosodies, the length of a line is entirely an arbitrary matter. We might divide the commencement of Byron's poem thus:

Know ye the | land where the. |

or thus:

Know ye the | land where the | cypress and. |

or thus:

Know ye the | land where the | cypress and | myrtle are. |

or thus:

Know ye the | land where the | cypress and | myrtle are |
emblems of. |

In short, we may give it any division we please, and the lines will be good – provided we have at least *two* feet in a line. As in mathematics two units are required to form number, so rhythm, (from the Greek αριθμος, number,) demands for its formation at least two feet. Beyond doubt, we often see such lines as

Know ye the –
Land where the –

lines of one foot; and our Prosodies admit such; but with impropriety; for common sense would dictate that every so obvious division of a poem as is made by a line, should include within itself all that is necessary for its own comprehension; but in a line of one foot we can have no appreciation of rhythm, which depends upon the equality between *two* or more pulsations. The false lines, consisting sometimes of a single cæsura, which are seen in mock Pindaric odes, are of course 'rhythmical' only in connection with some other line; and it is this want of independent rhythm which adapts them to the purposes of burlesque alone. Their effect is that of incongruity (the principle of mirth;) for they include the blankness of prose amid the harmony of verse.

My second object in quoting Byron's lines, was that of showing how absurd it often is to cite a single line from amid the body of a poem, for the purpose of instancing the perfection or imperfection of the line's rhythm. Were we to see by itself

Know ye the land where the cypress and myrtle,

we might justly condemn it as defective in the final foot, which is equal to only three, instead of being equal to four, short syllables.

In the foot (*flowers ever*) we shall find a further exemplification of the principle of the bastard iambus, bastard trochee, and quick trochee, as I have been at some pains in describing these feet above. All the Prosodies on English verse would insist upon making an elision in 'flowers,' thus (flow'rs,) but this is nonsense. In the quick trochee (māny ăre thĕ) occurring in Mr Cranch's *trochaic* line; we had to equalize the time of the three syllables (*ny*, *are*, *the*,) to that of the one *short* syllable whose position they usurp. Accordingly each of these syllables is equal to the third of a short syllable, that is to say, the *sixth of a long*. But in Byron's *dactylic* rhythm, we have to equalize the time of the three syllables (*ers*, *ev*, *er*), to that of the one *long* syllable whose position they usurp, or, (which is the same thing,) of the *two short*. Therefore the value of each of the syllables (*ers*, *ev*, and *er*) is the *third of a long*. We enunciate them with only half the rapidity we employ in enunciating the three final syllables of the quick trochee – which latter is a rare foot. The '*flowers ever*,' on the contrary, is as common in the dactylic rhythm as is the *bastard* trochee in the trochaic, or the bastard iambus in the iambic. We may as well accent it with the curve of the crescent to the right, and call it a *bastard dactyl*. A *bastard anapæst*, whose nature I now need be at no trouble in explaining, will of course occur, now and then, in an anapæstic rhythm.

In order to avoid any chance of that confusion which is apt to be introduced in an essay of this kind by too sudden and radical an alteration of the conventionalities to which the reader has been accustomed, I have thought it right to suggest for the accent marks of the bastard trochee, bastard iambus, etc., etc., certain characters which, in merely varying the direction of the ordinary short accent (˘) should imply, what is the fact, that the feet themselves are not *new* feet, in any proper sense, but simply modifications of the feet, respectively, from which they derive their names. Thus a bastard iambus is, in its essentiality, that is to say, in its time, an iambus. The variation lies only in the *distribution* of this time. The time, for example, occupied by the one short (or *half of long*) syllable, in the ordinary iambus, is, in the bastard, spread equally over two syllables, which are accordingly the *fourth of long*.

But this fact – the fact of the essentiality, or whole time, of the foot being unchanged, is now so fully before the reader, that I may venture to propose, finally, an accentuation which shall answer the real purpose – that is to say, what should be the real purpose of all accentuation – the purpose of expressing to the eye the exact relative value of every syllable employed in Verse.

I have already shown that enunciation, or *length*, is the point from which we start. In other words, we begin with a *long syllable*. This then is our unit; and there will be no need of accenting it at all. An unaccented syllable, in a system of accentuation, is to be regarded always as a long syllable. Thus a spondee would be without accent. In an iambus, the first syllable being 'short,' or the *half* of long, should be accented with a small 2, placed *beneath* the syllable; the last syllable, being long, should be unaccented; – the whole would be thus ($\underset{2}{\text{con}}\text{trol}$). In a trochee, these accents would be merely conversed, thus ($\text{man}\underset{2}{\text{ly}}$.) In a dactyl, each of the two final syllables, being the half of long, should, also, be accented with a small 2 beneath the syllable; and, the first syllable left unaccented, the whole would be thus ($\text{hap}\underset{2}{\text{pi}}\underset{2}{\text{ness}}$.) In an anapæst we should converse the dactyl thus, ($\underset{2}{\text{in}}\ \underset{2}{\text{the}}\ \text{land}$.) In the bastard dactyl, each of the three concluding syllables being the *third* of long, should be accented with a small 3 beneath the syllable and the whole foot would stand thus, ($\text{flow}\underset{3}{\text{ers}}\ \underset{3}{\text{ev}}\underset{3}{\text{er}}$.) In the bastard anapæst we should converse the bastard dactyl thus, (in the rebound.) In the bastard iambus, each of the two initial syllables, being the fourth of long, should be accented, below, with a small 4; the whole foot would be thus, (in the rain). In the bastard trochee, we should converse the bastard iambus thus, (many a). In the quick trochee, each of the three concluding syllables, being the *sixth* of long, should be accented, below, with a small 6; the whole foot would be thus, (many are the). The quick iambus is not yet created, and most probably never will be, for it will be excessively useless, awkward, and liable to misconception – as I have already shown that even the quick trochee is: – but, should it appear, we must accent it by conversing the quick trochee. The cæsura, being variable in length, but always *longer than 'long,'* should be accented, *above*, with a number expressing the length, or value, of the distinctive foot of the rhythm in which it occurs. Thus a cæsura, occurring in a spondaic rhythm, would be accented with a small 2 above the syllable, or, rather, foot. Occurring in a dactylic or anapæstic rhythm, we also accent it with the 2, above the foot. Occurring in an iambic rhythm, however, it must be accented, above, with 1½; for this is the relative value of the iambus. Occurring in the trochaic rhythm, we give it, of course, the same accentuation. For the complex 1½, however, it would be advisable to substitute the simpler expression 3/2 which amounts to the same thing.

In this system of accentuation Mr Cranch's lines, quoted above, would thus be written:

Many are the | thoughts that | come to | me
In my | lonely | musing, |
And they | drift so | strange and | swift
There's no | time for | choosing |
Which to | follow | for to | leave
Any, | seems a | losing. |

In the ordinary system the accentuation would be thus:

Māny arĕ thĕ | thōughts thăt | cōme tŏ | mē |
In my | lōnely | mŭsĭng, |
ānd thĕy | drīft sŏ | strānge ănd | swīft |
Therē's nŏ | timē fŏr | choōsĭng |
Whīch tŏ | fōllŏw, | fōr tŏ | lēave
āny, | seēms ă | lōsĭng. |

It must be observed, here, that I do not grant this to be the 'ordinary' *scansion*. On the contrary, I never yet met the man who had the faintest comprehension of the true scanning of these lines, or of such as these. But granting this to be the mode in which our Prosodies would divide the feet, they would accentuate the syllables as just above.

Now, let any reasonable person compare the two modes. The first advantage seen in my mode is that of simplicity – of time, labour, and ink saved. Counting the fractions as *two* accents, even, there will be found only *twenty-six* accents to the stanza. In the common accentuation there are *forty-one*. But admit that all this is a trifle, which it is *not*, and let us proceed to points of importance. Does the common accentuation express the truth, in particular, in general, or in any regard? Is it consistent with itself? Does it convey either to the ignorant or to the scholar a just conception of the rhythm of the lines? Each of these questions must be answered in the negative. The crescents, being precisely similar, must be understood as expressing, all of them, one and the same thing: and so all Prosodies have always understood them and wished them to be understood. They express, indeed, 'short' – but this word has all kinds of meanings. It serves to represent (the reader is left to guess *when*) sometimes the half, sometimes the third, sometimes the fourth, sometimes the sixth, of 'long' – while 'long' itself, in the books, is left undefined and undescribed. On the other hand, the horizontal accent, it may be said, expresses sufficiently well, and unvaryingly, the syllables which are meant to be long. It does nothing of the kind. This horizontal accent is placed over the cæsura (wherever, as in the Latin Prosodies, the cæsura is recognized) as well as over the ordinary long syllable, and implies anything and everything, just as the crescent. But grant that it does express the ordinary long syllables, (leaving the cæsura out of question,) have I not given the identical expression, by not employing any expression at all? In a word, while the Prosodies, with a certain number of accents, express *precisely nothing whatever*, I, with scarcely half the number, have expressed everything which, in a system of accentuation, demands expression. In glancing at my mode in the lines of Mr Cranch, it will be seen that it conveys not only the exact relation of the syllables and feet, among themselves, in those particular lines, but their precise value in relation to any other existing or conceivable feet or syllables, in any existing or conceivable system of rhythm.

The object of what we call *scansion* is the distinct marking of the rhythmical flow. Scansion with accents or perpendicular lines between the feet – that is to say scansion *by* the voice only – is scansion *to* the ear only; and all very good in its way. The written scansion addresses the ear through the eye. In either case the object is the distinct marking of the rhythmical, musical, or reading flow. There *can* be no other object and there is none. Of course, then, the scansion and the reading flow should go hand in hand. The former must agree with the latter. The former represents and expresses the latter; and is good or bad as it truly or falsely represents and expresses it. If by the written scansion of a line we are not enabled to perceive any rhythm or music in the line, then either the line is unrhythmical or the scansion false. Apply all this to the English lines which we have quoted, at various points, in the course of this article. It will be found that the scansion exactly conveys the rhythm, and thus thoroughly fulfils the only purpose for which scansion is required.

But let the scansion *of the schools* be applied to the Greek and Latin verse, and what result do we find? – that the verse is one thing and the scansion quite another. The ancient verse, *read* aloud, is in general musical, and occasionally *very* musical. *Scanned* by the Prosodial rules we can, for the most part, make nothing of it whatever. In the case of the English verse, the more emphatically we dwell on the divisions between the feet, the more distinct is our perception of the kind of rhythm intended. In the case of the Greek and Latin, the more we dwell the *less* distinct is this perception. To make this clear by an example:

Mæcenas, atavis edite regibus,
O, et præsidium et dulce decus meum,
Sunt quos curriculo pulverem Olympicum
Collegisse juvat, metaque fervidis
Evitata rotis, palmaque nobilis
Terrarum dominos evehit ad Deos.

Now in *reading* these lines, there is scarcely one person in a thousand who, if even ignorant of Latin, will not immediately feel and appreciate their flow – their music. A prosodist, however, informs the public that the *scansion* runs thus:

Mæce | nas ata | vis | edite | regibus |
O, et | præsidi' | et | dulce de | cus meum |
Sunt quos | curricu | lo | pulver' O | lympicum |
Colle | gisse ju | vat | metaque | fervidis |
Evi | tata ro | tis | palmaque | nobilis |
Terra | rum domi | nos | evehit | ad Deos. |

Now I do not deny that we get a *certain sort* of music from the lines if we read them according to this scansion, but I wish to call attention to the fact that this scansion and the certain sort of music which grows out of it, are entirely at war not only with the reading flow which any ordinary person would naturally give the lines, but with the reading flow universally given them, and never denied them, by even the most obstinate and stolid of scholars.

And now these questions are forced upon us – 'Why exists this discrepancy between the modern verse with its scansion, and the ancient verse with its scansion?' – 'Why, in the former case, are there agreement and representation, while in the latter there is neither the one nor the other?' or, to come to the point, – 'How are we to reconcile the ancient verse with the scholastic scansion of it?' This absolutely necessary conciliation – shall we bring it about by supposing the scholastic scansion wrong because the ancient verse is right, or by maintaining that the ancient verse is wrong because the scholastic scansion is not to be gainsaid?

Were we to adopt the latter mode of arranging the difficulty, we might, in some measure, at least simplify the expression of the arrangement by putting it thus – Because the pedants have no eyes, therefore the old poets had no ears.

'But,' say the gentlemen without the eyes, 'the scholastic scansion, although certainly not handed down to us in form from the old poets themselves (the gentlemen without the ears,) is nevertheless deduced from certain facts which are supplied us by careful observation of the old poems.'

And let us illustrate this strong position by an example from an American poet – who must be a poet of some eminence, or he will not answer the purpose. Let us take Mr Alfred B. Street. I remember these two lines of his:

> His sinuous path, by blazes, wound
> Among trunks grouped in myriads round.

With the *sense* of these lines I have nothing to do. When a poet is in a 'fine frenzy,' he may as well imagine a large forest as a small one – and 'by blazes!' is *not* intended for an oath. My concern is with the rhythm, which is iambic.

Now let us suppose that, a thousand years hence, when the 'American language' is dead, a learned prosodist should be deducing from 'careful observation' of our best poets, a system of scansion for our poetry. And let us suppose that this prosodist had so little dependence in the generality and immutability of the laws of Nature, as to assume in the outset, that, because we lived a thousand years before his time, and made use of steam-engines instead of mesmeric balloons, we must therefore have had a *very* singular fashion of mouthing our vowels, and altogether of hudsonizing our verse. And let us suppose that with these and other fundamental propositions carefully put away in his brain, he should arrive at the line, –

Among | trunks grouped | in my | riads round.

Finding it an obviously iambic rhythm, he would divide it as above; and observing that 'trunks' made the first member of an iambus, he would call it short, as Mr Street intended it to be. Now further: – if instead of admitting the possibility that Mr Street, (who by that time would be called Street simply, just as we say Homer,) – that Mr Street might have been in the habit of writing carelessly, as the poets of the prosodist's own era did, and as all poets will do (on account of being geniuses,) – instead of admitting this, suppose the learned scholar should make a 'rule' and put it in a book, to the effect that, in the American verse, the vowel *u*, *when found imbedded among nine consonants*, was *short*: what, under such circumstances, would the sensible people of the scholar's day have a right not only to think, but to say of that scholar? – why, that he was 'a fool – by blazes!'

I have put an extreme case, but it strikes at the root of the error. The 'rules' are grounded in 'authority'; and this 'authority' – can anyone tell us what it means? or can anyone suggest anything that it may *not* mean? Is it not clear that the 'scholar' above referred to, might as readily have deduced from authority a totally false system as a partially true one? To deduce from authority a consistent prosody of the ancient metres would indeed have been within the limits of the barest possibility; and the task has *not* been accomplished, for the reason that it demands a species of ratiocination altogether out of keeping with the brain of a bookworm. A rigid scrutiny will show that the very few 'rules' which have not as many exceptions as examples, are those which have, by accident, their true bases not in authority, but in the omniprevalent laws of syllabification; such, for example, as the rule which declares a vowel before two consonants to be long.

In a word, the gross confusion and antagonism of the scholastic prosody, as well as its marked inapplicability to the reading flow of the rhythms it pretends to illustrate, are attributable, first, to the utter absence of natural principle as a guide in the investigations which have been undertaken by inadequate men; and secondly, to the neglect of the obvious consideration that the ancient poems, which have been the *criteria* throughout, were the work of men who must have written as loosely, and with as little definitive system, as ourselves.

Were Horace alive to-day, he would divide for us his first Ode thus, and 'make great eyes' when assured by the prosodists that he had no business to make any such division!

> Mæcenas | atavis | edite | regibus |
> 2 2 2 2 2 2 2 2
>
> O et præ | sidium et | dulce de | cus meum |
> 2 2 3 3 3 2 2 2 2
>
> Sunt quos cur | riculo | pulverem O | lympicum |
> 2 2 2 2 3 3 3 2 2
>
> Collegisse | juvat | metaque | fervidis |
> 3 3 3 2 2 2 2
>
> Evitata | rotis | palmaque | nobilis |
> 3 3 3 2 2 2 2
>
> Terrarum | dominos | evehit | ad Deos. |
> 2 2 2 2 2 2 2 2

Read by this scansion, the flow is preserved; and the more we dwell on the divisions, the more the intended rhythm becomes apparent. Moreover, the feet have all the same time; while, in the scholastic scansion, trochees – admitted trochees – are absurdly employed as equivalents to spondees and dactyls. The books declare, for instance, that *Colle*, which begins the fourth line, is a trochee, and seem to be gloriously unconscious that to put a trochee in opposition with a longer foot is to violate the inviolable principle of all music, *time*.

It will be said, however, by 'some people,' that I have no business to make a dactyl out of such obviously long syllables as *sunt*, *quos*, *cur*. Certainly I have no business to do so. I *never* do so. And Horace should not have done so. But he did. Mr Bryant and Mr Longfellow do the same thing every day. And merely because these gentlemen, now and then, forget themselves in this way, it would be hard if some future prosodist should insist upon twisting the *Thanatopsis*, or the *Spanish Student*, into a jumble of trochees, spondees, and dactyls.

It may be said, also, by some other people, that in the word *decus*, I have succeeded no better than the books, in making the scansional agree with the reading flow; and that *decus* was not pronounced de*cus*. I reply, that there can be no doubt of the word having been pronounced, in this case, de*cus*. It must be observed, that the Latin inflection, or variation of a word in its terminating syllables, caused the Romans – *must* have caused them, to pay greater attention to the termination of a word than to its commencement, or than we do to the terminations of our words. The end of the Latin word established that relation of the word with other words which we establish by prepositions or auxiliary verbs. Therefore, it would seem infinitely less odd to them than it does to us, to dwell at any time, for any slight purpose, abnormally, on a terminating syllable. In verse, this licence – scarcely a licence – would be frequently admitted. These ideas unlock the secret of such lines as the

Litoreis ingens inventa sub ilici*bus sus*,

and the

Parturiunt montes et nascitur ridicu*lus mus*,

which I quoted, some time ago, while speaking of rhyme.

As regards the prosodial elisions, such as that of *rem* before O in *pulverem Olympicum*, it is really difficult to understand how so dismally silly a notion could have entered the brain even of a pedant. Were it demanded of me why the books cut off one *vowel* before another, I might say – It is, perhaps, because the books think that, since a bad reader is so apt to slide the one vowel into the other at any rate, it is just as well to print them *ready-slided*. But in the case of the terminating *m*, which is the most readily pronounced of all consonants, (as the infantile *mamma* will testify,) and the most impossible to cheat the ear of by any system of sliding – in the case of the *m*, I should be driven to reply that, to the best of my belief, the prosodists did the thing, because they had a fancy for doing it, and wished to see how funny it would look after it was done. The thinking reader will perceive that, from the great facility with which *em* may be enunciated, it is admirably suited to form one of the rapid short syllables in the bastard dactyl (pulv$\underset{3}{e}$r$\underset{3}{e}$m $\underset{3}{\text{O}}$;) but because the books had no conception of a bastard dactyl, they knocked it in the head at once – by cutting off its tail!

Let me now give a specimen of the true scansion of another Horatian measure – embodying an instance of proper elision.

Int$\underset{2}{e}$g$\underset{2}{e}$r | vitæ | sc$\underset{3}{e}$l$\underset{3}{e}$r$\underset{3}{i}$sque | purus |
Non $\underset{2}{e}$g$\underset{2}{e}$t | Mauri | jac$\underset{3}{u}$$\underset{3}{l}$is n$\underset{3}{e}$ | que arcu |
Nec v$\underset{2}{e}$n$\underset{2}{e}$ | natis | grav$\underset{3}{i}$d$\underset{3}{a}$ s$\underset{3}{a}$ | gittis,
Fus$\underset{2}{c}$e, ph$\underset{2}{a}$ | retrâ.

Here the regular recurrence of the bastard dactyl gives great animation to the rhythm. The *e* before the *a* in *que arcu*, is, almost of sheer necessity, cut off – that is to say, run into the *a* so as to preserve the spondee. But even this licence it would have been better not to take.

Had I space, nothing would afford me greater pleasure than to proceed with the scansion of *all* the ancient rhythms, and to show how easily, by the help of common sense, the intended music of each and all can be rendered instantaneously apparent. But I have already overstepped my limits, and must bring this paper to an end.

It will never do, however, to omit all mention of the heroic hexameter.

I began the 'processes' by a suggestion of the spondee as the first step towards verse. But the innate monotony of the spondee has caused its disappearance, as the basis of rhythm, from all modern poetry. We *may* say, indeed, that the French heroic – the most wretchedly monotonous verse in existence – is, to all intents and purposes, spondaic. But it is not designedly spondaic – and if the French were ever to examine it at all, they would no doubt pronounce it iambic. It must be observed, that the French language is strangely peculiar in this point – *that it is without accentuation, and consequently without verse.* The genius of the people, rather than the structure of the tongue, declares that their words are, for the most part, enunciated with an uniform dwelling on each syllable. For example – *we* say, 'syl*la*bifi*ca*tion.' A Frenchman would say, syl-la-bi-fi-ca-ti-on; dwelling on no one of the syllables with any noticeable particularity. Here again I put an extreme case, in order to be well understood; but the general fact is as I give it – that, comparatively, the French have *no* accentuation. And there can be nothing worth the name of verse without. Therefore, the French have no verse worth the name – which is the fact, put in sufficiently plain terms. Their iambic rhythm so superabounds in absolute spondees, as to warrant me in calling its basis spondaic; but French is the *only* modern tongue which has any rhythm with such basis; and even in the French, it is, as I have said, unintentional.

Admitting, however, the validity of my suggestion, that the spondee was the first approach to verse, we should expect to find, first, natural spondees (words each forming just a spondee,) most abundant in the most ancient languages; and, secondly, we should expect to find spondees forming the basis of the most ancient rhythms. These expecations are in both cases confirmed.

Of the Greek hexameter, the intentional basis is spondaic. The dactyls are the *variation* of the theme. It will be observed that there is no absolute certainty about *their* points of interposition. The penultimate foot, it is true, is usually a dactyl; but not uniformly so; while the ultimate, on which the ear *lingers*, is always a spondee. Even that the penultimate is usually a dactyl may be clearly referred to the necessity of winding up with the *distinctive* spondee. In corroboration of this idea, again, we should look to find the penultimate spondee most usual in the most ancient verse; and, accordingly, we find it more frequent in the Greek than in the Latin hexameter.

But besides all this, spondees are not only more prevalent in the heroic hexameter than dactyls, but occur to such an extent as is even unpleasant to modern ears, on account of monotony. What the modern chiefly appreciates and admires in the Greek hexameter, is the *melody of the abundant vowel sounds*. The Latin hexameters *really* please very few moderns – although so many pretend to fall into ecstasies about them. In the hexameters quoted, several pages ago, from Silius Italicus, the preponderance of the spondee is strikingly manifest. Besides the natural spondees of the Greek and Latin, numerous artificial ones arise in the verse of these tongues on account of the tendency which inflection has to throw full accentuation on terminal syllables; and the preponderance of the spondee is further ensured by the comparative infrequency of the small prepositions which *we* have to serve us *instead* of case, and also the absence of the diminutive auxiliary verbs with which *we* have to eke out the expression of our primary ones. These are the monosyllables whose abundance serves to stamp the poetic genius of a language as tripping or dactylic.

Now paying no attention to these facts, Sir Philip Sidney, Professor Longfellow, and innumerable other persons more or less modern, have busied themselves in constructing what they supposed to be 'English hexameters on the model of the Greek.' The only difficulty was that (even leaving out of question the melodious masses of vowel,) these gentlemen never could get their English hexameters to *sound* Greek. Did they *look* Greek? – that should have been the query; and the reply might have led to a solution of the riddle. In placing a copy of ancient hexameters side by side with a copy (in similar type) of such hexameters as Professor Longfellow, or Professor Felton, or the Frogpondian Professors collectively, are in the shameful practice of composing 'on the model of the Greek,' it will be seen that the latter (hexameters, not professors) are about one third longer *to the eye*, on an average, than the former. The more abundant dactyls make the difference. And it is the greater number of spondees in the Greek than in the English – in the ancient than in the modern tongue – which has caused it to fall out that while these eminent scholars were groping about in the dark for a Greek hexameter, which is a spondaic rhythm varied now and then by dactyls, they merely stumbled, to the lasting scandal of scholarship, over something which, on account of its long-leggedness, we may as well term a Feltonian hexameter, and which is a dactylic rhythm, interrupted, rarely, by artificial spondees which are no spondees at all, and which are curiously thrown in by the heels at all kinds of improper and impertinent points.

Here is a specimen of the Longfellownian hexameter:

Also the | church with | in was a | dorned for | this was the | season |
In which the | young their | parents' | hope and the | loved ones of | Heaven. |
Should at the | foot of the | altar re | new the | vows of their | baptism |
Therefore each | nook and | corner was | swept and | cleaned and the | dust was |
Blown from the | walls and | ceiling and | from the | oil-painted | benches. |

Mr Longfellow is a man of imagination – but *can* he imagine that any individual, with a proper understanding of the danger of lock-jaw, would make the attempt of twisting his mouth into the shape necessary for the emission of such spondees as 'par*ents*,' and 'from the,' or such dactyls as 'cleaned and the' and 'loved ones of'? 'Baptism' is by no means a bad spondee – perhaps because it happens to be a dactyl; – of all the rest, however, I am dreadfully ashamed.

But these feet – dactyls and spondees, all together, – should thus be put at once into their proper position:

> Also, the church within was adorned; for this was the season in which the young, their parents' hope, and the loved ones of Heaven, should, at the feet of the altar, renew the vows of their baptism. Therefore, each nook and corner was swept and cleaned; and the dust was blown from the walls and ceiling, and from the oil-painted benches.

There! – That is respectable prose; and it will incur no danger of ever getting its character ruined by anybody's mistaking it for verse.

But even when we let these modern hexameters go, as Greek, and merely hold them fast in their proper character of Longfellownian, or Feltonian, or Frogpondian, we must still condemn them as having been committed in a radical misconception of the philosophy of verse. The spondee, as I observed, is the *theme* of the Greek line. Most of the ancient hexameters *begin* with spondees, for the reason that the spondee *is* the theme; and the ear is filled with it as with a burden. Now the Feltonian dactylics have, in the same way, dactyls for the theme, and most of them begin with dactyls – which is all very proper if not very Greek – but, unhappily, the one point at which they *are* very Greek is that point, precisely, at which they should be nothing but Feltonian. They always *close* with what is meant for a spondee. To be consistently silly, they should die off in a dactyl.

That a truly Greek hexameter *cannot*, however, be readily composed in English, is a proposition which I am by no means inclined to admit. I think I could manage the point myself. For example:

Do tell! | when may we | hope to make | men of sense | out of the | Pundits |
Born and brought | up with their | snouts deep | down in the | mud of the | Frog-pond?
Why ask? | who ever | yet saw | money made | out of a | fat old |
Jew, or | downright | upright | nutmegs | out of a | pine-knot? |

The proper spondee predominance is here preserved. Some of the dactyls are not so good as I could wish – but, upon the whole, the rhythm is very decent – to say nothing of its excellent sense.

THE POETIC PRINCIPLE

In speaking of the Poetic Principle, I have no design to be either thorough or profound. While discussing, very much at random, the essentiality of what we call Poetry, my principal purpose will be to cite for consideration, some few of those minor English or American poems which best suit my own taste, or which, upon my own fancy, have left the most definite impression. 'By 'minor poems' I mean, of course, poems of little length. And here, in the beginning, permit me to say a few words in regard to a somewhat peculiar principle, which, whether rightfully or wrongfully, has always had its influence in my own critical estimate of the poem. I hold that a long poem does not exist. I maintain that the phrase, 'a long poem' is simply a flat contradiction in terms.

I need scarcely observe that a poem deserves its title only inasmuch as it excites, by elevating the soul. The value of the poem is in the ratio of this elevating excitement. But all excitements are, through a psychal necessity, transient. That degree of excitement which would entitle a poem to be so called at all, cannot be sustained throughout a composition of any great length. After the lapse of half an hour, at the very utmost, it flags – fails – a revulsion ensues – and then the poem is, in effect, and in fact, no longer such.

There are, no doubt, many who have found difficulty in reconciling the critical dictum that the *Paradise Lost* is to be devoutly admired throughout, with the absolute impossibility of maintaining for it, during perusal, the amount of enthusiasm which that critical dictum would demand. This great work, in fact, is to be regarded as poetical, only when, losing sight of that vital requisite in all works of Art, Unity, we view it merely as a series of minor poems. If, to preserve its Unity – its totality of effect or impression – we read it (as would be necessary) at a single sitting, the result is but a constant alternation of excitement and depression. After a passage of what we feel to be true poetry, there follows, inevitably, a passage of platitude which no critical pre-judgment can force us to admire; but if, upon completing the work, we read it again; omitting the first book – that is to say, commencing with the second – we shall be surprised at now finding that admirable which we before condemned – that damnable which we had previously so much admired. It follows from all this that the ultimate, aggregate, or absolute effect of even the best epic under the sun, is a nullity: – and this is precisely the fact.

In regard to the Iliad, we have, if not positive proof, at least very good reason, for believing it intended as a series of lyrics; but, granting the epic intention, I can say only that the work is based in an imperfect sense of Art. The modern epic is, of the suppositious ancient model, but an inconsiderate and blindfold imitation. But the day of these artistic anomalies is over. If, at any time, any very long poem *were* popular in reality – which I doubt – it is at least clear that no very long poem will ever be popular again.

That the extent of a poetical work is, *ceteris paribus*, the measure of its merit, seems undoubtedly, when we thus state it, a proposition sufficiently absurd – yet we are indebted for it to the quarterly Reviews. Surely there can be nothing in mere *size*, abstractly considered – there can be nothing in mere *bulk*, so far as a volume is concerned, which has so continuously elicited admiration from these saturnine pamphlets! A mountain, to be sure, by the mere sentiment of physical magnitude which it conveys, *does* impress us with a sense of the sublime – but no man is impressed after *this* fashion by the material grandeur of even *The Columbiad*. Even the Quarterlies have not instructed us to be so impressed by it. *As yet*, they have not *insisted* on our estimating Lamartine by the cubic foot, or Pollock by the pound – but what else are we to *infer* from their continual prating about 'sustained effort?' If, by 'sustained effort,' any little gentleman has accomplished an epic, let us frankly commend him for the effort – if this indeed be a thing commendable – but let us forbear praising the epic on the effort's account. It is to be hoped that common sense, in the time to come, will prefer deciding upon a work of Art, rather by the impression it makes – by the effect it produces – than by the time it took to impress the effect, or by the amount of 'sustained effort' which had been found necessary in effecting the impression. The fact is, that perseverance is one thing and genius quite another – nor can all the Quarterlies in Christendom confound them. By-and-by, this proposition, with many which I have been just urging, will be received as self-evident. In the meantime, by being generally condemned as falsities, they will not be essentially damaged as truths.

On the other hand, it is clear that a poem may be improperly brief. Undue brevity degenerates into mere epigrammatism. A *very* short poem, while now and then producing a brilliant or vivid, never produces a profound or enduring effect. There must be the steady pressing down of the stamp upon the wax. De Béranger has wrought innumerable things, pungent and spirit-stirring; but, in general, they have been too imponderous to stamp themselves deeply into the public attention; and thus, as so many feathers of fancy, have been blown aloft only to be whistled down the wind.

A remarkable instance of the effect of undue brevity in depressing a poem – in keeping it out of the popular view – is afforded by the following exquisite little Serenade:

> I arise from dreams of thee
>   In the first sweet sleep of night,
> When the winds are breathing low,
>   And the stars are shining bright.
> I arise from dreams of thee,
>   And a spirit in my feet
> Has led me – who knows how? –
>   To thy chamber-window, sweet!
>
> The wandering airs they faint
>   On the dark, the silent stream –
> The champak odours fail
>   Like sweet thoughts in a dream;
> The nightingale's complaint,
>   It dies upon her heart,
> As I must die on thine,
>   O, beloved as thou art!
>
> O, lift me from the grass!
>   I die, I faint, I fail!
> Let thy love in kisses rain
>   On my lips and eyelids pale.
> My cheek is cold and white, alas!
>   My heart beats loud and fast:
> Oh! press it close to thine again,
>   Where it will break at last!

Very few, perhaps, are familiar with these lines – yet no less a poet than Shelley is their author. Their warm, yet delicate and ethereal imagination will be appreciated by all – but by none so thoroughly as by him who has himself arisen from sweet dreams of one beloved, to bathe in the aromatic air of a southern midsummer night.

One of the finest poems by Willis – the very best, in my opinion, which he has ever written – has, no doubt, through this same defect of undue brevity, been kept back from its proper position, not less in the critical than in the popular view.

The shadows lay along Broadway,
'Twas near the twilight-tide –
And slowly there a lady fair
Was walking in her pride.
Alone walk'd she; but, viewlessly,
Walk'd spirits at her side.

Peace charm'd the street beneath her feet,
And Honour charm'd the air;
And all astir looked kind on her,
And call'd her good as fair –
For all God ever gave to her
She kept with chary care.

She kept with care her beauties rare
From lovers warm and true –
For her heart was cold to all but gold,
And the rich came not to woo –
But honour'd well are charms to sell
If priests the selling do.

Now walking there was one more fair –
A slight girl, lily-pale;
And she had unseen company
To make the spirit quail –
'Twixt Want and Scorn she walk'd forlorn,
And nothing could avail.

No mercy now can clear her brow
For this world's peace to pray;
For, as love's wild prayer dissolved in air,
Her woman's heart gave way! –
But the sin forgiven by Christ in Heaven
By man is cursed alway!

In this composition we find it difficult to recognize the Willis who has written so many mere 'verses of society.' The lines are not only richly ideal, but, full of energy; while they breathe an earnestness – an evident sincerity of sentiment – for which we look in vain throughout all the other works of this author.

While the epic mania – while the idea that, to merit in poetry, prolixity is indispensable – has, for some years past, been gradually dying out of the public mind, by mere dint of its own absurdity – we find it succeeded by a heresy too palpably false to be long tolerated, but one which, in the brief period it has already endured, may be said to have accomplished more in the corruption of our Poetical Literature than all its other enemies combined. I allude to the heresy of *The Didactic*. It has been assumed, tacitly and avowedly, directly and indirectly, that the ultimate object of all Poetry is Truth. Every poem, it is said, should inculcate a moral; and by this moral is the poetical merit of the work to be adjudged. We Americans especially have patronized this happy idea; and we Bostonians, very especially, have developed it in full. We have taken it into our heads that to write a poem simply for the poem's sake, and to acknowledge such to have been our design, would be to confess ourselves radically wanting in the true Poetic dignity and force: – but the simple fact is, that, would we but permit ourselves to look into our own souls, we should immediately there discover that under the sun there neither exists nor *can* exist any work more thoroughly dignified – more supremely noble than this very poem – this poem *per se* – this poem which is a poem and nothing more – this poem written solely for the poem's sake.

With as deep a reverence for the True as ever inspired the bosom of man, I would, nevertheless, limit, in some measure, its modes of inculcation. I would limit to enforce them. I would not enfeeble them by dissipation. The demands of Truth are severe. She has no sympathy with the myrtles. All *that* which is so indispensable in Song, is precisely all *that* with which *she* has nothing whatever to do. It is but making her a flaunting paradox, to wreathe her in gems and flowers. In enforcing a truth, we need severity rather than efflorescence of language. We must be simple, precise, terse. We must be cool, calm, unimpassioned. In a word, we must be in that mood which, as nearly as possible, is the exact converse of the poetical. *He* must be blind indeed who does not perceive the radical and chasmal differences between the truthful and the poetical modes of inculcation. He must be theory-mad beyond redemption who, in spite of these differences, shall still persist in attempting to reconcile the obstinate oils and waters of Poetry and Truth.

Dividing the world of mind into its three most immediately obvious distinctions, we have the Pure Intellect, Taste, and the Moral Sense. I place Taste in the middle, because it is just this position which, in the mind, it occupies. It holds intimate relations with either extreme; but from the Moral Sense is separated by so faint a difference that Aristotle has not hesitated to place some of its operations among the virtues themselves. Nevertheless, we find the *offices* of the trio marked with a sufficient distinction. Just as the

Intellect concerns itself with Truth, so Taste informs us of the Beautiful while the Moral Sense is regardful of Duty. Of this latter, while Conscience teaches the obligation, and Reason the expediency, Taste contents herself with displaying the charms: – waging war upon Vice solely on the ground of her deformity – her disproportion – her animosity to the fitting, to the appropriate, to the harmonious –in a word, to Beauty.

An immortal instinct, deep within the spirit of man, is thus, plainly, a sense of the Beautiful. This it is which administers to his delight in the manifold forms, and sounds, and odours, and sentiments amid which he exists. And just as the lily is repeated in the lake, or the eyes of Amaryllis in the mirror, so is the mere oral or written repetition of these forms, and sounds, and colours, and odours, and sentiments, a duplicate source of delight. But this mere repetition is not poetry. He who shall simply sing, with however glowing enthusiasm, or with however vivid a truth of description, of the sights, and sounds, and odours, and colours, and sentiments, which greet *him* in common with all mankind – he, I say, has yet failed to prove his divine title. There is still a something in the distance which he has been unable to attain. We have still a thirst unquenchable, to allay which he has not shown us the crystal springs. This thirst belongs to the immortality of Man. It is at once a consequence and an indication of his perennial existence. It is the desire of the moth for the star. It is no mere appreciation of the Beauty before us – but a wild effort to reach the Beauty above. Inspired by an ecstatic prescience of the glories beyond the grave, we struggle, by multiform combinations among the things and thoughts of Time, to attain a portion of that Loveliness whose very elements, perhaps, appertain to eternity alone. And thus when by Poetry – or when by Music, the most entrancing of the Poetic moods – we find ourselves melted into tears – we weep then – not as the Abbaté Gravina supposes – through excess of pleasure, but through a certain, petulant, impatient sorrow at our inability to grasp *now*, wholly, here on earth, at once and for ever, those divine and rapturous joys, of which *through* the poem, or *through* the music, we attain to but brief and indeterminate glimpses.

The struggle to apprehend the supernal Loveliness – this struggle, on the part of souls fittingly constituted – has given to the world all *that* which it (the world) has ever been enabled at once to understand and *to feel* as poetic.

The Poetic Sentiment, of course, may develop itself in various modes – in Painting, in Sculpture, in Architecture, in the Dance – very especially in Music – and very peculiarly, and with a wide field, in the composition of the Landscape Garden. Our present theme, however, has regard only to its manifestation in words. And here let me speak briefly on the topic of rhythm. Contenting myself with the certainty that Music, in its various modes of metre, rhythm, and rhyme, is of so vast a moment in Poetry as never to be wisely rejected – is so vitally important an adjunct, that he is simply silly who declines its assistance, I will not now pause to maintain its absolute essentiality. It is in Music, perhaps, that the soul most nearly attains the great end for which, when inspired by the Poetic Sentiment, it struggles – the creation of supernal Beauty. It *may* be, indeed, that here this sublime end is, now and then, attained *in fact*. We are often made to feel, with a shivering delight, that from an earthly harp are stricken notes which *cannot* have been unfamiliar to the angels. And thus there can be little doubt that in the union of Poetry with Music in its popular sense, we shall find the widest field for the Poetic development. The old Bards and Minnesingers had advantages which we do not possess – and Thomas Moore, singing his own songs, was, in the most legitimate manner, perfecting them as poems.

To recapitulate, then: – I would define, in brief, the Poetry of words as *The Rhythmical Creation of Beauty*. Its sole arbiter is Taste. With the Intellect or with the Conscience, it has only collateral relations. Unless incidentally, it has no concern whatever either with Duty or with Truth.

A few words, however, in explanation. *That* pleasure which is at once the most pure, the most elevating, and the most intense, is derived, I maintain, from the contemplation of the Beautiful. In the contemplation of Beauty we alone find it possible to attain that pleasurable elevation, or excitement, *of the soul*, which we recognize as the Poetic Sentiment, and which is so easily distinguished from Truth, which is the satisfaction of the Reason, or from Passion, which is the excitement of the heart. I make Beauty, therefore – using the word as inclusive of the sublime – I make Beauty the province of the poem, simply because it is an obvious rule of Art that effects should be made to spring as directly as possible from their causes: – no one as yet having been weak enough to deny that the peculiar elevation in question is at least *most readily* attainable in the poem. It by no means follows, however, that the incitements of Passion, or the precepts of Duty, or even the lessons of Truth, may not be introduced into a poem, and with advantage; for they may subserve, incidentally, in various ways, the general purposes of the work: – but the true artist will always contrive to tone them down in proper subjection to that *Beauty* which is the atmosphere and the real essence of the poem.

I cannot better introduce the few poems which I shall present for your consideration, than by the citation of the Pröem to Mr Longfellow's *Waif*.

The day is done, and the darkness
  Falls from the wings of Night,
As a feather is wafted downward
  From an Eagle in his flight.

I see the lights of the village
  Gleam through the rain and the mist,
And a feeling of sadness comes o'er me,
  That my soul cannot resist;

A feeling of sadness and longing,
  That is not akin to pain,
And resembles sorrow only
  As the mist resembles the rain.

Come, read to me some poem,
  Some simple and heartfelt lay,
That shall soothe this restless feeling,
  And banish the thoughts of day.

Not from the grand old masters,
  Not from the bards sublime,
Whose distant footsteps echo
  Through the corridors of time.

For, like strains of martial music,
  Their mighty thoughts suggest
Life's endless toil and endeavour;
  And to-night I long for rest.

Read from some humbler poet,
  Whose songs gushed from his heart,
As showers from the clouds of summer,
  Or tears from the eyelids start;

Who through long days of labour,
  And nights devoid of ease,
Still heard in his soul the music
  Of wonderful melodies.

Such songs have power to quiet
The restless pulse of care,
And come like the benediction
That follows after prayer.

Then read from the treasured volume
The poem of thy choice,
And lend to the rhyme of the poet
The beauty of thy voice.

And the night shall be filled with music,
And the cares, that infest the day,
Shall fold their tents, like the Arabs,
And as silently steal away.

With no great range of imagination, these lines have been justly admired for their delicacy of expression. Some of the images are very effective. Nothing can be better than –

—— The bards sublime,
Whose distant footsteps echo
Down the corridors of Time.

The idea of the last quatrain is also very effective. The poem, on the whole, however, is chiefly to be admired for the graceful *insouciance* of its metre, so well in accordance with the character of the sentiments, and especially for the *ease* of the general manner. This 'ease,' or naturalness, in a literary style, it has long been the fashion to regard as ease in appearance alone – as a point of really difficult attainment. But not so: – a natural manner is difficult only to him who should never meddle with it – to the unnatural. It is but the result of writing with the understanding, or with the instinct, that *the tone*, in composition, should always be that which the mass of mankind would adopt – and must perpetually vary, of course, with the occasion. The author who, after the fashion of *The North American Review*, should be, upon *all* occasions, merely 'quiet,' must necessarily upon *many* occasions, be simply silly, or stupid; and has no more right to be considered 'easy,' or 'natural,' than a Cockney exquisite, or than the sleeping Beauty in the wax-works.

Among the minor poems of Bryant, none has so much impressed me as the one which he entitles *June*. I quote only a portion of it:

There, through the long, long summer hours,
The golden light should lie,

And thick, young herbs and groups of flowers
    Stand in their beauty by.
The oriole should build and tell
His love-tale, close beside my cell;
    The idle butterfly
Should rest him there, and there be heard
The housewife-bee and humming bird.

And what, if cheerful shouts, at noon,
    Come, from the village sent,
Or songs of maids, beneath the moon,
    With fairy laughter blent?
And what if, in the evening light,
Betrothed lovers walk in sight
    Of my low monument!
I would the lovely scene around
Might know no sadder sight nor sound.

I know, I know I should not see
    The season's glorious show,
Nor would its brightness shine for me,
    Nor its wild music flow;
But if, around my place of sleep,
The friends I love should come to weep,
    They might not haste to go.
Soft airs, and song, and light, and bloom
Should keep them lingering by my tomb.

These to their soften'd hearts should bear
    The thought of what has been,
And speak of one who cannot share
    The gladness of the scene;
Whose part in all the pomp that fills
The circuit of the summer hills,
    Is – that his grave is green;
And deeply would their hearts rejoice
To hear again his living voice.

The rhythmical flow, here, is even voluptuous – nothing could be more melodious. The poem has always affected me in a remarkable manner. The intense melancholy which seems to well up, perforce, to the surface of all the poet's cheerful sayings about his grave, we find thrilling us to the soul – while there is the truest poetic elevation in the thrill. The impression left is one of a pleasurable sadness. And if, in the remaining compositions which I shall introduce to you, there be more or less of a similar tone always apparent, let me remind you that (how or why we know not) this certain taint of sadness is inseparably connected with all the higher manifestations of true Beauty. It is, nevertheless,

> A feeling of sadness and longing
> That is not akin to pain,
> And resembles sorrow only
> As the mist resembles the rain.

The taint of which I speak is clearly perceptible even in a poem so full of brilliancy and spirit as the *Health* of Edward Coote Pinkney:

> I fill this cup to one made up
> Of loveliness alone,
> A woman, of her gentle sex
> The seeming paragon;
> To whom the better elements
> And kindly stars have given
> A form so fair, that, like the air,
> 'Tis less of earth than heaven.
>
> Her every tone is music's own,
> Like those of morning birds,
> And something more than melody
> Dwells ever in her words;
> The coinage of her heart are they,
> And from her lips each flows
> As one may see the burden'd bee
> Forth issue from the rose.
>
> Affections are as thoughts to her,
> The measures of her hours;
> Her feelings have the fragrancy,
> The freshness of young flowers,
> And lovely passions, changing oft,
> So fill her, she appears
> The image of themselves by turns, –
> The idol of past years!
>
> Of her bright face one glance will trace
> A picture on the brain,
> And of her voice in echoing hearts
> A sound must long remain;

But memory, such as mine of her,
So very much endears,
When death is nigh, my latest sigh
Will not be life's, but hers.

I fill'd this cup to one made up
Of loveliness alone,
A woman, of her gentle sex
The seeming paragon –
Her health! and would on earth there stood,
Some more of such a frame,
That life might be all poetry,
And weariness a name.

It was the misfortune of Mr Pinkney to have been born too far south. Had he been a New Englander, it is probable that he would have been ranked as the first of American lyricists, by that magnanimous cabal which has so long controlled the destinies of American Letters, in conducting the thing called *The North American Review*. The poem just cited is especially beautiful; but the poetic elevation which it induces, we must refer chiefly to our sympathy in the poet's enthusiasm. We pardon his hyperboles for the evident earnestness with which they are uttered.

It was by no means my design, however, to expatiate upon the *merits* of what I should read you. These will necessarily speak for themselves. Boccalini, in his *Advertisements from Parnassus*, tells us that Zoilus once presented Apollo a very caustic criticism upon a very admirable book: – whereupon the god asked him for the beauties of the work. He replied that he only busied himself about the errors. On hearing this, Apollo, handing him a sack of unwinnowed wheat, bade him pick out *all the chaff* for his reward.

Now this fable answers very well as a hit at the critics – but I am by no means sure that the god was in the right. I am by no means certain that the true limits of the critical duty are not grossly misunderstood. Excellence, in a poem especially, may be considered in the light of an axiom, which need only be properly *put*, to become self-evident. It is *not* excellence if it require to be demonstrated as such: – and thus, to point out too particularly the merits of a work of Art, is to admit that they are *not* merits altogether.

Among the *Melodies* of Thomas Moore, is one whose distinguished character as a poem proper, seems to have been singularly left out of view. I allude to his lines beginning – 'Come rest in this bosom.' The intense energy of their expression is not surpassed by anything in Byron. These are two of the lines in which a sentiment is conveyed that embodies the *all in all* of the divine passion of Love – a sentiment which, perhaps, has found its echo in more, and in more passionate, human hearts than any other single sentiment ever embodied in words:

Come, rest in this bosom, my own stricken deer,
Though the herd have fled from thee, thy home is still here;
Here still is the smile, that no cloud can o'ercast,
And a heart and a hand all thy own to the last.

Oh! what was love made for, if 'tis not the same
Through joy and through torment, through glory and shame?
I know not, I ask not, if guilt's in that heart,
I but know that I love thee, whatever thou art.

Thou hast call'd me thy Angel in moments of bliss,
And thy Angel I'll be, 'mid the horrors of this, –
Through the furnace, unshrinking, thy steps to pursue,
And shield thee, and save thee, – or perish there too!

It has been the fashion, of late days, to deny Moore Imagination, while granting him Fancy – a distinction originating with Coleridge – than whom no man more fully comprehended the great powers of Moore. The fact is, that the fancy of this poet so far predominates over all his other faculties, and over the fancy of all other men, as to have induced, very naturally, the idea that he is fanciful *only*. But never was there a greater mistake. Never was a grosser wrong done the fame of a true poet. In the compass of the English language I can call to mind no poem more profoundly – more weirdly *imaginative*, in the best sense, than the lines commencing – 'I would I were by that dim lake' – which are the composition of Thomas Moore. I regret that I am unable to remember them.

One of the noblest – and, speaking of Fancy, one of the most singularly fanciful of modern poets, was Thomas Hood. His *Fair Ines* had always, for me, an inexpressible charm:

O saw ye not fair Ines?
  She's gone into the West,
To dazzle when the sun is down,
  And rob the world of rest;
She took our daylight with her,
  The smiles that we love best,

With morning blushes on her cheek,
  And pearls upon her breast.

O turn again, fair Ines,
  Before the fall of night,
For fear the moon should shine alone,
  And stars unrivall'd bright;
And blessed will the lover be
  That walks beneath their light,
And breathes the love against thy cheek
  I dare not even write!

Would I had been, fair Ines,
  That gallant cavalier,
Who rode so gaily by thy side,
  And whisper'd thee so near!
Were there no bonny dames at home,
  Or no true lovers here,
That he should cross the seas to win
  The dearest of the dear?

I saw thee, lovely Ines,
  Descend along the shore,
With bands of noble gentlemen,
  And banners wav'd before;
And gentle youth and maidens gay,
  And snowy plumes they wore;
It would have been a beauteous dream,
  – If it had been no more!

Alas, alas, fair Ines,
  She went away with song,
With Music waiting on her steps,
  And shoutings of the throng;
But some were sad and felt no mirth,
  But only Music's wrong,
In sounds that sang Farewell, Farewell,
  To her you've loved so long.

Farewell, farewell, fair Ines,
  That vessel never bore
So fair a lady on its deck,
  Nor danced so light before, –
Alas, for pleasure on the sea,
  And sorrow on the shore!

The smile that blest one lover's heart
Has broken many more!

The Haunted House, by the same author, is one of the truest poems ever written – one of the *truest* – one of the most unexceptionable – one of the most thoroughly artistic, both in its theme and in its execution. It is, moreover, powerfully ideal – imaginative. I regret that its length renders it unsuitable for the purposes of this Lecture. In place of it, permit me to offer the universally appreciated *Bridge of Sighs*.

One more Unfortunate,
Weary of breath,
Rashly importunate,
Gone to her death!

Take her up tenderly,
Lift her with care; –
Fashion'd so slenderly,
Young, and so fair!

Look at her garments
Clinging like cerements;
Whilst the wave constantly
Drips from her clothing;
Take her up instantly,
Loving, not loathing. –

Touch her not scornfully;
Think of her mournfully,
Gently and humanly;
Not of the stains of her,
All that remains of her
Now, is pure womanly.

Make no deep scrutiny
Into her mutiny
Rash and undutiful;
Past all dishonour,
Death has left on her
Only the beautiful.

Still, for all slips of hers,
One of Eve's family –
Wipe those poor lips of hers
Oozing so clammily.

Loop up her tresses
Escaped from the comb,
Her fair auburn tresses;
Whilst wonderment guesses
Where was her home?

Who was her father?
Who was her mother?
Had she a sister?
Had she a brother?
Or was there a dearer one
Still, and a nearer one
Yet, than all other?

Alas! for the rarity
Of Christian charity
Under the sun!
Oh! it was pitiful!
Near a whole city full,
Home she had none.

Sisterly, brotherly,
Fatherly, motherly,
Feelings had changed;
Love, by harsh evidence,
Thrown from its eminence;
Even God's providence
Seeming estranged.

Where the lamps quiver
So far in the river,
With many a light
From window and casement
From garret to basement,
She stood, with amazement,
Houseless by night.

The bleak wind of March
Made her tremble and shiver;
But not the dark arch,
Or the black flowing river:

Mad from life's history,
Glad of death's mystery,
Swift to be hurl'd –
Anywhere, anywhere
Out of the world!

In she plunged boldly,
No matter how coldly
The rough river ran, –
Over the brink of it,
Picture it, – think of it,
Dissolute Man!
Lave in it, drink of it
Then, if you can!

Take her up tenderly,
Lift her with care;
Fashion'd so slenderly,
Young, and so fair!
Ere her limbs frigidly
Stiffen too rigidly,
Decently, – kindly, –
Smooth and compose them
And her eyes, close them,
Staring so blindly!

Dreadfully staring
Through muddy impurity,
As when with the daring
Last look of despairing
Fixed on futurity.

Perishing gloomily,
Spurred by contumely,
Cold inhumanity,
Burning insanity,
Into her rest, –
Cross her hands humbly,
As if praying dumbly,
Over her breast!
Owning her weakness,
Her evil behaviour,
And leaving, with meekness,
Her sins to her Saviour!

The vigour of this poem is no less remarkable than its pathos. The versification, although carrying the fanciful to the very verge of the fantastic, is nevertheless admirably adapted to the wild insanity which is the thesis of the poem.

Among the minor poems of Lord Byron, is one which has never received from the critics the praise which it undoubtedly deserves:

Though the day of my destiny's over,
  And the star of my fate hath declined,
Thy soft heart refused to discover
  The faults which so many could find;
Though thy soul with my grief was acquainted,
  It shrunk not to share it with me,
And the love which my spirit hath painted
  It never hath found but in *thee*.

Then when nature around me is smiling,
  The last smile which answers to mine,
I do not believe it beguiling,
  Because it reminds me of thine;
And when winds are at war with the ocean,
  As the breasts I believed in with me,
If their billows excite an emotion,
  It is that they bear me from *thee*.

Though the rock of my last hope is shivered,
  And its fragments are sunk in the wave,
Though I feel that my soul is delivered
  To pain – it shall not be its slave.
There is many a pang to pursue me:
  They may crush, but they shall not contemn –
They may torture, but shall not subdue me –
  'Tis of *thee* that I think – not of them.

Though human, thou didst not deceive me,
  Though woman, thou didst not forsake,
Though loved, thou forborest to grieve me,
  Though slandered, thou never couldst shake, –
Though trusted, thou didst not disclaim me,
  Though parted, it was not to fly,
Though watchful, 'twas not to defame me,
  Nor mute, that the world might belie.

Yet I blame not the world, nor despise it,
  Nor the war of the many with one –
If my soul was not fitted to prize it,
  'Twas folly not sooner to shun:
And if dearly that error hath cost me,

And more than I once could foresee,
I have found that whatever it lost me,
It could not deprive me of *thee*.

From the wreck of the past, which hath perished,
Thus much I at least may recall,
It hath taught me that which I most cherished
Deserved to be dearest of all:
In the desert a fountain is springing,
In the wide waste there still is a tree,
And a bird in the solitude singing,
Which speaks to my spirit of *thee*.

Although the rhythm, here, is one of the most difficult, the versification could scarcely be improved. No nobler *theme* ever engaged the pen of poet. It is the soul-elevating idea, that no man can consider himself entitled to complain of Fate while, in his adversity, he still retains the unwavering love of woman.

From Alfred Tennyson – although in perfect sincerity I regard him as the noblest poet that ever lived – I have left myself time to cite only a very brief specimen. I call him, and *think* him the noblest of poets – *not* because the impressions he produces are, at *all* times, the most profound – *not* because the poetical excitement which he induces is, at *all* times, the most intense – but because it *is*, at all times, the most ethereal – in other words, the most elevating and the most pure. No poet is so little of the earth, earthy. What I am about to read is from his last long poem, *The Princess*:

Tears, idle tears, I know not what they mean,
Tears from the depth of some divine despair
Rise in the heart, and gather to the eyes,
In looking on the happy Autumn-fields,
And thinking of the days that are no more.

Fresh as the first beam glittering on a sail,
That brings our friends up from the underworld,
Sad as the last which reddens over one
That sinks with all we love below the verge;
So sad, so fresh, the days that are no more.

Ah, sad and strange as in dark summer dawns
The earliest pipe of half-awaken'd birds
To dying ears, when unto dying eyes

The casement slowly grows a glimmering square;
So sad, so strange, the days that are no more.

Dear as remember'd kisses after death,
And sweet as those by hopeless fancy feign'd
On lips that are for others; deep as love,
Deep as first love, and wild with all regret;
O death in Life, the days that are no more.

Thus, although in a very cursory and imperfect manner, I have endeavoured to convey to you my conception of the Poetic Principle. It has been my purpose to suggest that, while this Principle itself is, strictly and simply, the Human Aspiration for Supernal Beauty, the manifestation of the Principle is always found in *an elevating excitement of the Soul* – quite independent of that passion which is the intoxication of the Heart – or of that Truth which is the satisfaction of the Reason. For, in regard to Passion, alas! its tendency is to degrade, rather than to elevate the Soul. Love, on the contrary – Love – the true, the divine Eros – the Uranian, as distinguished from the Dionæan Venus – is unquestionably the purest and truest of all poetical themes. And in regard to Truth – if, to be sure, through the attainment of a truth, we are led to perceive a harmony where none was apparent before, we experience, at once, the true poetical effect – but this effect is referable to the harmony alone, and not in the least degree to the truth which merely served to render the harmony manifest.

We shall reach, however, more immediately a distinct conception of what the true Poetry is, by mere reference to a few of the simple elements which induce in the Poet himself the true poetical effect. He recognizes the ambrosia which nourishes his soul, in the bright orbs that shine in Heaven – in the volutes of the flower – in the clustering of low shrubberies – in the waving of the grain-fields – in the slanting of tall, Eastern trees – in the blue distance of mountains – in the grouping of clouds – in the twinkling of half-hidden brooks – in the gleaming of silver rivers – in the repose of sequestered lakes – in the star-mirroring depths of lonely wells. He perceives it in the songs of birds – in the harp of Æolus – in the sighing of the night-wind – in the repining voice of the forest – in the surf that complains to the shore – in the fresh breath of the woods – in the scent of the violet – in the voluptuous perfume of the hyacinth – in the suggestive odour that comes to him, at eventide, from far-distant, undiscovered islands, over dim oceans, illimitable and unexplored. He owns it in all noble thoughts – in all unworldly motives – in all holy impulses – in all chivalrous, generous, and self-sacrificing deeds. He feels it in the beauty of woman – in the grace of her step – in the lustre of her eye – in the melody of her voice – in her soft laughter – in her sigh – in the harmony of the rustling of her robes. He deeply feels it in her winning endearments – in her burning enthusiasms – in her gentle charities – in her meek and devotional endurances – but above all – ah, far above all – he kneels to it – he worships it in the faith, in the purity, in the strength, in the altogether divine majesty – of her *love*.

Let me conclude – by the recitation of yet another brief poem – one very different in character from any that I have before quoted. It is by Motherwell, and is called *The Song of the Cavalier*. With our modern and altogether rational ideas of the absurdity and impiety of warfare, we are not precisely in that frame of mind best adapted to sympathize with the sentiments, and thus to appreciate the real excellence of the poem. To do this fully, we must identify ourselves, in fancy, with the soul of the old cavalier.

Then mounte! then mounte, brave gallants, all
And don your helmes amaine:
Deathe's couriers, Fame and Honour, call
Us to the field againe.

No shrewish tears shall fill our eye
When the sword-hilt's in our hand, –
Heart-whole we'll part, and no whit sighe
For the fayrest of the land;

Let piping swaine, and craven wight
Thus weepe and puling crye,
Our business is like men to fight,
And hero-like to die!

GEORGIA SCENES[1]

This book has reached us anonymously – not to say anomalously – yet it is most heartily welcome. The author, whoever he is, is a clever fellow, imbued with a spirit of the truest humour, and endowed, moreover, with an exquisitely discriminative and penetrating understanding of *character* in general, and of Southern character in particular. And we do not mean to speak of *human* character exclusively. To be sure, our Georgian is *au fait* here too – he is learned in all things appertaining to the biped without feathers. In regard, especially, to that class of southwestern mammalia who come under the generic appellation of 'savagerous wild cats,' he is a very Theophrastus in duodecimo. But he is not the less at home in other matters. Of geese and ganders he is the La Bruyère, and of good-for-nothing horses the Rochefoucault.

Seriously – if this book were printed in England it would make the fortune of its author. We positively mean what we say – and are quite sure of being sustained in our opinion by all proper judges who may be so fortunate as to obtain a copy of the *'Georgia Scenes,'* and who will be at the trouble of sifting their peculiar merits from amid the *gaucheries* of a Southern publication. Seldom – perhaps never in our lives – have we laughed as immoderately over any book as over the one now before us. If these *scenes* have produced such effect upon *our* cachinnatory nerves – upon *us* who are not 'of the merry mood,' and, moreover, have not been used to the perusal of somewhat similar things – we are at no loss to imagine what a hubbub they would occasion in the uninitiated regions of Cockaigne. And what would Christopher North say to them? – ah, what would Christopher North say? that is the question. Certainly not a word. But we can fancy the pursing up of his lips, and the long, loud, and jovial resonation of his wicked, uproarious ha! ha's!

From the Preface to the Sketches before us we learn that although they are, generally, nothing more than fanciful combinations of real incidents and characters, still, in some instances, the narratives are literally true. We are told also that the publication of these pieces was commenced, rather more than a year ago, in one of the Gazettes of the State, and that they were favourably received. 'For the last six

[1] *Georgia Scenes, Characters, Incidents, &c. in the First Half Century of the Republic. By a Native Georgian* [A. B. Longstreet]. Augusta, Georgia, 1836.

months,' says the author, 'I have been importuned by persons from all quarters of the State to give them to the public in the present form.' This speaks well for the Georgian taste. But that the publication will *succeed*, in the bookselling sense of the word, is problematical. Thanks to the long-indulged literary supineness of the South, her presses are not as apt in putting forth a *saleable* book as her sons are in concocting a wise one.

From a desire of concealing the author's name, two different signatures, Baldwin and Hall, were used in the original *Sketches*, and, to save trouble, are preserved in the present volume. With the exception, however, of one scene, '*The Company Drill*,' all the book is the production of the same pen. The first article in the list is '*Georgia Theatrics*.' Our friend *Hall*, in this piece, represents himself as ascending, about eleven o'clock in the forenoon of a June day, 'a long and gentle slope in what was called the Dark Corner of Lincoln County, Georgia.' Suddenly his ears are assailed by loud, profane, and boisterous voices, proceeding, apparently, from a large company of ragamuffins, concealed in a thick covert of undergrowth about a hundred yards from the road.

. . . . .

And now the sounds assume all the discordant intonations inseparable from a Georgia 'rough and tumble' fight. Our traveller listens in dismay to the indications of a quick, violent, and deadly struggle. With the intention of acting as pacificator, he dismounts in haste, and hurries to the scene of action. Presently, through a gap in the thicket, he obtains a glimpse of one, at least, of the combatants. This one appears to have his antagonist beneath him on the ground, and to be dealing on the prostrate wretch the most unmerciful blows. Having overcome about half the space which separated him from the combatants, our friend Hall is horror-stricken at seeing 'the uppermost make a heavy plunge with both his thumbs, and hearing, at the same instant, a cry in the accent of keenest torture, "Enough! my eye's out!"'

Rushing to the rescue of the mutilated wretch the traveller is surprised at finding that all the accomplices in the hellish deed have fled at his approach – at least so he supposes, for none of them are to be seen.

. . . . .

All that had been seen or heard was nothing more nor less than a Lincoln rehearsal; in which all the parts of all the characters of a Georgian Court-House fight had been sustained by the youth of the plough *solus*. The whole anecdote is told with a raciness and vigour which would do honour to the pages of Blackwood.

The second Article is '*The Dance, a Personal Adventure of the Author*' in which the oddities of a backwood reel are depicted with inimitable force, fidelity and picturesque effect. '*The Horse-swap*' is a vivid narration of an encounter between the wits of two Georgian horse-jockies. This is most excellent in every respect – but especially so in its delineations of Southern bravado, and the keen sense of the ludicrous evinced in the portraiture of the steeds. We think the following free and easy sketch of a *hoss* superior, in joint humour and verisimilitude, to any thing of the kind we have ever seen.

. . . . .

'*The Character of a Native Georgian*' is amusing, but not so good as the scenes which precede and succeed it. Moreover the character described (a practical humorist) is neither very original, nor appertaining exclusively to Georgia.

'*The Fight*' although involving some horrible and disgusting details of southern barbarity is a sketch unsurpassed in dramatic vigour, and in the vivid truth to nature of one or two of the personages introduced. *Uncle Tommy Loggins*, in particular, an oracle in 'rough and tumbles,' and Ransy Sniffle, a misshapen urchin 'who in his earlier days had fed copiously upon red clay and blackberries,' and all the pleasures of whose life concentre in a love of fisticuffs – are both forcible, accurate and original generic delineations of real existences to be found sparsely in Georgia, Mississippi and Louisiana, and very plentifully in our more remote settlements and territories. This article would positively make the fortune of any British periodical.

'*The Song*' is a burlesque somewhat overdone, but upon the whole a good caricature of Italian bravura singing. The following account of Miss Aurelia Emma Theodosia Augusta Crump's execution on the piano is inimitable.

. . . . .

The '*Turn Out*' is an excellent – a second edition of Miss Edgeworth's '*Barring Out,*' and full of fine touches of the truest humour. The scene is laid in Georgia, and in the good old days of *fescues*, *abbiselfas*, and *anpersants* – terms in very common use, but whose derivation we have always been at a loss to understand. Our author thus learnedly explains the riddle.

> The *fescue* was a sharpened wire, or other instrument, used by the preceptor, to point out the letters to the children. *Abbiselfa* is a contraction of the words 'a, by itself, a.' It was usual, when either of the vowels constituted a syllable of a word, to pronounce it, and denote its independent character, by the words first mentioned, thus: 'a by itself *a*, c-o-r-n corn, *acorn*' – e by itself *e*, v-i-l vil, evil. The character which stands for the word *and* (&) was probably pronounced with the same accompaniment, but in terms borrowed from the Latin language, thus: '*& per se* (by itself) &.' Hence '*anpersant.*'

This whole story forms an admirable picture of school-boy democracy in the woods. The *master* refuses his pupils an Easter holiday; and upon repairing, at the usual hour of the fatal day, to his school house, 'a log pen about twenty feet square,' finds every avenue to his ingress fortified and barricadoed. He advances, and is assailed by a whole wilderness of sticks from the cracks. Growing desperate, he seizes a fence rail, and finally succeeds in effecting an entrance by demolishing the door. He is soundly flogged however for his pains, and the triumphant urchins suffer him to escape with his life, solely upon condition of their being allowed to do what they please as long as they shall think proper.

'The Charming Creature as a Wife,' is a very striking narrative of the evils attendant upon an ill-arranged marriage – but as it has nothing about it peculiarly Georgian, we pass it over without further comment.

'The Gander Pulling' is a gem worthy, in every respect, of the writer of '*The Fight*,' and '*The Horse Swap*.' What a '*Gander Pulling*' is, however, may probably not be known by a great majority of our readers. We will therefore tell them. It is a piece of unprincipled barbarity not infrequently practised in the South and West. A circular horse path is formed of about forty or fifty yards in diameter. Over this path, and between two posts about ten feet apart, is extended a rope which, swinging loosely, vibrates in an arc of five or six feet. From the middle of this rope, lying directly over the middle of the path, a gander, whose neck and head are well greased, is suspended by the feet. The distance of the fowl from the ground is generally about ten feet – and its neck is consequently just within reach of a man on horseback. Matters being thus arranged, and the mob of vagabonds assembled, who are desirous of entering the chivalrous

lists of the 'Gander Pulling,' a hat is handed round, into which a quarter or half dollar, as the case may be, is thrown by each competitor. The money thus collected is the prize of the victor in the game – and the game is thus conducted. The ragamuffins mounted on horseback, gallop round the circle in Indian file. At a word of command, given by the proprietor of the gander, the pulling, properly so called, commences. Each villain as he passes under the rope, makes a grab at the throat of the devoted bird – the end and object of the tourney being to pull off his head. This of course is an end not easily accomplished. The fowl is obstinately bent upon retaining his caput if possible – in which determination he finds a powerful adjunct in the grease. The rope, moreover, by the efforts of the human devils, is kept in a troublesome and tantalizing state of vibration, while two assistants of the proprietor, one at each pole, are provided with a tough cowhide, for the purpose of preventing any horse from making too long a sojourn beneath the gander. Many hours, therefore, not unfrequently elapse before the contest is decided.

'The Ball' – a Georgia ball – is done to the life. Some passages, in a certain species of sly humour, wherein intense observation of character is disguised by simplicity of relation, put us forcibly in mind of the Spectator. For example.

. . . . .

'The Mother and her Child,' we have seen before – but read it a second time with zest. It is a laughable burlesque of the baby gibberish so frequently made use of by mothers in speaking to their children. This sketch evinces, like all the rest of the Georgia scenes – a fine dramatic talent.

'The Debating Society' is the best thing in the book – and indeed one among the best things of the kind we have ever read. It has all the force and freedom of some similar articles in the Diary of a Physician – without the evident straining for effect which so disfigures that otherwise admirable series. We will need no apology for copying *The Debating Society* entire.

. . . . .

'The Militia Company Drill,' is not by the author of the other pieces but has a strong family resemblance, and is very well executed. Among the innumerable descriptions of Militia musters which are so

rife in the land, we have met with nothing at all equal to this in the matter of broad farce.

'The Turf' is also capital, and bears with it a kind of dry and sarcastic morality which will recommend it to many readers.

'An Interesting Interview' is another specimen of exquisite dramatic talent. It consists of nothing more than a facsimile of the speech, actions, and *thoughts* of two drunken old men – but its air of truth is perfectly inimitable.

'The Fox-Hunt,' 'The Wax Works,' and *'A Sage Conversation,'* are all good – but neither *as* good as many other articles in the book.

'The Shooting Match,' which concludes the volume, may rank with the best of the Tales which precede it. As a portraiture of the manners of our South-Western peasantry, in especial, it is perhaps better than any.

Altogether this very humorous, and very clever book forms an æra in our reading. It has reached us per mail, and without a cover. We will have it bound forthwith, and give it a niche in our library as a sure omen of better days for the literature of the South.

FANCY AND IMAGINATION[1]

Amid the vague mythology of Egypt, the voluptuous scenery of her Nile, and the gigantic mysteries of her pyramids, Anacreon Moore has found all of that striking *matériel* which he so much delights in working up, and which he has embodied in the poem before us. The design of the story (for plot it has none) has been a less consideration than its facilities, and is made subservient to its execution. The subject is comprised in five epistles. In the first, Alciphron, the head of the Epicurean sect at Athens, writes, from Alexandria, to his friend Cleon, in the former city. He tells him (assigning a reason for quitting Athens and her pleasures) that, having fallen asleep one night after protracted festivity, he beholds, in a dream, a spectre, who tells him that, beside the sacred Nile, he, the Epicurean, shall find that Eternal Life for which he had so long been sighing. In the second, from the same to the same, the traveller speaks, at large and in rapturous terms, of the scenery of Egypt; of the beauty of her maidens; of an approaching Festival of the Moon; and of a wild hope entertained that amid the subterranean chambers of some huge pyramid lies the secret which he covets, the secret of Life Eternal. In the third letter he relates a love adventure at the Festival. Fascinated by the charms of one of the nymphs of a procession, he is first in despair at losing sight of her, then overjoyed at again seeing her in Necropolis, and finally traces her steps untill they are lost near one of the smaller pyramids. In epistle the fourth, (still from the same to the same,) he enters and explores the pyramid, and, passing through a complete series of Eleusinian mysteries, is at length successfully initiated into the secrets of Memphian priestcraft; we learning this latter point from letter the fifth, which concludes the poem, and is addressed by Orcus, high priest of Memphis, to Decius, a prætorian prefect.

A new poem from Moore calls to mind that critical opinion respecting him which had its origin, we believe, in the dogmatism of Coleridge – we mean the opinion that he is essentially the poet of *fancy* – the term being employed in contradistinction to *imagination*. 'The Fancy,' says the author of the *Ancient Mariner*, in his *Biographia Literaria*, 'the fancy combines, the imagination creates.' And this was intended, and has been received, as a distinction. If so at

[1] '*Alciphron, a Poem*. By Thomas Moore, Esq., author of *Lalla Rookh*, etc., etc. Carey and Hart, Philadelphia.

all, it is one without a difference; without even a difference of *degree*. The fancy as nearly creates as the imagination; and neither creates in any respect. All novel conceptions are merely unusual combinations. The mind of man can *imagine* nothing which has not really existed; and this point is susceptible of the most positive demonstration – see the Baron de Bielfeld, in his *Premiers Traits de L'Érudition Universelle*, 1767. It will be said, perhaps, that we can imagine a *griffin*, and that a griffin does not exist. Not the griffin certainly, but its component parts. It is a mere compendium of known limbs and features – of known qualities. Thus with all which seems to be *new* – which appears to be a *creation* of intellect. It is re-soluble into the old. The wildest and most vigorous effort of mind cannot stand the test of this analysis.

We might make a distinction, *of degree*, between the fancy and the imagination, in saying that the latter is the former *loftily employed*. But experience proves this distinction to be unsatisfactory. What we *feel* and *know* to be fancy, will be found still only *fanciful*, whatever be the theme which engages it. It retains its idiosyncrasy under all circumstances. No *subject* exalts it into the ideal. We might exemplify this by reference to the writings of one whom our patriotism, rather than our judgment, has elevated to a niche in the Poetic Temple which he does not becomingly fill, and which he cannot long uninterruptedly hold. We allude to the late Dr Rodman Drake, whose puerile abortion, *The Culprit Fay*, we examined, at some length, in a *critique* elsewhere; proving it, we think, beyond all question, to belong to that class of the pseudo-ideal, in dealing with which we find ourselves embarrassed between a kind of half-consciousness that we ought to admire, and the certainty that we do not. Dr Drake was employed upon a good subject – at least it is a subject precisely identical with those which Shakspeare was wont so happily to treat, and in which, especially, the author of *Lilian* has so wonderfully succeeded. But the American has brought to his task a mere *fancy*, and has grossly failed in doing what many suppose him to have done – in writing an ideal or imaginative poem. There is not one particle of the true ποιησις about *The Culprit Fay*. We say that the subject, even at its best points, did not aid Dr Drake in the slightest degree. He was never more than *fanciful*. The passage, for example, chiefly cited by his admirers, is the account of the 'Sylphid Queen'; and to show the difference between the false and true ideal, we collated, in the review just alluded to, this, the most admired passage, with one upon a similar topic by Shelley. We shall be pardoned for repeating here, as nearly as we remember them, some words of what we then said.

The description of the Sylphid Queen runs thus:

But oh, how fair the shape that lay
  Beneath a rainbow bending bright;
She seemed to the entranced Fay,
  The loveliest of the forms of light;
Her mantle was the purple rolled
  At twilight in the west afar;
'Twas tied with threads of dawning gold,
  And buttoned with a sparkling star.
Her face was like the lily roon
  That veils the vestal planet's hue;
Her eyes two beamlets from the moon
  Set floating in the welkin blue.
Her hair is like the sunny beam,
And the diamond gems which round it gleam
Are the pure drops of dewy even
That ne'er have left their native heaven.

In the *Queen Mab* of Shelley, a Fairy is thus introduced:

Those who had looked upon the sight,
Passing all human glory,
Saw not the yellow moon,
Saw not the mortal scene,
Heard not the night-wind's rush,
Heard not an earthly sound,
Saw but the fairy pageant,
Heard but the heavenly strains
That filled the lonely dwellings –

And thus described –

The Fairy's frame was slight; yon fibrous cloud
That catches but the palest tinge of even,
And which the straining eye can hardly seize
When melting into eastern twilight's shadow,
Were scarce so thin, so slight; but the fair star
That gems the glittering coronet of morn,
Sheds not a light so mild, so powerful,
As that which, bursting from the Fairy's form,
Spread a purpureal halo round the scene,
  Yet with an undulating motion,
  Swayed to her outline gracefully.

In these exquisite lines the faculty of mere comparison is but little exercised – that of ideality in a wonderful degree. It is probable that in a similar case Dr Drake would have formed the face of the fairy of the 'fibrous cloud,' her arms of the 'pale tinge of even,' her eyes of the 'fair stars,' and her body of the 'twilight shadow.' Having so done, his admirers would have congratulated him upon his *imagination*, not taking the trouble to think that they themselves could at any moment *imagine* a fairy of materials equally as good, and conveying an equally distinct idea. Their mistake would be precisely analogous to that of many a schoolboy who admires the imagination displayed in *Jack the Giant-Killer*, and is finally rejoiced at discovering his own imagination to surpass that of the author, since the monsters destroyed by Jack are only about forty feet in height, and he himself has no trouble in imagining some of one hundred and forty. It will be seen that the fairy of Shelley is not a mere compound of incongruous natural objects, inartificially put together, and unaccompanied by any *moral* sentiment – but a being, in the illustration of whose nature some physical elements are used collaterally as adjuncts, while the main conception springs immediately, *or thus apparently springs*, from the brain of the poet, enveloped in the moral sentiments of grace, of colour, of motion – of the beautiful, of the *mystical*, of the august – in short, of the ideal.

The truth is, that the just distinction between the fancy and the imagination (and which is still but a distinction *of degree*) is involved in the consideration of the *mystic*. We give this as an idea of our own altogether. We have no authority for our opinion – but do not the less firmly hold it. The term *mystic* is here employed in the sense of Augustus William Schlegel, and of most other German critics. It is applied by them to that class of composition in which there lies beneath the transparent upper-current of meaning, an under or *suggestive* one. What we vaguely term the *moral* of any sentiment is its mystic or secondary expression. It has the vast force of an accompaniment in music. This vivifies the air; that spiritualizes the *fanciful* conception, and lifts it into the *ideal*.

This theory will bear, we think, the most rigorous test which can be made applicable to it, and will be acknowledged as tenable by all who are themselves imaginative. If we carefully examine those poems, or portions of poems, or those prose romances, which mankind have been accustomed to designate as *imaginative*, (for an instinctive feeling leads us to employ properly the term whose full import we have still never been able to define,) it will be seen that all so designated are remarkable for the *suggestive* character which we have discussed. They are strongly *mystic* – in the proper sense of the word. We will here only call to the reader's mind the *Prometheus Vinctus* of Æschylus; the *Inferno* of Dante; the *Destruction of Numantia* by Cervantes; the *Comus* of Milton; the *Ancient Mariner*, the *Christabel*, and the *Kubla Khan*, of Coleridge; the *Nightingale* of Keats; and, most especially, the *Sensitive Plant* of Shelley, and the *Undine* of De la Motte Fouqué. These two latter poems (for we call them both such) are the finest possible examples of the purely *ideal*. There is little of fancy here, and everything of imagination. With each note of the lyre is heard a ghostly, and not always a distinct, but an august and soul-exalting *echo*. In every glimpse of beauty presented, we catch, through long and wild vistas, dim bewildering visions of a far more ethereal beauty *beyond*. But not so in poems which the world has always persisted in terming *fanciful*. Here the upper-current is often exceedingly brilliant and beautiful; but then men *feel* that this upper-current *is all*. No Naiad voice addresses them *from below*. The notes of the air of the song do not tremble with the according tones of the accompaniment.

It is the failure to perceive these truths which has occasioned the embarrassment experienced by our critics while discussing the topic of Moore's station in the poetic world – that hesitation with which we are obliged to refuse him the loftiest rank among the most noble. The popular voice, and the popular heart, have denied him that happiest quality, imagination – and here the popular voice (*because* for once it is gone with the popular heart) is right – but yet only relatively so. Imagination is not the leading feature of the poetry of Moore; but he possesses it in no little degree.

We will quote a few instances from the poem now before us – instances which will serve to exemplify the distinctive feature which we have attributed to ideality.

It is the *suggestive* force which exalts and etherealizes the passages we copy.

> Or is it that there lurks, indeed,
> Some truth in man's prevailing creed,
> And that our guardians from on high,
>   Come, in that pause from toil and sin,
> To put the senses' curtain by,
>   And on the wakeful soul look in!

Again –

> The eternal pyramids of Memphis burst
> Awfully on my sight – standing sublime
> 'Twixt earth and heaven, the watch-towers of time,
> From whose lone summit, when his reign hath past,
> From earth forever, he will look his last.

And again –

> Is there for man no hope – but this which dooms
> His only lasting trophies to be tombs!
> But 'tis not so – earth, heaven, all nature shows
> He *may* become immortal, *may* unclose
> The wings within him wrapt, and proudly rise
> Redeemed from earth a creature of the skies!

And here –

> The pyramid shadows, stretching from the light,
> Look like the first colossal steps of night,
> Stalking across the valley to invade
> The distant hills of porphyry with their shade!

And once more –

> There Silence, thoughtful God, who loves
> The neighbourhood of Death, in groves
> Of asphodel lies hid, and weaves
> His hushing spell among the leaves.

Such lines as these, we must admit, however, are not of frequent occurrence in the poem – the sum of whose great beauty is composed of the several sums of a world of minor excellences.

Moore has always been renowned for the number and appositeness, as well as novelty, of his similes; and the renown thus acquired is strongly indicial of his deficiency in that nobler merit – the noblest of them all. No poet thus distinguished was ever richly ideal. Pope and Cowper are remarkable instances in point. Similes (so much insisted upon by the critics of the reign of Queen Anne) are never, in our opinion, strictly in good taste, whatever may be said to the contrary, and certainly can never be made to accord with other high qualities, except when naturally arising from the subject in the way of illustration – and, when thus arising, they have seldom the merit of novelty. To be novel, they must fail in essential particulars. The higher minds will avoid their frequent use. They form no portion of the ideal, and appertain to the fancy alone.

We proceed with a few random observations upon *Alciphron*. The poem is distinguished throughout by a very happy facility which has never been mentioned in connexion with its author, but which has much to do with the reputation he has obtained. We allude to the facility with which he recounts a poetical story in a *prosaic* way. By this is meant that he preserves the tone and method of arrangement of a prose relation, and thus obtains great advantages over his more stilted compeers. His is no poetical *style*, (such, for example, as the French have – a distinct style for a distinct purpose,) but an easy and ordinary prose manner, *ornamented into poetry*. By means of this he is enabled to enter, with ease, into details which would baffle any other versifier of the age, and at which Lamartine would stand aghast. For anything that we see to the contrary, Moore might solve a cubic equation in verse. His facility in this respect is truly admirable, and is, no doubt, the result of long practice after mature deliberation. We refer the reader to page 50 of the pamphlet now reviewed; where the minute and conflicting incidents of the descent into the pyramid are detailed with absolutely *more* precision than we have ever known a similar relation detailed with in prose.

In general dexterity and melody of versification the author of *Lalla Rookh* is unrivalled; but he is by no means at all times accurate, falling occasionally into the common foible of throwing accent upon syllables too unimportant to sustain it. Thus, in the lines which follow, where we have italicized the weak syllables:

> And mark 'tis nigh; already *the* sun bids . .
> While hark from all the temples *a* rich swell . . .
> I rushed in*to* the cool night air.

He also too frequently draws out the word Heaven into two syllables – a protraction which it *never* will support.

His English is now and then objectionable, as, at page 26, where he speaks of

> lighted barks
> That down Syene's cataract *shoots*,

making *shoots* rhyme with flutes, below; also, at page 6, and elsewhere, where the word *none* has improperly a singular, instead of a plural force. But such criticism as this is somewhat captious, for in general he is most highly polished.

At page 27, he has stolen his 'woven snow' from the *ventum textilem* of Apuleius.

At page 8, he either himself has misunderstood the tenets of Epicurus, or wilfully misrepresents them through the voice of Alciphron. We incline to the former idea, however; as the philosophy of that most noble of the sophists is habitually perverted by the moderns. Nothing could be more spiritual and less sensual than the doctrines we so torture into wrong. But we have drawn out this notice at somewhat too great length, and must conclude. In truth the exceeding beauty of *Alciphron* has bewildered and detained us. We could not point out a poem in any language which, as a whole, greatly excels it. It is far superior to *Lalla Rookh*. While Moore does not reach, except in rare snatches, the height of the loftiest qualities of some whom we have named, yet he has written finer poems than any, of equal length, by the greatest of his rivals. His radiance, not always as bright as some flashes from other pens, is yet a radiance of equable glow, whose total amount of light exceeds, by very much, we think, that total amount in the case of any contemporary writer whatsoever. A vivid fancy; an epigrammatic spirit; a fine taste; vivacity, dexterity, and a musical ear; have made him very easily what he is, the most popular poet now living – if not the most popular that ever lived – and perhaps, a slight modification at birth of that which phrenologists have agreed to term *temperament*, might have made him the truest and noblest votary of the muse of any age or clime. As it is, we have only casual glimpses of that *mens divinior* which is assuredly enshrined within him.

CHARLES DICKENS[1]

We often hear it said, of this or of that proposition, that it may be good in theory, but will not answer in practice; and in such assertions we find the substance of all the sneers at critical art which so gracefully curl the upper lips of a tribe which is beneath it. We mean the small geniuses – the literary Titmice – animalculæ which judge of merit solely by *result*, and boast of the solidity, tangibility, and infallibility of the test which they employ. The worth of a work is most accurately estimated, they assure us, by the number of those who peruse it; and 'does a book sell?' is a query embodying, in their opinion, all that need be said or sung on the topic of its fitness for sale. We should as soon think of maintaining, in the presence of these creatures, the *dictum* of Anaxagoras, that snow is black, as of disputing, for example, the profundity of that genius which, in a run of five hundred nights, has rendered itself evident in *London Assurance*. 'What,' cry they, 'are critical precepts to us, or to anybody? Were we to observe all the critical rules in creation we should still be unable to write a good book' – a point, by the way, which we shall not now pause to deny. 'Give us *results*,' they vociferate, 'for we are plain men of common sense. We contend for fact instead of fancy – for practice in opposition to theory.'

The mistake into which the Titmice have been innocently led, however, is precisely that of dividing the practice which they would uphold from the theory to which they would object. They should have been told in infancy, and thus prevented from exposing themselves in old age, that theory and practice are in so much *one*, that the former implies or includes the latter. A theory is only good as such, in proportion to its reducibility to practice. If the practice fail, it is because the theory is imperfect. To say what they are in the daily habit of saying – that such or such a matter may be good in theory but is false in practice, – is to perpetrate a bull – to commit a paradox – to state a contradiction in terms – in plain words, to tell a lie *which is a lie at sight* to the understanding of anything bigger than a Titmouse.

But we have no idea, just now, of persecuting the Tittlebats by too close a scrutiny into their little opinions. It is not our purpose, for example, to press them with so grave a weapon as the *argumentum*

[1] *Barnaby Rudge*. By Charles Dickens, (Boz). Author of *The Old Curiosity Shop*, *Pickwick*, *Oliver Twist*, etc. Lea & Blanchard: Philadelphia.

ad absurdum, or to ask them why, if the popularity of a book be in fact the measure of its worth, we should not be at once in condition to admit the inferiority of *Newton's Principia* to *Hoyle's Games*; of *Ernest Maltravers* to *Jack-the-Giant-Killer*, or *Jack Sheppard*, or *Jack Brag*; and of *Dick's Christian Philosopher* to *Charlotte Temple*, or the *Memoirs of de Grammont*, or to one or two dozen other works which must be nameless. Our present design is but to speak, at some length, of a book which in so much concerns the Titmice, that it affords them the very kind of demonstration which they chiefly affect – *practical* demonstration – of the fallacy of one of their favourite dogmas; we mean the dogma that no work of fiction can fully suit, at the same time, the critical and the popular taste; in fact, that the disregarding or contravening of critical rule is absolutely essential to success, beyond a certain and very limited extent, with the public at large. And if, in the course of our random observations – for we have no space for systematic review – it should appear, incidentally, that the vast popularity of *Barnaby Rudge* must be regarded less as the measure of its value, than as the legitimate and inevitable result of certain well-understood critical propositions reduced by genius into practice, there will appear nothing more than what has before become apparent in the *Vicar of Wakefield* of Goldsmith, or in the *Robinson Crusoe* of De Foe – nothing more, in fact, than what is a truism to all but the Titmice.

Those who know us will not, from what is here premised, suppose it our intention to enter into any wholesale laudation of *Barnaby Rudge*. In truth, our design may appear, at a cursory glance, to be very different indeed. Boccalini, in his *Advertisements from Parnassus*, tells us that a critic once presented Apollo with a severe censure upon an excellent poem. The god asked him for the beauties of the work. He replied that he only troubled himself about the errors. Apollo presented him with a sack of unwinnowed wheat, and bade him pick out all the chaff for his pains. Now we have not fully made up our minds that the god was in the right. We are not sure that the limit of critical duty is not very generally misapprehended. *Excellence* may be considered an axiom, or a proposition which becomes self-evident just in proportion to the clearness or precision with which it is *put*. If it fairly exists, in this sense, it requires no further elucidation. It is not excellence if it need to be demonstrated as such. To point out too particularly the beauties of a work, is to admit, tacitly, that these beauties are not wholly admirable. Regarding, then, excellence as that which is capable of self-manifestation, it but remains for the critic to show when, where, and how it fails in becoming manifest; and, in this showing, it will be the fault of the book itself if what of beauty it contains be not, at least, placed in the fairest light. In a word, we may assume, notwithstanding a vast deal of pitiable cant upon this topic, that in pointing out frankly the errors of a work, we do nearly all that is critically necessary, in displaying its merits. In teaching what perfection *is*, how, in fact, shall we more rationally proceed than in specifying what it *is not*?

The plot of *Barnaby Rudge* runs thus: About a hundred years ago, Geoffrey Haredale and John Chester were schoolmates in England – the former being the scapegoat and drudge of the latter. Leaving school, the boys become friends, with much of the old understanding. Haredale loves; Chester deprives him of his mistress. The one cherishes the most deadly hatred; the other merely contemns and avoids. By routes widely different both attain mature age. Haredale, remembering his old love, and still cherishing his old hatred, remains a bachelor and is poor. Chester, among other crimes, is guilty of the seduction and heartless abandonment of a gipsy-girl, who, after the desertion of her lover, gives birth to a son, and, falling into evil courses, is finally hung at Tyburn. The son is received and taken charge of, at an inn called the Maypole, upon the borders of Epping Forest, and about twelve miles from London. This inn is kept by one John Willet, a burly-headed and very obtuse little man, who has a son, Joe, and who employs his *protégé*, under the single name of Hugh, as perpetual hostler at the inn. Hugh's father marries, in the meantime, a rich *parvenue*, who soon dies, but not before having presented Mr Chester with a boy, Edward. The father, (a thoroughly selfish man-of-the-world, whose model is Chesterfield,) educates this son at a distance, seeing him rarely, and calling him to the paternal residence, at London, only when he has attained the age of twenty-four or five. He, the father, has, long ere this time, spent the fortune brought him by his wife, having been living upon his wits and a small annuity for some eighteen years. The son is recalled chiefly that by marrying an heiress, on the strength of his own personal merit and the reputed wealth of old Chester, he may enable the latter to continue his gayeties in old age. But of this design, as well as of his poverty, Edward is kept in ignorance for some three or four years after his recall; when the father's discovery of what he considers an inexpedient love-entanglement on the part of the son, induces him to disclose the true state of his affairs, as well as the real tenor of his intentions.

Now the love-entanglement of which we speak, is considered inexpedient by Mr Chester for two reasons – the first of which is, that the lady beloved is the orphan niece of his old enemy, Haredale, and the second is, that Haredale (although in circumstances which have been much and very unexpectedly improved during the preceding twenty-two years) is still insufficiently wealthy to meet the views of Mr Chester.

We say that, about twenty-two years before the period in question, there came an unlooked-for change in the worldly circumstances of Haredale. This gentleman has an elder brother, Reuben, who has long possessed the family inheritance of the Haredales, residing at a mansion called The Warren not far from the Maypole Inn, which is itself a portion of the estate. Reuben *is a widower*, with one child, a daughter, Emma. Besides this daughter, there are living with him a gardener, a steward (whose name is Rudge) and *two* women servants, one of whom is the wife of Rudge. On the night of the nineteenth of March, 1733, Rudge murders his master for the sake of a large sum of money which he is known to have in possession. During the struggle, Mr Haredale grasps the cord of an alarm-bell which hangs within his reach, but succeeds in sounding it only once or twice, when it is severed by the knife of the ruffian, who then, completing his bloody business, and securing the money, proceeds to quit the chamber. While doing this, however, he is disconcerted by meeting the gardener, whose pallid countenance evinces suspicion of the deed committed. The murderer is thus forced to kill his fellow-servant. Having done so, the idea strikes him of transferring the burden of the crime from himself. He dresses the corpse of the gardener in his own clothes, puts upon its finger his own ring, and in its pocket his own watch – then drags it to a pond in the grounds, and throws it in. He now returns to the house, and, disclosing all to his wife, requests her to become a partner in his flight. Horror-stricken, she falls to the ground. He attempts to raise her. She seizes his wrist, *staining her hand with blood in the attempt*. She renounces him for ever; yet promises to conceal the crime. Alone, he flees the country. The next morning, Mr Haredale being found murdered, and the steward and gardener being both missing, both are suspected. Mrs Rudge leaves The Warren, and retires to an obscure lodging in London (where she lives upon an annuity allowed her by Haredale), having given birth, *on the very day after the murder*, to a son, Barnaby Rudge, who proves an idiot, who bears upon his wrist a red mark, and who is born possessed with a maniacal horror of blood.

Some months since the assassination having elapsed, what appears to be the corpse of Rudge is discovered, and the outrage is attributed to the gardener. Yet not universally: – for, as Geoffrey Haredale comes into possession of the estate, there are not wanting suspicions (fomented by Chester) of his own participation in the deed. This taint of suspicion, acting upon his hereditary gloom, together with the natural grief and horror of the atrocity, embitters the whole life of Haredale. He secludes himself at The Warren, and acquires a monomaniac acerbity of temper relieved only by love of his beautiful niece.

Time wears away. Twenty-two years pass by. The niece has ripened into womanhood, and loves young Chester without the knowledge of her uncle or the youth's father. Hugh has grown a stalwart man – the type of man *the animal*, as his father is of man the ultra-civilized. Rudge, the murderer, returns, urged to his undoing by Fate. He appears at the Maypole and inquires stealthily of the circumstances which have occurred at The Warren in his absence. He proceeds to London, discovers the dwelling of his wife, threatens her with the betrayal of her idiot son into vice and extorts from her the bounty of Haredale. Revolting at such appropriation of such means, the widow, with Barnaby, again seeks The Warren, renounces the annuity, and, refusing to assign any reason for her conduct, states her intention of quitting London for ever, and of burying herself in some obscure retreat – a retreat which she begs Haredale not to attempt discovering. When he seeks her in London the next day, she is gone; and there are no tidings, either of herself or of Barnaby; *until the expiration of five years* – which brings the time up to that of the celebrated 'No Popery' Riots of Lord George Gordon.

In the meanwhile, and immediately subsequent to the reappearance of Rudge, Haredale and the elder Chester, each heartily desirous of preventing the union of Edward and Emma, have entered into a covenant, the result of which is that, by means of treachery on the part of Chester, permitted on that of Haredale, the lovers misunderstand each other and are estranged. Joe, also, the son of the innkeeper, Willet, having been coquetted with, to too great an extent, by Dolly Varden, (the pretty daughter of one Gabriel Varden, a locksmith of Clerkenwell, London) and having been otherwise maltreated at home, enlists in his Majesty's army and is carried beyond seas, to America; not returning until towards the close of the riots. Just before their commencement, Rudge, in a midnight prowl about the scene of his atrocity, is encountered by an individual who had been familiar with him in earlier life, while living at The Warren. This individual, terrified at what he supposes, very naturally, to be the ghost of the murdered Rudge, relates his adventure to his companions at the Maypole, and John Willet conveys the intelligence, forthwith, to Mr Haredale. Connecting the apparition, in his own mind, with the peculiar conduct of Mrs Rudge, this gentleman imbibes a suspicion, at once, of the true state of affairs. This suspicion (which he mentions to no one) is, moreover, very strongly confirmed by an occurrence happening to Varden, the locksmith, who, visiting the woman late one night, finds her in communion, of a nature apparently most confidential, with a ruffian whom the locksmith knows to be such, without knowing the man himself. Upon an attempt, on the part of Varden, to seize this ruffian, he is thwarted by Mrs R.; and upon Haredale's inquiring minutely into the personal appearance of the man, he is found to accord with Rudge. We have already shown that the ruffian was in fact Rudge himself. Acting upon the suspicion thus aroused, Haredale watches, by night, alone, in the deserted house formerly occupied by Mrs R. in hope of here coming upon the murderer, and makes other exertions with the view of arresting him; but all in vain.

It is, also, at the conclusion *of the five years*, that the hitherto uninvaded retreat of Mrs Rudge is disturbed by a message from her husband, demanding money. He has discovered her abode by accident. Giving him what she has at the time, she afterwards eludes him, and hastens, with Barnaby, to bury herself in the crowd of London, until she can find opportunity again to seek retreat in some more distant region of England. But the riots have now begun. The idiot is beguiled into joining the mob, and, becoming separated from his mother (who, growing ill through grief, is borne to a hospital) meets with his old playmate Hugh, and becomes with him a ringleader in the rebellion.

The riots proceed. A conspicuous part is borne in them by one Simon Tappertit, a fantastic and conceited little apprentice of Varden's, and a sworn enemy to Joe Willet, who has rivalled him in the affection of Dolly. A hangman, Dennis, is also very busy amid the mob. Lord George Gordon, and his secretary, Gashford, with John Grueby, his servant, appear, of course, upon the scene. Old Chester, who, during the five years, has become Sir John, instigates Gashford, who has received personal insult from Haredale, (a Catholic and consequently obnoxious to the mob) instigates Gashford to procure the burning of The Warren, and to abduct Emma during the excitement ensuing. The mansion is burned, (Hugh, who also fancies himself wronged by Haredale, being chief actor in the outrage) and Miss H. carried off, in company with Dolly, who had long lived with her, and whom Tappertit abducts upon his own responsibility. Rudge, in the meantime, finding the eye of Haredale upon him, (since he has become aware of the watch kept nightly at his wife's,) goaded by the dread of solitude, and fancying that his sole chance of safety lies in joining the rioters, hurries upon their track to the doomed Warren. He arrives too late – the mob have departed. Skulking about the ruins, he is discovered by Haredale, and finally captured without a struggle, within the glowing walls of the very chamber in which the deed was committed. He is conveyed to prison, where he meets and recognizes Barnaby, who had been captured as a rioter. The mob assail and burn the jail. The father and son escape. Betrayed by Dennis, both are again retaken, and Hugh shares their fate. In Newgate, Dennis, through accident, discovers the parentage of Hugh, and an effort is made in vain to interest Chester in behalf of his son. Finally, Varden procures the pardon of Barnaby; but Hugh, Rudge, and Dennis are hung. At the eleventh hour, Joe returns from abroad with one arm. In company with Edward Chester, he performs prodigies of valour (during the last riots) on behalf of the Government. The two, with Haredale and Varden, rescue Emma and Dolly. A double marriage, of course, takes place; for Dolly has repented her fine airs, and the prejudices of Haredale are overcome. Having killed Chester in a duel, he quits England for ever, and ends his days in the seclusion of an Italian convent. Thus, after summary disposal of the understrappers, ends the drama of *Barnaby Rudge*.

We have given, as may well be supposed, but a very meagre outline of the story, and we have given it in the simple or natural sequence. That is to say, we have related the events, as nearly as might be, in the order of their occurrence. But this order would by no means have suited the purpose of the novelist, whose design has been to maintain the secret of the murder, and the consequent mystery which encircles Rudge, and the actions of his wife, until the catastrophe of his discovery by Haredale. The *thesis* of the novel may thus be regarded as based upon curiosity. Every point is so arranged as to perplex the reader, and whet his desire for elucidation: – for example, the first appearance of Rudge at the Maypole; his questions; his persecution of Mrs R.; the ghost seen by the frequenter of the Maypole; and Haredale's impressive conduct in consequence. What *we* have told, in the very beginning of our digest, in regard to the shifting of the gardener's dress, is sedulously kept from the reader's knowledge until he learns it from Rudge's own confession in jail. We say sedulously; for, *the intention once known*, the *traces* of the design can be found upon every page. There is an amusing and exceedingly ingenious instance at page 145, where Solomon Daisy describes his adventure with the ghost.

> 'It was a ghost – a spirit,' cried Daisy.
>
> 'Whose?' they all three asked together.
>
> In the excess of his emotion (for he fell back trembling in his chair and waved his hand as if entreating them to question him no further) *his answer was lost upon all* but old John Willet, who happened to be seated close beside him.
>
> 'Who!' cried Parkes and Tom Cobb – 'Who was it?'
>
> 'Gentlemen,' said Mr Willet, after a long pause, 'you needn't ask. The likeness of a murdered man. This is the nineteenth of March.'
>
> A profound silence ensued.

The impression here skilfully conveyed is, that the ghost seen is that of Reuben Haredale; and the mind of the not-too-acute reader is at once averted from the true state of the case – from the murderer, Rudge, living in the body.

Now there can be no question that, by such means as these, many points which are comparatively insipid in the natural sequence of our digest, and which would have been comparatively insipid even if given in full detail in a natural sequence, are endued with the interest of mystery; but neither can it be denied that a vast many more points are at the same time deprived of all effect, and become null, through the impossibility of comprehending them without the key. The author, who, cognizant of his plot, writes with this cognizance continually operating upon him, and thus *writes to himself* in spite of himself, does not, of course, feel that much of what is effective to his own informed perception, must necessarily be lost upon his uninformed readers, and he himself is never in condition, as regards his own work, to bring the matter to test. But the reader may easily satisfy himself of the validity of our objection. Let him *re-peruse Barnaby Rudge*, and with a pre-comprehension of the mystery, these points of which we speak break out in all directions like stars, and throw quadruple brilliance over the narrative – a brilliance which a correct taste will at once declare unprofitably sacrificed at the shrine of the keenest interest of mere mystery.

The design of *mystery*, however, being once determined upon by an author, it becomes imperative first, that no undue or inartistical means be employed to conceal the secret of the plot; and, secondly, that the secret be well kept. Now, when at page 16, we read that 'the body of *poor Mr Rudge, the steward, was found*' months after the outrage, etc., we see that Mr Dickens has been guilty of no misdemeanour against Art in stating what was not the fact; since the falsehood is put into the mouth of Solomon Daisy, and given merely as the impression of this individual and of the public. The writer has not asserted it in his own person, but ingeniously conveyed an idea (false in itself, yet a belief in which is necessary for the effect of the tale) by the mouth of one of his characters. The case is different, however, when Mrs Rudge is repeatedly denominated 'the widow.' It is the author who, himself, frequently so terms her. This is disingenuous and inartistical: accidentally so, of course. We speak of the matter merely by way of illustrating our point, and as an oversight on the part of Mr Dickens.

That the secret be well kept is obviously necessary. A failure to preserve it until the proper moment of *dénouement* throws all into confusion, so far as regards the *effect* intended. If the mystery leaks out, against the author's will, his purposes are immediately at odds and ends; for he proceeds upon the supposition that certain impressions *do* exist, which do *not* exist in the mind of his readers. We are not prepared to say, so positively as we could wish, whether, by the public at large, the whole *mystery* of the murder committed by Rudge, with the identity of the Maypole ruffian with Rudge himself, was fathomed at any period previous to the period intended, or, if so, whether at a period so early as materially to interfere with the interest designed; but we are forced, through sheer modesty, to suppose this the case; since, by ourselves individually, the secret was distinctly understood immediately upon the perusal of the story of Solomon Daisy, which occurs at the seventh page of this volume of three hundred and twenty-three. In the number of the *Philadelphia Saturday Evening Post*, for May the first, 1841, (the tale having then only begun) will be found a *prospective notice* of some length, in which we made use of the following words:

> That Barnaby is the son of the murderer may not appear evident to our readers – but we will explain. The person murdered is Mr Reuben Haredale. He was found assassinated in his bed-chamber. His steward, (Mr Rudge, senior,) and his gardener (name not mentioned) are missing. At first both are suspected. 'Some months afterward' – here we use the words of the story –' the steward's body, scarcely to be

recognized but by his clothes, and the watch and ring he wore – was found at the bottom of a piece of water in the grounds, with a deep gash in the breast, where he had been stabbed by a knife. He was only partly dressed; and all people agreed that he had been sitting up reading in his own room, where there were many traces of blood, and was suddenly fallen upon and killed, before his master.'

Now, be it observed, it is not the author himself who asserts that *the steward's body was found*; he has put the words in the mouth of one of his characters. His design is to make it appear, in the *dénouement*, that the steward, Rudge, first murdered the gardener, then went to his master's chamber, murdered *him*, was interrupted by his (Rudge's) wife, whom he seized and held *by the wrist*, to prevent her giving the alarm – that he then, after possessing himself of the booty desired, returned to the gardener's room, exchanged clothes with him, put upon the corpse his own watch and ring, and secreted it where it was afterwards discovered at so late a period that the features could not be identified.

The differences between our pre-conceived ideas, as here stated, and the actual facts of the story, will be found immaterial. The gardener was murdered, not before but after his master; and that Rudge's wife seized *him* by the wrist, instead of his seizing *her*, has so much the air of a mistake on the part of Mr Dickens, that we can scarcely speak of our own version as erroneous. The grasp of a murderer's bloody hand on the wrist of a woman *enceinte*, would have been more likely to produce the effect described (and, this every one will allow) than the grasp of the hand of the woman upon the wrist of the assassin. We may therefore say of our supposition as Talleyrand said of some cockney's bad French – *que s'il ne soit pas Français, assurément donc il le doit être* – that if we did not rightly prophesy, yet, at least, our prophecy *should have been* right.

We are informed in the Preface to *Barnaby Rudge* that 'no account of the Gordon Riots having been introduced into any work of fiction, and the subject presenting very extraordinary and remarkable features,' our author 'was led to project this tale.' But for this distinct announcement (for Mr Dickens can scarcely have deceived himself) we should have looked upon the riots as altogether an afterthought. It is evident that they have no necessary connexion with the story. In our digest, which carefully includes all *essentials* of the plot, we have dismissed the doings of the mob in a paragraph. The whole event of the drama would have proceeded as well without as with them. They have even the appearance of being *forcibly* introduced. In our compendium above, it will be seen that we emphasized several allusions to an interval of *five years*. The action is brought up to a certain point. The train of events is so far uninterrupted – nor is there any apparent need of interruption – yet all the characters are now thrown forward for a period of *five years*. And why? We ask in vain. It is not to bestow upon the lovers a more decorous maturity of age – for this is the only possible idea which suggests itself – Edward Chester is already eight-and-twenty, and Emma Haredale would, in America at least, be upon the list of old maids. No – there is no such reason; nor does there appear to be any one more plausible than that, as it is now the year of our Lord 1775, an advance of five years will bring the *dramatis personæ* up to a very remarkable period, affording an admirable opportunity for their display – the period, in short, of the 'No Popery' riots. This was the idea with which we were forcibly impressed in perusal, and which nothing less than Mr Dickens' positive assurance to the contrary would have been sufficient to eradicate.

It is, perhaps, but one of a thousand instances of the disadvantages, both to the author and the public, of the present absurd fashion of periodical novel-writing, that our author had not sufficiently considered or determined upon *any* particular plot when he began the story now under review. In fact, we see, or fancy that we see, numerous traces of indecision – traces which a dexterous supervision of the complete work might have enabled him to erase. We have already spoken of the intermission of a lustrum. The opening speeches of old Chester are by far too *truly* gentlemanly for his subsequent character. The wife of Varden, also, is too wholesale a shrew to be converted into the quiet wife – the original design was to punish her. At page 16 we read thus – Solomon Daisy is telling his story:

> 'I put as good a face upon it as I could, and muffling myself up, started out with a lighted lantern in one hand and the key of the church in the other' – at this point of the narrative, the dress of the strange man rustled as if he had turned to hear more distinctly.

Here the design is to call the reader's attention to a *point* in the tale; but no subsequent explanation is made. Again, a few lines below –

> The houses were all shut up, and the folks indoors, and perhaps there is only one man in the world who knows how dark it really was.

Here the intention is still more evident, but there is no result. Again, at page 54, the idiot draws Mr Chester to the window, and directs his attention to the clothes hanging upon the lines in the yard –

> 'Look down,' he said softly; 'do you mark how they whisper in each other's ears, then dance and leap to make believe they are in sport? Do you see how they stop for a moment, when they think there is no one looking, and mutter among themselves again; and then how they roll and gambol, delighted with the mischief they've been plotting? Look at 'em now! See how they whirl and plunge. And now they stop again, and whisper cautiously together – little thinking, mind, how often I have lain upon the ground and watched them. I say – what is it that they plot and hatch? Do you know?'

Upon perusal of these ravings, we at once supposed them to have allusion to some *real* plotting; and even now we cannot force ourselves to believe them not so intended. They suggested the opinion that Haredale himself would be implicated in the murder, and that the counsellings alluded to might be those of that gentleman with Rudge. It is by no means impossible that some such conception wavered in the mind of the author. At page 32 we have a confirmation of our idea, when Varden endeavours to arrest the murderer in the house of his wife –

> 'Come back – come back!' exclaimed the woman, wrestling with and clasping him. 'Do not touch him on your life. *He carries other lives beside his own.*'

The *dénouement* fails to account for this exclamation.

In the beginning of the story much emphasis is placed upon the *two* female servants of Haredale, and upon his journey to and from London, as well as upon his wife. We have merely said, in our digest, that he was a widower, italicizing the remark. All these other points are, in fact, singularly irrelevant, in the supposition that the original design has not undergone modification.

Again, at page 57, when Haredale talks of 'his dismantled and beggared hearth' we cannot help fancying that the author had in view some different wrong, or series of wrongs, perpetrated by Chester, than any which appear in the end. This gentleman, too, takes extreme and frequent pains to acquire dominion over the rough Hugh – this matter is particularly insisted upon by the novelist – we look, of course, for some important result – but the filching of a letter is nearly all that is accomplished. That Barnaby's delight in the desperate scenes of the Rebellion, is inconsistent with his horror of blood, will strike every reader; and this inconsistency seems to be the consequence of the *after-thought* upon which we have already commented. In fact, the title of the work, the elaborate and pointed manner of the commencement, the impressive description of The Warren, and especially of Mrs Rudge, go far to show that Mr Dickens has really deceived himself – that the soul of the plot, as originally conceived, was the murder of Haredale, with the subsequent discovery of the murderer in Rudge – but that this idea was afterwards abandoned, or rather suffered to be merged in that of the Popish riots. The result has been most unfavourable. That which, of itself, would have proved highly effective, has been rendered nearly null by its situation. In the multitudinous outrage and horror of the Rebellion, the *one* atrocity is utterly whelmed and extinguished.

The reasons of this deflection from the first purpose appear to us self-evident. One of them we have already mentioned. The other is that our author discovered, when too late, that *he had anticipated, and thus rendered valueless, his chief effect*. This will be readily understood. The particulars of the assassination being withheld, the strength of the narrator is put forth, in the beginning of the story, to *whet curiosity* in respect to these particulars and, so far, he is but in proper pursuance of his main design. But from this intention he unwittingly passes into the error of *exaggerating anticipation*. And error though it be, it is an error wrought with consummate skill. What, for example, could more vividly enhance our impression of the unknown horror enacted, than the deep and enduring gloom of Haredale – than the idiot's inborn awe of blood – or, especially, than the expression of countenance so imaginatively attributed to Mrs Rudge – 'the capacity for expressing terror – something only dimly seen, but never absent for a moment – the shadow of some look to which an instant of intense and most unutterable horror only could have given rise'? But it is a condition of the human fancy that the promises of such words are irredeemable. In the notice before mentioned we thus spoke upon this topic:

> This is a conception admirably adapted to whet curiosity in respect to the character of that event which is hinted at as forming the basis of the story. But this observation should not fail to be made – that the anticipation must surpass the reality; that no matter how terrific be the circumstances which, in the *dénouement*, shall appear to have occasioned the expression of countenance worn habitually by Mrs Rudge, still they will not be able to satisfy the mind of the reader. He will surely be disappointed. The skilful intimation of horror held out

> by the artist, produces an effect which will deprive his conclusion of all. These intimations – these dark hints of some uncertain evil – are often rhetorically praised as effective – but are only justly so praised where there is *no dénouement* whatever – where the reader's imagination is left to clear up the mystery for itself – and this is not the design of Mr Dickens.

And, in fact, our author was not long in seeing his precipitancy. He had placed himself in a dilemma from which even his high genius could not extricate him. He at once shifts the main interest – and in truth we do not see what better he could have done. The reader's attention becomes absorbed in the riots, and he fails to observe that what should have been the true catastrophe of the novel is exceedingly feeble and ineffective.

A few cursory remarks: – Mr Dickens fails peculiarly in *pure* narration. See, for example, page 296, where the connexion of Hugh and Chester is detailed by Varden. See also in *The Old Curiosity Shop*, where, when the result is fully known, so many words are occupied in explaining the relationship of the brothers. The effect of the present narrative might have been materially increased by confining the action within the limits of London. The *Notre-Dame* of Hugo affords a fine example of the force which can be gained by concentration, or unity of place. The unity of time is also sadly neglected, to no purpose, in *Barnaby Rudge*. That Rudge should so long and so deeply feel the sting of conscience is inconsistent with his brutality. On page 15, the interval elapsing between the murder and Rudge's return is variously stated at twenty-two and twenty-four years. It may be asked why the inmates of The Warren failed to hear the alarm-bell which was heard by Solomon Daisy. The idea of persecution by being tracked, as by blood-hounds, from one spot of quietude to another, is a favourite one with Mr Dickens. Its effect cannot be denied. The stain upon Barnaby's wrist, caused by fright in the mother at so late a period of gestation as one day before mature parturition, is shockingly at war with all medical experience. When Rudge, escaped from prison, unshackled, with money at command, is in agony at his wife's refusal to perjure herself for his salvation – is it not *queer* that he should demand any other salvation than lay in his heels?

Some of the conclusions of chapters – see pages 40 and 100 – seem to have been written for the mere purpose of illustrating tail-pieces.

The leading idiosyncrasy of Mr Dickens' remarkable humour is to be found in his *translating the language of gesture, or action, or tone.* For example –

> The cronies nodded to each other, and Mr Parkes remarked in an undertone, shaking his head meanwhile, *as who should say 'let no man contradict me, for I won't believe him,'* that Willet was in amazing force to-night.

The riots form a series of vivid pictures never surpassed. At page 17, the road between London and the Maypole is described as a horribly rough and dangerous, and at page 97, as an uncommonly smooth and convenient one. At page 116, how comes Chester in possession of the key of Mrs Rudge's vacated house?

Mr Dickens' English is usually pure. His most remarkable error is that of employing the adverb 'directly' in the sense of 'as soon as.' For example – 'Directly he arrived, Rudge said,' etc. Bulwer is uniformly guilty of the same blunder.

It is observable that so original a stylist as our author should occasionally lapse into a gross imitation of what, itself, is a gross imitation. We mean the manner of Lamb – a manner based in the Latin construction. For example –

> In summer time its pumps suggest to thirsty idlers springs cooler and more sparkling and deeper than other wells; and as they trace the spillings of full pitchers on the heated ground, they snuff the freshness, and, sighing, cast sad looks towards the Thames, and think of baths and boats, and saunter on, despondent.

The wood-cut *designs* which accompany the edition before us are occasionally good. The copper engravings are pitiably ill-conceived and ill-drawn; and not only this, but are in broad contradiction of the wood-designs and text.

There are many *coincidences* wrought into the narrative – those, for example, which relate to the nineteenth of March; the dream of Barnaby, respecting his father, at the very period when his father is actually in the house; and the dream of Haredale previous to his final meeting with Chester. These things are meant to *insinuate* a fatality which, very properly, is not expressed in plain terms – but it is questionable whether the story derives more in ideality from their introduction, than it might have gained of verisimilitude from their omission.

The *dramatis personæ* sustain the high fame of Mr Dickens as a delineator of character. Miggs, the disconsolate handmaiden of Varden; Tappertit, his chivalrous apprentice; Mrs Varden, herself; and Dennis, a hangman – may be regarded as original caricatures, of the highest merit as such. Their traits are founded in acute observation of nature, but are exaggerated to the utmost admissible extent. Miss Haredale and Edward Chester are commonplaces – no effort has been made in their behalf. Joe Willet is a naturally drawn country youth. Stagg is a mere make-weight. Gashford and Gordon are truthfully copied. Dolly Varden is truth itself. Haredale, Rudge and Mrs Rudge, are impressive only through the circumstances which surround them. Sir John Chester, is, of course, not original, but is a vast improvement upon all his predecessors – his heartlessness is rendered somewhat too amusing, and his end too much that of a man of honour. Hugh is a noble conception. His fierce exultation in his animal powers; his subserviency to the smooth Chester; his mirthful contempt and patronage of Tappertit, and his *brutal* yet firm courage in the hour of death – form a picture to be set in diamonds. Old Willet is not surpassed by any character even among those of Dickens. He is nature itself – yet a step farther would have placed him in the class of caricatures. His combined conceit and obtusity are indescribably droll, and his peculiar misdirected energy when aroused is one of the most exquisite touches in all humorous painting. We shall never forget how heartily we laughed at his shaking Solomon Daisy and threatening to put him behind the fire, because the unfortunate little man was too much frightened to articulate. Varden is one of those free, jovial, honest fellows, at charity with all mankind, whom our author is so fond of depicting. And lastly, Barnaby, the hero of the tale – in him we have been somewhat disappointed. We have already said that his delight in the atrocities of the Rebellion is at variance with his horror of blood. But this horror of blood is *inconsequential*; and of this we complain. Strongly insisted upon in the beginning of the narrative, it produces no adequate result. And here how fine an opportunity has Mr Dickens missed! The conviction of the assassin, after the lapse of twenty-two years, might easily have been brought about through his son's mysterious awe of blood – *an awe created in the unborn by the assassination itself* – and this would have been one of the finest possible embodiments of the idea which we are accustomed to attach to 'poetical justice.' The raven, too, intensely amusing as it is, might have been made, more than we now see it, a portion of the conception of the fantastic Barnaby. Its croakings might have been *prophetically* heard in the course of the drama. Its character might have performed, in regard to that of the idiot, much the same part as does, in music, the accompaniment in respect to the air. Each might have been distinct. Each might have differed remarkably from the other. Yet between them there might have been wrought an analogical resemblance, and although each might have existed apart, they might have formed together a whole which would have been imperfect in the absence of either.

From what we have here said – and, perhaps, said without due deliberation – (for alas! the hurried duties of the journalist preclude it) – there will not be wanting those who will accuse us of a mad design to detract from the pure fame of the novelist. But to such we merely say in the language of heraldry, 'ye should wear a plain point sanguine in your arms.' If this be understood, well; if not, well again. There lives no man feeling a deeper reverence for genius than ourself. If we have not dwelt so specially upon the high merits as upon the trivial defects of *Barnaby Rudge* we have already given our reasons for the omission, and these reasons will be sufficiently understood by all whom we care to understand them. The work before us is not, we think, equal to the tale which immediately preceded it; but there are few – very few others to which we consider it inferior. Our chief objection has not, perhaps, been so distinctly stated as we could wish. That this fiction, or indeed that any fiction written by Mr Dickens, should be based in the excitement and maintenance of curiosity we look upon as a misconception, on the part of the writer, of his own very great yet very peculiar powers. He has done this thing well, to be sure – he would do anything well in comparison with the herd of his contemporaries – but he has not done it so thoroughly well as his high and just reputation would demand. We think that the whole book has been an effort to him – solely through the nature of its design. He has been smitten with an untimely desire for a novel path. The idiosyncrasy of his intellect would lead him, naturally, into the most fluent and simple style of narration. In tales of ordinary sequence he may and will long reign triumphant. He has a *talent* for all things, but no positive *genius* for *adaptation*, and still less for that metaphysical art in which the souls of all *mysteries* lie. *Caleb Williams* is a far less noble work than *The Old Curiosity Shop*; but Mr Dickens could no more have constructed the one than Mr Goodwin could have dreamed of the other.

LONGFELLOW[1]

'Il y a à parier,' says Chamfort, *'que toute idée publique, toute convention reçue, est une sottise, car elle a convenue au plus grand nombre.'* – One would be safe in wagering that any given public idea is erroneous, for it has been yielded to the clamour of the majority; – and this strictly philosophical, although somewhat French assertion, has especial bearing upon the whole race of what are termed maxims and popular proverbs; nine-tenths of which are the quintessence of folly. One of the most deplorably false of them is the antique adage, *De gustibus non est disputandum* – there should be no disputing about taste. Here the idea designed to be conveyed is that any one person has as just right to consider his own taste *the true*, as has any one other – that taste itself, in short, is an arbitrary something, amenable to no law, and measurable by no definite rules. It must be confessed, however, that the exceedingly vague and impotent treatises which are alone extant, have much to answer for as regards confirming the general error. Not the least important service which, hereafter, mankind will owe to *Phrenology*, may, perhaps, be recognized in an analysis of the real principles, and a digest of the resulting laws of taste. These principles, in fact, are as clearly traceable, and these laws as readily susceptible of system, as are any whatever.

In the meantime, the insane adage above mentioned is in no respect more generally, more stupidly, and more pertinaciously quoted than by the admirers of what is termed the 'good old Pope,' or the 'good old Goldsmith' of poetry, in reference to the bolder, more natural, and *more ideal* compositions of such authors as Coëtlogon and Lamartine[2] in France; Herder, Körner, and Uhland in Germany; Brun and Baggesen in Denmark; Bellman, Tegnér, and Nyberg[3] in Sweden; Keats, Shelley, Coleridge, and Tennyson in England; Lowell and Longfellow in America. *'De gustibus non,'* say these 'good-old-school' fellows; and we have no doubt that their mental translation of the phrase is – 'We pity your taste – we pity everybody's taste but our own.'

[1] *Ballads and other Poems.* By Henry Wadsworth Longfellow, Author of *Voices of the Night*, *Hyperion*, etc. Second Edition, John Owen, Cambridge.
[2] We allude here chiefly to the *David* of Coëtlogon, and *only* to the *Chute d'un Ange* of Lamartine.
[3] C. Julia Nyberg, author of the *Dikter von Euphrosyne*.

It is our purpose to controvert the popular idea that the poets just mentioned owe to novelty, to trickeries of expression, and to other meretricious effects, their appreciation by certain readers: – to demonstrate (for the matter is susceptible of demonstration) that such poetry and *such alone* has fulfilled the legitimate office of the muse; has thoroughly satisfied an earnest and unquenchable desire existing in the heart of man.

This volume of Ballads and Tales includes, with several brief original pieces, a translation from the Swedish of Tegnér. In attempting (what never should be attempted) a literal version of both the words and the metre of this poem, Professor Longfellow has failed to do justice either to his author or himself. He has striven to do what no man ever did well, and what, from the nature of language itself, never *can* be well done. Unless, for example, we shall come to have an influx of *spondees* in our English tongue, it will always be impossible to construct an English hexameter. Our spondees, or, we should say, our spondaic words, are rare. In the Swedish they are nearly as abundant as in the Latin and Greek. We have only '*compound*,' '*context*,' '*footfall*,' and a few other similar ones. This is the difficulty; and that it *is* so will become evident upon reading *The Children of the Lord's Supper*, where the sole *readable* verses are those in which we meet with the rare spondaic dissyllables. We mean to say *readable as hexameters*; for many of them will read very well as mere English dactylics with certain irregularities.

Much as we admire the genius of Mr Longfellow, we are fully sensible of his many errors of affectation and imitation. His artistical skill is great, and his ideality high. But his conception of the *aims* of poesy *is all wrong*; and this we shall prove at some future day – to our own satisfaction, at least. His didactics are all *out of place*. He has written brilliant poems – by accident; that is to say when permitting his genius to get the better of his conventional habit of thinking – a habit deduced from German study. We do not mean to say that a didactic moral may not be well made the *under-current* of a poetical thesis; but that it can never be well put so obtrusively forth, as in the majority of his compositions.

. . . . .

We have said that Mr Longfellow's conception of the *aims* of poesy is erroneous; and that thus, labouring at a disadvantage, he does violent wrong to his own high powers; and now the question is, what *are* his ideas of the aims of the Muse, as we gather these ideas from the *general* tendency of his poems? It will be at once evident that, imbued with the peculiar spirit of German song (in pure conventionality) he regards the inculcation of a *moral* as essential. Here we find it necessary to repeat that we have reference only to the *general* tendency of his compositions; for there are some magnificent exceptions, where, as if by accident, he has permitted his genius to get the better of his conventional prejudice. But didacticism is the prevalent *tone* of his song. His invention, his imagery, his all, is made subservient to the elucidation of some one or more points (but rarely of more than one) which he looks upon as *truth*. And that this mode of procedure will find stern defenders should never excite surprise, so long as the world is full to overflowing with cant and conventicles. There are men who will scramble on all fours through the muddiest sloughs of vice to pick up a single apple of virtue. There are things called men who, so long as the sun rolls, will greet with snuffling huzzas every figure that takes upon itself the semblance of truth, even although the figure, in itself only a 'stuffed Paddy,' be as much out of place as a toga on the statue of Washington, or out of season as rabbits in the days of the dog-star.

. . . .

We say this with little fear of contradiction. Yet the spirit of our assertion must be more heeded than the letter. Mankind have *seemed* to define Poesy in a thousand, and in a thousand conflicting definitions. But the war is one only of words. Induction is as well applicable to this subject as to the most palpable and utilitarian; and by its sober processes we find that, in respect to compositions which have been really received as poems, the *imaginative*, or, more popularly, the creative portions *alone* have ensured them to be so received. Yet these works, on account of these portions, having once been so received and so named, it has happened, naturally and inevitably, that other portions totally unpoetic have not only come to be regarded by the popular voice as poetic, but have been made to serve as false standards of perfection, in the adjustment of other poetical claims. Whatever has been found in whatever has been received as a poem has been blindly regarded as *ex statû* poetic. And this is a species of gross error which scarcely could have made its way into any less intangible topic. In fact that licence which appertains to the Muse herself, it has been thought decorous, if not sagacious to indulge, in all examination of her character . . .

Poesy is a response – unsatisfactory it is true – but still in some measure a response, to a natural and irrepressible demand. Man being what he is, the time could never have been in which Poesy was not. Its first element is the thirst for supernal BEAUTY – a beauty which is not afforded the soul by any existing collocation of earth's forms – a beauty which, perhaps, *no possible* combination of these forms would fully produce. Its second element is the attempt to satisfy this thirst by *novel* combinations among those forms of beauty which already exist – or by novel combinations *of those combinations which our predecessors, toiling in chase of the same phantom, have already set in order.* We thus clearly deduce the *novelty*, the *originality*, the *invention*, the *imagination*, or lastly the *creation* of BEAUTY, (for the terms as here employed are synonymous,) as the essence of all Poesy. Nor is this idea so much at variance with ordinary opinion as, at first sight, it may appear. A multitude of antique dogmas on this topic will be found, when divested of extrinsic speculation, to be easily resoluble into the definition now proposed. We do nothing more than present tangibly the vague clouds of the world's idea. We recognize the idea itself floating, unsettled, indefinite, in every attempt which has yet been made to circumscribe the conception of 'Poesy' in words. A striking instance of this is observable in the fact that no definition exists, in which either 'the beautiful,' or some one of those qualities which we have above designated synonymously with 'creation,' has not been pointed out as the *chief* attribute of the Muse. 'Invention,' however, or 'imagination,' is by far more commonly insisted upon. The word ποιησις itself (creation) speaks volumes upon this point. Neither will it be amiss here to mention Count Bielfeld's definition of poetry as *'L'art d'exprimer les pensées par la fiction.'* With this definition (of which the philosophy is profound to a certain extent) the German terms *Dichtkunst*, the art of fiction, and *Dichten*, to feign, which are used for '*poetry*' and '*to make verses*,' are in full and remarkable accordance. It is, nevertheless, in the *combination* of the two omni-prevalent ideas that the novelty, and, we believe, the force of our own proposition is to be found.

. . . . .

The elements of that beauty, which is felt in sound, *may be* the mutual or common heritage of Earth and Heaven. Contenting ourselves with the firm conviction, that music (in its modifications of rhythm and rhyme) is of so vast a moment to Poesy, as *never* to be neglected by him who is truly poetical – is of so mighty a force in furthering the great aim intended, that he is mad who rejects its assistance – content with this idea we shall not pause to maintain its absolute essentiality, for the mere sake of rounding a definition. That our definition of poetry will necessarily exclude much of what, through a supine toleration, has been hitherto ranked as poetical, is a matter which affords us not even momentary concern. We address but the thoughtful, and heed only their approval – with our own. If our suggestions are truthful, then 'after many days' shall they be understood as truth, even though found in contradiction of *all* that has been hitherto so understood. If false, shall we not be the first to bid them die?

We would reject, of course, all such matters as *Armstrong on Health*, a revolting production; Pope's *Essay on Man*, which may well be content with the title of an 'Essay in Rhyme'; *Hudibras* and other merely humorous pieces. We do not gainsay the peculiar merits of either of these latter compositions – but deny them the position held. In a notice of Brainard's Poems, we took occasion to show that the common use of a certain instrument, (rhythm,) had tended, more than aught else, to confound humorous verse with poetry. The observation is now recalled to corroborate what we have just said in respect to the vast effect or force of melody in itself – an effect which could elevate into even momentary confusion with the highest efforts of mind, compositions such as are the greater number of satires or burlesques . . .

We have shown our ground of objection to the general *themes* of Professor Longfellow. In common with all who claim the sacred title of poet, he should limit his endeavours to the creation of novel moods of beauty, in form, in colour, in sound, in sentiment; for over all this wide range has the poetry of words dominion. To what the world terms *prose* may be safely and properly left all else. The artist who doubts of his thesis may always resolve his doubt by the single question – 'might not this matter be as well or better handled in *prose*?' If it *may*, then is it no subject for the Muse. In the general acceptation of the term *Beauty* we are content to rest; being careful only to suggest that, in our peculiar views, it must be understood as inclusive of *the sublime*.

Of the pieces which constitute the present volume, there are not more than one or two thoroughly fulfilling the ideas we have proposed; although the volume, as a whole, is by no means so chargeable with didacticism as Mr Longfellow's previous book. We would mention as poems *nearly true*, *The Village Blacksmith*; *The Wreck of the Hesperus*, and especially *The Skeleton in Armour*. In the first-mentioned we have the *beauty* of simple-mindedness as a genuine thesis; and this thesis is inimitably handled until the concluding stanza, where the spirit of legitimate poesy is aggrieved in the pointed antithetical deduction of a *moral* from what has gone before. In *The Wreck of the Hesperus* we have the *beauty* of child-like confidence and innocence, with that of the father's stern courage and affection. But, with slight exception, those particulars of the storm here detailed are not poetic subjects. Their thrilling *horror* belongs to prose, in which it could be far more effectively discussed, as Professor Longfellow may assure himself at any moment by experiment. There *are* points of a tempest which afford the loftiest and truest poetical themes – points in which pure beauty is found, or, better still, beauty heightened into the sublime, by terror. But when we read, among other similar things, that

> The salt sea was frozen on her breast,
> The salt tears in her eyes,

we feel, if not positive disgust, at least a chilling sense of the inappropriate. In the *Skeleton in Armour* we find a pure and perfect thesis artistically treated. We find the beauty of bold courage and self-confidence, of love and maiden devotion, of reckless adventure, and finally of life-contemning grief. Combined with all this, we have numerous *points* of beauty apparently insulated, but all aiding the main effect or impression. The heart is stirred, and the mind does not lament its mal-instruction. The metre is simple, sonorous, well-balanced, and fully adapted to the subject. Upon the whole, there are few truer poems than this. It has but one defect – an important one. The prose remarks prefacing the narrative are really *necessary*. But every work of art should contain within itself all that is requisite for its own comprehension. And this remark is especially true of the ballad. In poems of magnitude the mind of the reader is not, at all times, enabled to include, in one comprehensive survey, the proportions and proper adjustment of the whole. He is pleased, if at all, with particular passages; and the sum of his pleasure is compounded of the sums of the pleasurable sentiments inspired by these individual passages in the progress of perusal. But, in pieces of less extent, the pleasure is *unique*, in the proper acceptation of this term – the understanding is employed, without difficulty, in the contemplation of the picture *as a whole*; and thus its effect will depend, in great measure, upon the perfection of its finish, upon the nice adaptation of its constituent parts, and especially, upon what is rightly termed by Schlegel *the unity or totality of interest*. But the practice of prefixing explanatory passages is utterly at variance with such unity. By the prefix, we are either put in possession of the subject of the poem, or some hint, historic fact, or suggestion, is thereby afforded, not included in the body of the piece, which, without the hint, is incomprehensible. In the latter case, while perusing the poem, the reader must revert, in mind at least, to the prefix, for the necessary explanation. In the former, the poem being a mere paraphrase of the prefix, the interest is divided between the prefix and the paraphrase. In either instance the totality of effect is destroyed.

Of the other original poems in the volume before us, there is none in which the aim of instruction, or *truth*, has not been too obviously substituted for the legitimate aim, *beauty*. We have heretofore taken occasion to say that a didactic moral might be happily made the *under-current* of a poetical theme, and we have treated this point at length, in a review of Moore's *Alciphron*; but the moral thus conveyed is invariably an ill effect when obtruding beyond the upper-current of the thesis itself. Perhaps the worst specimen of this obtrusion is given us by our poet in *Blind Bartimeus* and *The Goblet of Life*, where it will be observed that the *sole* interest of the upper-current of meaning depends upon its relation or reference to the under. What we read upon the surface would be *vox et preterea nihil* in default of the moral beneath. The Greek *finales* of *Blind Bartimeus* are an affectation altogether inexcusable. What the small, second-hand, Gibbonish pedantry of Byron introduced, is unworthy the imitation of Longfellow.

Of the translations we scarcely think it necessary to speak at all. We regret that our poet will persist in busying himself about such matters. *His* time might be better employed in original conception. Most of these versions are marked with the error upon which we have commented. This error is in fact essentially Germanic. *The Luck of Edenhall*, however, is a truly beautiful poem; and we say this with all that deference which the opinion of the *Democratic Review* demands. This composition appears to us *one of the very finest*. It has all the free, hearty, *obvious* movement of the true ballad-legend. The greatest force of language is combined in it with the richest imagination, acting in its most legitimate province. Upon the whole, we prefer it even to the *Sword-Song* of Körner. The pointed moral with which it terminates is so exceedingly natural – so perfectly fluent from the incidents – that we have hardly heart to pronounce it in ill taste. We may observe of this ballad, in conclusion, that its subject is more *physical* than is usual in Germany. Its images are rich rather in physical than in moral beauty. And this tendency, in Song, is the true one. It is chiefly, if we are not mistaken – it is chiefly amid forms of physical loveliness (we use the word *forms* in its widest sense as embracing modifications of sound and colour) that the soul seeks the realization of its dreams of BEAUTY. It is to her demand in this sense especially that the poet, who is wise, will most frequently and most earnestly respond.

The Children of the Lord's Supper is, beyond doubt, a true and most beautiful poem in great part, while, in some particulars, it is too metaphysical to have any pretension to the name. We have already objected, briefly, to its metre – the ordinary Latin or Greek Hexameter – dactyls and spondees at random, with a spondee in conclusion. We maintain that the hexameter can never be introduced into our language, from the nature of that language itself. This rhythm demands, *for English ears*, a preponderance of natural spondees. Our tongue has few. Not only does the Latin and Greek, with the Swedish, and some others, abound in them; but the Greek and Roman ear had become reconciled (why or how is unknown) to the reception of artificial spondees – that is to say, spondaic words formed partly of one word and partly of another, or from an excised part of one word. In short, the ancients were content to read *as they scanned*, or nearly so. It may be safely prophesied that we shall never do this; and thus we shall never admit English hexameters. The attempt to introduce them, after the repeated failures of Sir Philip Sidney, and others, is, perhaps, somewhat discreditable to the scholarship of Professor Longfellow. The *Democratic Review*, in saying that he has triumphed over difficulties in this rhythm, has been deceived, it is evident, by the facility with which some of these verses may be read. In glancing over the poem, we do not observe a single verse which can be read, *to English ears, as a Greek hexameter*. There are many, however, which can be well read as mere English dactylic verses; such, for example, as the well-known lines of Byron, commencing

Know ye the | land where the | cypress and | myrtle.

These lines (although full of irregularities) are, in their perfection, formed of three dactyls and a cæsura – just as if we should cut short the initial verse of the *Bucolics* thus –

Tityre | tu patu | læ recu | bans –

The 'myrtle,' at the close of Byron's line, is a double rhyme, and must be understood as one syllable.

Now a great number of Professor Longfellow's hexameters are merely these dactylic lines, *continued for two feet*. For example –

Whispered the | race of the | flowers and | merry on | balancing | branches.

In this example, also, 'branches,' which is a double ending, must be regarded as the cæsura, or one syllable, of which alone it has the force.

As we have already alluded, in one or two regards, to a notice of these poems which appeared in the *Democratic Review*, we may as well here proceed with some few further comments upon the article in question – with whose general tenor we are happy to agree.

The *Review* speaks of *Maidenhood* as a poem, 'not to be understood but at the expense of more time and trouble than a song can justly claim.' We are scarcely less surprised at this opinion from Mr Langtree than we were at the condemnation of *The Luck of Edenhall*.

Maidenhood is faulty, it appears to us, only on the score of its theme, which is somewhat didactic. Its *meaning* seems simplicity itself. A maiden on the verge of womanhood, hesitating to enjoy life (for which she has a strong appetite) through a false idea of duty, is bidden to fear nothing, having purity of heart as her lion of Una.

What Mr Langtree styles 'an unfortunate peculiarity' in Mr Longfellow, resulting from 'adherence to a false system,' has really been always regarded by us as one of his idiosyncratic merits. 'In each poem,' says the critic, 'he has but *one* idea, which, in the progress of his song, is gradually unfolded, and at last reaches its full development in the concluding lines; this singleness of thought might lead a harsh critic to suspect intellectual barrenness.' It leads *us*, individually, only to a full sense of the artistical power and knowledge of the poet. We confess that now, for the first time, we hear unity of conception objected to as a defect. But Mr Langtree seems to have fallen into the singular error of supposing the poet to have absolutely *but one idea* in each of his ballads. Yet how 'one idea' can be 'gradually unfolded' without other ideas, is, to us, a mystery of mysteries. Mr Longfellow, very properly, has but one *leading* idea which forms the basis of his poem; but to the aid and development of this one there are innumerable others, of which the rare excellence is, that all are in keeping, that none could be well omitted, that each tends to the one general effect. It is unnecessary to say another word upon this topic.

In speaking of *Excelsior*, Mr Langtree (are we wrong in attributing the notice to his very forcible pen?) seems to labour under some similar misconception. 'It carries along with it,' says he, 'a false moral which greatly diminishes its merit in our eyes. The great merit of a picture, whether made with the pencil or pen, is its *truth*; and this merit does not belong to Mr Longfellow's sketch. Men of genius may, and probably do, meet with greater difficulties in their struggles with the world than their fellow-men who are less highly gifted; but their power of overcoming obstacles is proportionately greater, and the result of their laborious suffering is not death but immortality.'

That the chief merit of a picture is its *truth*, is an assertion deplorably erroneous. Even in Painting, which is, more essentially than Poetry, a mimetic art, the proposition cannot be sustained. Truth is not even *the aim*. Indeed, it is curious to observe how very slight a degree of truth is sufficient to satisfy the mind, which acquiesces in the absence of numerous essentials in the thing depicted. An outline frequently stirs the spirit more pleasantly than the most elaborate picture. We need only refer to the compositions of Flaxman and of Retzch. Here all details are omitted – nothing can be farther from *truth*. Without even colour the most thrilling effects are produced. In statues we are rather pleased than disgusted with *the want of the eyeball*. The hair of the Venus de Medicis *was gilded*. Truth indeed! The grapes of Zeuxis as well as the curtain of Parrhasius were received as indisputable evidence of the truthful ability of these artists – but they were not even *classed among their pictures*. If truth is the highest aim of either Painting or Poesy, then Jan Steen was a greater artist than Angelo, and Crabbe is a more noble poet than Milton. But we have not quoted the observation of Mr Langtree to deny its philosophy; our design was simply to show that he has misunderstood the poet. *Excelsior* has not even a remote tendency to the interpretation assigned it by the critic. It depicts the *earnest upward impulse of the soul* – an impulse not to be subdued even in Death. Despising danger, resisting pleasure, the youth, bearing the banner inscribed '*Excelsior!*' (higher still!), struggles through all difficulties to an Alpine summit. Warned to be content with the elevation attained, his cry is still '*Excelsior!*' and, even in falling dead on the highest pinnacle, his cry is *still* '*Excelsior!*' There is yet an immortal height to be surmounted – an ascent in Eternity. The poet holds in view the idea of never-ending *progress.* That he is misunderstood is rather the misfortune of Mr Langtree than the fault of Mr Longfellow. There is an old adage about the difficulty of one's furnishing an auditor both with matter to be comprehended and brains for its comprehension.

ELIZABETH BARRETT BARRETT[1]

'A well-bred *man*,' says Sir James Puckle, in his *Gray Cap for a Green Head*, 'will never give himself the liberty to speak ill of women.' We emphasize the 'man.' Setting aside, for the present, certain rare commentators and compilers of the species – creatures neither precisely men, women, nor Mary Wollstonecrafts – setting these aside as unclassifiable, we may observe that the race of critics are masculine – men. With the exception, perhaps, of Mrs Anne Royal, we can call to mind no female who has occupied, even temporarily, the Zoilus throne. And this, the Salic law, is an evil; for the inherent chivalry of the critical *man* renders it not only an unpleasant task to him 'to speak ill of a woman,' (and a woman and her book are identical,) but an almost impossible task not to laud her *ad nauseam*. In general, therefore, it is the unhappy lot of the authoress to be subjected, time after time, to the downright degradation of mere puffery. On her own side of the Atlantic, Miss Barrett has indeed, in one instance at least, escaped the infliction of this lamentable contumely and wrong; but if she had been really solicitous of its infliction in America, she could not have adopted a more effectual plan than that of saying a few words about 'the great American people,' in an American edition of her work, published under the superintendence of an American author.[2] Of the innumerable 'native' notices of *The Drama of Exile*, which have come under our observation, we can call to mind *not one* in which there is anything more remarkable than the critic's dogged determination to find *nothing* barren, from Beersheba to Dan. Another in the *Democratic Review* has proceeded so far, it is true, as to venture a *very* delicate insinuation to the effect that the poetess 'will not fail to speak her mind *though it bring upon her a bad rhyme*'; beyond this, nobody has proceeded: and as for the elaborate paper in the new *Whig Monthly*, all that anybody can say or think, and all that Miss Barrett can *feel* respecting it is, that it is an eulogy as well written as it is an insult well

[1] *The Drama of Exile, and other Poems*. By Elizabeth Barrett Barrett, Author of *The Seraphim*, and other Poems. Henry G. Langley: New York.

[2] We are sorry to notice, in the American edition, a multitude of typographical errors, many of which affect the sense, and should therefore be corrected in a second impression, if called for. How far they are chargeable to the London copy, we are not prepared to say. 'Froze,' for instance, is printed 'frore.' 'Foregone,' throughout, is printed 'forgone.' 'Wordless' is printed 'worldless' – 'worldly,' 'wordly' – 'spilt,' 'split,' etc., etc., – while transpositions, false accents, and mis-punctuations abound.

intended. Now of all the friends of the fair author, we doubt whether one exists, with more profound – with more enthusiastic reverence and admiration of her genius, than the writer of these words. And it is for this very reason, beyond all others, that he intends to speak of her *the truth*. Our chief regret is, nevertheless, that the limits of this work will preclude the possibilities of our speaking this truth so fully, and so much in detail, as we could wish. By far the most valuable criticism that we, or that any one could give, of the volumes now lying before us, would be the quotation of three-fourths of their contents. But we have this advantage – that the work has been long published, and almost universally read – and thus, in some measure, we may proceed, concisely, as if the text of our context were an understood thing.

In her preface to this, the 'American edition' of her late poems, Miss Barrett, speaking of *The Drama of Exile*, says: – 'I decided on publishing it, after considerable hesitation and doubt. Its subject rather fastened on me than was chosen; and the form, approaching the model of the Greek tragedy, shaped itself under my hand rather by force of pleasure than of design. But when the compositional excitement had subsided, I felt afraid of my position. My own object was the new and strange experiment of the fallen Humanity, as it went forth from Paradise in the Wilderness, with a peculiar reference to Eve's allotted grief, which, considering that self-sacrifice belonged to her womanhood, and the consciousness of being the organ of the Fall to her offence, appeared to me imperfectly apprehended hitherto, and more expressible by a woman than by a man.' In this abstract announcement of the theme, it is difficult to understand the ground of the poet's hesitation to publish; for the theme in itself seems admirably adapted to the purposes of the closet drama. The poet, nevertheless, is, very properly, conscious of failure – a failure which occurs not in the general, but in the particular conception, and which must be placed to the account of 'the model of the Greek tragedies.' The Greek tragedies *had* and even *have* high merits; but we act wisely in now substituting for the external and typified human sympathy of the antique Chorus, a direct, internal, living and moving sympathy itself; and although Æschylus might have done service as 'a model,' to either Euripides or Sophocles, yet were Sophocles and Euripides in London to-day, they would, perhaps, while granting a certain formless and shadowy grandeur, indulge a quiet smile at the shallowness and uncouthness of that Art, which, in the old amphitheatres, had beguiled them into applause of the *Œdipus at Colonos.*

It would have been better for Miss Barrett if, throwing herself independently upon her own very extraordinary resources and forgetting that a Greek had ever lived, she had involved her Eve in a series of adventures merely natural, or if not this, of adventures preternatural within the limits of at least a conceivable relation – a relation of matter to spirit and spirit to matter, that should have left room for something like palpable action and comprehensible emotion – that should not have utterly precluded the development of that womanly character which is admitted as the principal object of the poem. As the case actually stands, it is only in a few snatches of verbal intercommunication with Adam and Lucifer, that we behold her as a woman at all. For the rest, she is a mystical something or nothing, enwrapped in a fog of rhapsody about Transfiguration, and the Seed, and the Bruising of the Heel, and other talk of a nature that no man ever pretended to understand in plain prose, and which, when solar-microscoped into poetry 'upon the model of the Greek drama,' is about as convincing as the Egyptian Lectures of Mr Silk Buckingham – about as much to any purpose under the sun as the *hi presto!* conjurations of Signor Blitz. What are we to make, for example, of dramatic colloquy such as this? – the words are those of a Chorus of Invisible Angels addressing Adam:

> Live, work on, O Earthy!
> By the Actual's tension
> Speed the arrow worthy
> Of a pure ascension.
> From the low earth round you
> Reach the heights above you;
> From the stripes that wound you
> Seek the loves that love you!
> God's divinest burneth plain
> Through the crystal diaphane
> Of our loves that lovè you.

Now we do not mean to assert that, by excessive 'tension' of the intellect, a reader accustomed to the cant of the transcendentalists (or of those who degrade an ennobling philosophy by styling themselves such) may not succeed in ferreting from the passage quoted, and indeed from each of the thousand similar ones throughout the book, something that shall bear the aspect of an absolute idea – but we do mean to say, first, that in nine cases out of ten, the thought when dug out will be found very poorly to repay the labour of the digging; – for it is the nature of thought in general, as it is the nature of some ores in particular, to be richest when most superficial. And we do mean to say, secondly, that, in nineteen cases out of twenty, the reader will suffer the most valuable ore to remain unmined to all eternity, before he will be put to the trouble of digging for it one inch. And we do mean to assert, thirdly, that no reader is to be condemned for *not* putting himself to the trouble of digging even the one inch; for no writer has the right to impose any such necessity upon him. What is worth thinking is distinctly thought: what is distinctly thought, can and should be distinctly expressed or should not be expressed at all. Nevertheless, there is no more appropriate opportunity than the present for admitting and maintaining, at once, what has never before been either maintained or admitted – that there is a justifiable exception to the rule for which we contend. It is where the design is to convey the fantastic – not the obscure. To give the idea of the latter we need, as in general, the most precise and definitive terms, and those who employ other terms but confound obscurity of expression with the expression of obscurity. The fantastic in itself, however, – phantasm – may be materially furthered in its development by the *quaint* in phraseology: – a proposition which any moralist may examine at his leisure for himself.

The *Drama of Exile* opens with a very palpable *bull*: – 'Scene, the outer side of the gate of Eden, shut fast with clouds' – [a scene out of sight!] – 'from the depth of which revolves the sword of fire, self-moved. A watch of innumerable angels, rank above rank, slopes up from around it to the zenith; and the glare cast from their brightness and from the sword, extends many miles into the wilderness. Adam and Eve are seen in the distance, flying along the glare. The angel Gabriel and Lucifer are beside the gate.' – These are the 'stage directions' which greet us on the threshold of the book. We complain first of the bull: secondly, of the blue-fire melodramatic aspect of the revolving sword; thirdly, of the duplicate nature of the sword, which, if steel, and sufficiently inflamed to do service in burning, would, perhaps, have been in no temper to cut; and on the other hand, if sufficiently cool to have an edge, would have accomplished little in the way of scorching a personage so well accustomed to fire and brimstone and all that, as we have very good reason to believe Lucifer was. We cannot help objecting, too, to the 'innumerable angels,' as a force altogether disproportioned to the one enemy to be kept out:

either the self-moving sword itself, we think, or the angel Gabriel alone, or five or six of the 'innumerable' angels, would have sufficed to keep the devil (or is it Adam?) outside of the gate which, after all, he might not have been able to discover, on account of the clouds.

Far be it from us, however, to dwell irreverently on matters which have venerability in the faith or in the fancy of Miss Barrett. We allude to these *niaiseries* at all – found here in the very first paragraph of her poem, – simply by way of putting in the clearest light the mass of inconsistency and antagonism in which her *subject* has inextricably involved her. She has made allusion to Milton, and no doubt felt secure in her theme (as a theme merely) when she considered his *Paradise Lost*. But even in Milton's own day, when men had the habit of believing all things, the more nonsensical the more readily, and of worshipping, in blind acquiescence, the most preposterous of impossibilities – even *then*, there were not wanting individuals who would have read the great epic with more zest, could it have been explained to their satisfaction, how and why it was, not only that a snake quoted Aristotle's *Ethics*, and behaved otherwise pretty much as he pleased, but that bloody battles were continually being fought between bloodless 'innumerable angels,' that found no inconvenience in losing a wing one minute and a head the next, and if pounded up into puff-paste late in the afternoon, were as good 'innumerable angels' as new the next morning, in time to be at *réveillé* roll-call. And now – at the present epoch – there are few people who do not occasionally *think*. This is emphatically the thinking age; – indeed, it may very well be questioned whether mankind ever substantially thought before. The fact is, if the *Paradise Lost* were written to-day (assuming that it had never been written when it was,) not even its eminent, although over-estimated merits, would counterbalance, either in the public view, or in the opinion of any critic at once intelligent and honest, the multitudinous incongruities which are part and parcel of its plot.

But in the plot of the drama of Miss Barrett it is something even worse than incongruity which affronts: – a continuous mystical strain of ill-fitting and exaggerated allegory – if, indeed, allegory is not much too respectable a term for it. We are called upon, for example, to sympathize in the whimsical woes of two Spirits, who, upspringing from the bowels of the earth, set immediately to bewailing their miseries in jargon such as this:

I am the spirit of the harmless earth;
God spake me softly out among the stars,
As softly as a blessing of much worth –
And then his smile did follow unawares,
That all things, fashioned, so, for use and duty,
Might shine anointed with his chrism of beauty –
Yet I wail!
I drave on with the worlds exultingly,
Obliquely down the Godlight's gradual fall –
Individual aspect and complexity
Of gyratory orb and interval,
Lost in the fluent motion of delight
Toward the high ends of Being, beyond Sight –
Yet I wail!

Innumerable other spirits discourse successively after the same fashion, each ending every stanza of his lamentation with the 'yet I wail!' When at length they have fairly made an end, Eve touches Adam upon the elbow, and hazards, also, the profound and pathetic observation – 'Lo, Adam, they wail!' – which is nothing more than the simple truth – for they *do* – and God deliver us from any such wailing again!

It is not our purpose, however, to demonstrate what every reader of these volumes will have readily seen self-demonstrated – the utter indefensibility of *The Drama of Exile*, considered uniquely, as a work of art. We have none of us to be told that a medley of metaphysical recitatives sung out of tune, at Adam and Eve, by all manner of inconceivable abstractions, is not exactly the best material for a poem. Still it may very well happen that among this material there shall be individual passages of great beauty. But should anyone doubt the possibility, let him be satisfied by a single extract such as follows:

On a mountain peak
Half sheathed in primal woods and glittering
In *spasms of awful sunshine*, at that hour
A lion couched, – part raised upon his paws,
With his calm massive face turned full on thine,
And his mane listening. When the ended curse
Left silence in the world, right suddenly
He sprang up rampant, and stood straight and stiff,
As if the new reality of death
Were dashed against his eyes, – and roared so fierce,

(Such thick carnivorous passion in his throat
Tearing a passage through the wrath and fear) –
And roared so wild, and smote from all the hills
Such *fast keen echoes crumbling down the vales*
To distant silence, – that the forest beasts,
One after one, did mutter a response
In savage and in sorrowful complaint
Which trailed along the gorges.

There is an Homeric force here – a vivid picturesqueness which all men will appreciate and admire. It is, however, the longest quotable passage in the drama, not disfigured with blemishes of importance; – although there are many – very many passages of a far loftier order of excellence, so disfigured, and which, therefore, it would not suit our immediate purpose to extract. The truth is, – and it may be as well mentioned at this point as elsewhere – that we are not to look in Miss Barrett's works for any examples of what has been occasionally termed 'sustained effort'; for neither are there, in any of her poems, any long commendable paragraphs, nor are there any individual compositions which will bear the slightest examination as consistent Art-products. Her wild and magnificent genius seems to have contented itself with points – to have exhausted itself in flashes; – but it is the profusion – the unparalleled number and close propinquity of these points and flashes which render her book *one flame*, and justify us in calling her, unhesitatingly, the greatest – the most glorious of her sex.

The *Drama of Exile* calls for little more, in the way of comment, than what we have generally said. Its finest particular feature is, perhaps, the rapture of Eve – rapture bursting through despair – upon discovering that she still possesses in the unwavering love of Adam an undreamed-of and priceless treasure. The poem ends, as it commences, with a bull. The last sentence gives us to understand that 'there is a sound through the silence, as of the falling tears of an angel.' How there can be sound during silence, and how an audience are to distinguish by such sound, angel tears from any other species of tears, it may be as well, perhaps, not too particularly to inquire.

Next, in length, to the Drama is, *The Vision of Poets*. We object to the didacticism of its design, which the poetess thus states: 'I have attempted to express here my view of the mission of the veritable poet – of the self-abnegation implied in it, of the uses of sorrow suffered in it, of the great work accomplished in it through suffering, and of the duty and glory of what Balzac has beautifully and truly called "*la patience angélique du génie.*"' This 'view' may be correct, but neither its correctness nor its falsity has anything to do with a poem. If a thesis is to be demonstrated, we need *prose* for its demonstration. In this instance, so far as the allegorical instruction and argumentation are lost sight of, in the upper current – so far as the main admitted intention of the work is kept out of view – so far only is the work a poem, and so far only is the poem worth notice, or worthy of its author. Apart from its poetical character, the composition is thoughtful, vivid, epigrammatic, and abundant in just observation – although the critical opinions introduced are not always our own. A reviewer in *Blackwood's Magazine*, quoting many of these critical portraits, takes occasion to find fault with the grammar of this tristich:

> Here Æschylus – the women swooned
> To see so awful when he frowned
> As the Gods did – he standeth crowned.

'What on earth,' says the critic, 'are we to make of the words "the women swooned to see so awful"? . . . The syntax will punish future commentators as much as some of his own corrupt choruses.' In general, we are happy to agree with this reviewer, whose decisions respecting the book are, upon the whole, so nearly coincident with ours that we hesitated, through fear of repetition, to undertake a *critique* at all, until we considered that we might say a very great deal in simply supplying his omissions; but he frequently errs through mere hurry, and never did he err more singularly than at the point now in question. He evidently supposes that 'awful' has been misused as an adverb and made referable to 'women.' But not so; and although the construction of the passage is unjustifiably involute, its grammar is intact. Disentangling the construction, we make this evident at once: 'Here Æschylus (he) standeth crowned, (whom) the women swooned to see so awful, when he frowned as the Gods did.' The 'he' is excessive, and the 'whom' is understood. Respecting the lines,

> Euripides, with close and mild
> Scholastic lips, that could be wild,
> And laugh or sob out like a child
> Right in the classes,

the critic observes: – '"Right in the classes" throws our intellect completely upon its beam-ends.' But, if so, the fault possibly lies in the crankness of the intellect; for the words themselves mean merely that Sophocles laughed or cried like a schoolboy – like a child right (or just) in his classes – one who had not yet left school. The phrase is affected, we grant, but quite intelligible. A still more remarkable misapprehension occurs in regard to the triplet,

> And Goethe, with that reaching eye
> His soul reached out from, far and high,
> And fell from inner entity.

The reviewer's remarks upon this are too preposterous not to be quoted in full; – we doubt if any commentator of equal dignity ever so egregiously committed himself before. 'Goethe,' he says, 'is a perfect enigma; what does the word "fell" mean? δεωος we suppose – that is, "not to be trifled with." But surely it sounds very strange, although it may be true enough, to say that his "fellness" is occasioned by "inner entity." But perhaps the line has some deeper meaning which we are unable to fathom.' Perhaps it has: and this is the criticism – the British criticism – the *Blackwood* criticism – to which we have so long implicitly bowed down! As before, Miss Barrett's verses are needlessly involved, but their meaning requires no Œdipus. Their construction is thus intended: – 'And Goethe, with that reaching eye from which his soul reached out, far and high, and (in so reaching) fell from inner entity.' The plain prose is this: – Goethe, (the poet would say,) in involving himself too far and too profoundly in external speculations – speculations concerning the world without him – neglected, or made miscalculations concerning, his inner entity, or being, – concerning the world within. This idea is involved in the metaphor of a person leaning from a window so far that finally he falls from it – the person being the soul, the window the eye.

Of the twenty-eight *Sonnets*, which immediately succeed the *Drama of Exile*, and which receive the especial commendation of *Blackwood*, we have no very enthusiastic opinion. The *best* sonnet is objectionable from its extreme artificiality; and, to be effective, this species of composition requires a minute management – a well-controlled dexterity of touch – compatible neither with Miss Barrett's deficient constructiveness, nor with the fervid rush and whirl of her genius. Of the particular instances here given, we prefer *The Prisoner*, of which the conclusion is particularly beautiful. In general, the themes are obtrusively metaphysical, or didactic.

The Romaunt of the Page, an imitation of the old English ballad, is neither very original in subject, nor very skilfully put together. We speak comparatively, of course: – It is not very good – for Miss Barrett: – and what we have said of this poem will apply equally to a very similar production, *The Rhyme of the Duchess May*. The *Poet and the Bird – A Child Asleep – Crowned and Wedded – Crowned and Buried – To Flush my Dog – The Fourfold Aspect – A Flower in a Letter – A Lay of the Early Rose – That Day – L. E. L.'s Questio – Catarina to Camoëns – Wine of Cyprus – The Dead Pan – Sleeping and Watching – A Portrait – The Mournful Mother* – and *A Valediction* – although all burning with divine fire, manifested only in scintillations, have nothing in them idiosyncratic. *The House of Clouds* and *The Last Bower* are superlatively lovely, and show the vast powers of the poet in the field best adapted to their legitimate display: – the *themes*, here, could not be improved. The former poem is purely imaginative; the latter is unobjectionably because unobtrusively suggestive of a moral, and is, perhaps, upon the whole, the most admirable composition in the two volumes: – or, if it is not, then *The Lay of the Brown Rosarie* is. In this last the ballad-character is elevated – etherealized – and thus made to afford scope for an ideality at once the richest and most vigorous in the world. The peculiar foibles of the author are here, too, dropped bodily, as a mantle, in the tumultuous movement and excitement of the narrative.

Miss Barratt has need only of *real* self-interest in her subjects, to do justice to her subjects and to herself. On the other hand, *A Rhapsody of Life's Progress*, although gleaming with cold corruscations, is the least meritorious, because the most philosophical, effusion of the whole: – this, we say, in flat contradiction of the *'spoudiotaton kai philosophikotaton genos'* of Aristotle. *The Cry of the Human* is singularly effective, not more from the vigour and ghastly passion of its thought, than from the artistically-conceived *arabesquerie* of its rhythm. *The Cry of the Children*, similar, although superior in tone and handling, is full of a nervous unflinching energy – a horror sublime in its simplicity – of which a far greater than Dante might have been proud. *Bertha in the Lane*, a rich ballad, very singularly excepted from the wholesale commendation of the *Democratic Review*, as 'perhaps not one of the best,' and designated by *Blackwood*, on the contrary, as 'decidedly the finest poem of the collection,' is *not* the *very* best, we think, only because mere pathos, however exquisite, cannot be ranked with the loftiest exhibitions of the ideal. Of *Lady Geraldine's Courtship*, the magazine last quoted observes that 'some pith is put forth in its passionate parts.' We will not pause to examine the delicacy or lucidity of the metaphor embraced in the '*putting forth* of some pith'; but unless by 'some pith' itself, is intended the utmost conceivable intensity and vigour, then the critic is merely damning with faint praise. With the exception of Tennyson's *Locksley Hall*, we have never perused a poem combining so much of the fiercest passion with so much of the most ethereal fancy, as the *Lady Geraldine's Courtship*, of Miss Barrett. We are forced to admit, however, that the latter work *is* a very palpable imitation of the former, which it surpasses in plot, or rather in thesis, as much as it falls below it in artistical management, and a certain calm energy – lustrous and indomitable – such as we might imagine in a broad river of molten gold.

It is in the *Lady Geraldine* that the critic of *Blackwood* is again put at fault in the comprehension of a couple of passages. He confesses his inability 'to make out the construction of the words, "all that spirits pure and ardent are cast out of love and reverence, because chancing not to hold."' There are comparatively few American schoolboys who could not parse it. The prosaic construction would run thus: – 'all *that* (wealth understood) because chancing not to hold *which*, (or on account of not holding which) all pure and ardent spirits are cast out of love and reverence.' The 'which' is involved in the relative pronoun 'that' – the second word of the sentence. *All that we know is, that Miss Barrett is right:* – here is a parallel phrase, meaning – 'all that (which) we know,' etc. The fact is, that the accusation of imperfect grammar would have been more safely, if more generally, urged: in descending to particular exceptions, the reviewer has been doing little more than exposing himself at all points.

Turning aside, however, from grammar, he declares his incapacity to fathom the meaning of

She has halls and she has castles, and the resonant steam-eagles
Follow far on the directing of her floating dove-like hand –
With a thunderous vapour trailing underneath the starry vigils,
So to mark upon the blasted heaven the measure of her land.

Now it must be understood that he is profoundly serious in his declaration – he really *does not* apprehend the thought designed – and he is even more than profoundly serious, too, in intending these his own comments upon his own stolidity, for wit: – 'We thought that steam-coaches generally followed the directing of no hand except the stoker's, but *it*, certainly, is always much *liker* a raven than a dove.' After this, who shall question the infallibility of Christopher North? We presume there are very few of *our* readers who will not easily appreciate the richly imaginative conception of the poetess: – The Lady Geraldine is supposed to be standing in her own door, (positively *not* on the top of an engine), and thence pointing, 'with her floating dove-like hand,' to the lines of vapour, from the 'resonant steam-eagles,' that designate upon the 'blasted heaven,' the remote boundaries of her domain. – But, perhaps, we are guilty of a very gross absurdity ourselves, in commenting *at all* upon the whimsicalities of a reviewer who can deliberately *select* for special animadversion the second of the four verses we here copy:

Eyes, he said, now throbbing through me! are ye eyes that did undo me?
Shining eyes like antique jewels set in Parian statue-stone!
Underneath that calm white forehead are ye ever burning torrid
O'er the desolate sand desert of my heart and life undone?

The ghost of the Great Frederick might, to be sure, quote at us, in his own Latin, his favourite adage, 'De gustibus non est disputand*us*'; – but, when we take into consideration the moral designed, the weirdness of effect intended, and the historical adaptation of the fact alluded to, in the line italicized, (a fact of which it is by no means impossible that the critic is ignorant,) we cannot refrain from expressing our conviction – and we here *express it* in the teeth of the whole horde of the Ambrosianians – that from the entire range of poetical literature there shall not, in a century, be produced a more sonorous – a more vigorous verse – a juster – a nobler – a more ideal – a more magnificent image – than this very image, in this very verse, which the most noted magazine of Europe has so especially and so contemptuously condemned.

The Lady Geraldine is, we think, the only poem of its author which is not deficient, considered as an artistical whole. Her constructive ability, as we have already suggested, is either not very remarkable, or has never been properly brought into play: – in truth, her genius is too impetuous for the minuter technicalities of that elaborate *Art* so needful in the building up of pyramids for immortality. This deficiency, then – if there be any such – is her chief weakness. Her other foibles, although some of them are, in fact, glaring, glare, nevertheless, to no very material ill purpose. There are none which she will not readily dismiss in her future works. She retains them now, perhaps, because unaware of their existence.

Her affectations are unquestionably many, and generally inexcusable. We may, perhaps, tolerate such words as 'blé,' 'chrysm,' 'nympholeptic,' 'œnomel,' and 'chrysopras' – they have at least the merit either of distinct meaning, or of terse and sonorous expression; but what can be well said in defence of the unnecessary nonsense of ''ware' for 'aware' – of ''bide,' for 'abide' – of ''gins,' for 'begins' – of ''las' for 'alas' – of 'oftly,' 'ofter,' and 'oftest' for 'often,' 'more often,' and 'most often' – or of 'erelong' in the sense of 'long ago'? That there is *authority* for the mere words proves nothing; those who employed them in their day would not employ them if writing *now*. Although we grant, too, that the poetess is very usually Homeric in her compounds, there is no intelligibility of construction, and therefore no force of meaning in 'dew-pallid,' 'pale-passioned,' and 'silver-solemn.' Neither have we any partiality for 'drave' or '*su*preme,' or '*la*ment'; and while upon this topic, we may as well observe that there are few readers who do anything but laugh or stare at such phrases as 'L. E. L.'s Last Questio' – 'The Cry of the Human' – 'Leaning from my Human' – 'Heaven assist the human' – 'the full sense of your mortal' – 'a grave for your divine' – 'falling off from our created' – 'he sends this gage for thy pity's counting' – 'they could not press their futures on the present of her courtesy' – or 'could another fairer lack to thee, lack to thee?' There are few, at the same time, who do not feel disposed to weep outright, when they hear of such things as 'Hope withdrawing her peradventure' – 'spirits dealing in pathos of antithesis' – 'angels in antagonism to God and his reflex beatitudes' – 'songs of glories ruffling down doorways' – 'God's possibles' – and 'rules of Mandom.'

We have already said, however, that mere *quaintness* within reasonable limit is not only *not* to be regarded as affectation, but has its proper artistic uses in aiding a fantastic effect. We quote, from the lines *To my Dog Flush*, a passage in exemplification:

> Leap! thy broad tail waves a light!
> Leap! thy slender feet are bright,
>   Canopied in fringes!
> Leap! those tasselled ears of thine
> Flicker strangely, fair and fine,
>   *Down their golden inches!*

And again – from the song of a tree-spirit, in the *Drama of Exile*:

The Divine impulsion cleaves
In dim movements to the leaves
Dropt and lifted, dropt and lifted,
In the sun-light greenly sifted, –
In the sun-light and the moon-light
Greenly sifted through the trees.
Ever wave the Eden trees,
In the night-light and the noon-light,
With a ruffling of green branches,
Shaded off to resonances,
Never stirred by rain or breeze.

The thoughts, here, belong to the highest order of poetry, but they could not have been wrought into effective impression, without the instrumentality of those repetitions – those unusual phrases – in a word, those *quaintnesses*, which it has been too long the fashion to censure, indiscriminately, under the one general head of 'affectation.' No true poet will fail to be enraptured with the two extracts above quoted – but we believe there are few who would not find a difficulty in reconciling the psychal impossibility of refraining from admiration, with the too-hastily attained mental conviction that, critically, there is nothing to admire.

Occasionally, we meet in Miss Barrett's poems a certain *far-fetchedness* of imagery, which is reprehensible in the extreme. What, for example, are we to think of

Now he hears the angel voices
Folding silence in the room? –

undoubtedly, that it is nonsense, and no more; or of

How the silence round you shivers
While our voices through it go? –

again, unquestionably, that it is nonsense, and nothing beyond.

Sometimes we are startled by knotty paradoxes; and it is not acquitting their perpetrator of all blame on their account to admit that, in some instances, they are susceptible of solution. It is really difficult to discover anything for approbation in enigmas such as

That bright impassive, passive angel-hood,

or –

The silence of my heart is full of sound.

At long intervals, we are annoyed by specimens of repulsive imagery, as where the children cry:

> How long, O cruel nation,
> Will you stand, to move the world, *on a child's heart* –
> *Stifle down with a mailed heel its palpitation*? etc.

Now and then, too, we are confounded by a pure platitude, as when Eve exclaims:

> Leave us not
> In agony beyond what we can bear,
> And in abasement *below thunder-mark!*

or, when the Saviour is made to say:

> So, at last,
> He shall look round on you *with lids too straight*
> *To hold the grateful tears.*

'Strait' was, no doubt, intended, but does not materially elevate, although it slightly elucidates, the thought. A very remarkable passage is that, also, wherein Eve bids the infant voices

> Hear the steep generations, how they fall
> Adown the visionary stairs of Time,
> Like supernatural thunders – far yet near,
> Sowing their fiery echoes through the hills!

Here, saying nothing of the affectation in 'adown'; not alluding to the insoluble paradox of 'far yet near'; not mentioning the inconsistent metaphor involved in the 'sowing of *fiery* echoes'; adverting but slightly to the misusage of 'like,' in place of 'as,' and to the impropriety of making anything fall like *thunder*, which has never been known to fall at all; merely hinting, too, at the misapplication of 'steep,' to the 'generations,' instead of to the 'stairs' – a perversion in no degree to be justified by the fact that so preposterous a figure as *synecdoche* exists in the school-books; – letting these things pass, for the present, we shall still find it difficult to understand how Miss Barrett should have been led to think the principal idea itself – the abstract idea – the idea of *tumbling downstairs*, in any shape, or under any circumstances – either a poetical or a decorous conception. And yet we have seen this very passage quoted as 'sublime,' by a critic who seems to take it for granted, as a general rule, that Nat-Leeism is the loftiest order of literary merit. That the lines very *narrowly missed* sublimity, we grant; that they came within a step of it, we admit; – but, unhappily, the step is that *one* step which, time out of mind, has intervened between the sublime and the ridiculous. So true is this, that any person – that even *we* – with a very partial modification of the imagery – a modification that shall not interfere with its richly spiritual *tone* – may elevate the quotation into unexceptionability. For example: and we offer it with profound deference –

> Hear the far generations – how they crash,
> From crag to crag, down the precipitous Time,
> In multitudinous thunders that upstartle,
> Aghast, the echoes from their cavernous lairs
> In the visionary hills!

We have no doubt that our version has its faults – but it has, at least, the merit of consistency. Not only is a mountain more poetical than a pair of stairs; but echoes are more appropriately typified as wild beasts than as seeds; and echoes and wild beasts agree better with a mountain, than does a pair of stairs with the *sowing* of seeds – even admitting that these seeds be seeds of fire, and be sown broadcast 'among the hill,' by a steep generation, while in the act of tumbling down the stairs – that is to say, of coming down the stairs – in too violent a hurry to be capable of sowing the seeds as accurately as all seeds should be sown; nor is the matter rendered any better for Miss Barrett, even if the construction of her sentence is to be understood as implying that the fiery seeds were sown, not immediately by the steep generations that tumbled down the stairs, but mediately, through the intervention of the 'supernatural thunders' that were *occasioned* by the 'steep generations' that tumbled down the stairs.

The poetess is not unfrequently guilty of repeating herself. The 'thunder cloud veined by lightning' appears, for instance, on pages 34 of the first, and 228 of the second volume. The 'silver clash of wings' is heard at pages 53 of the first, and 269 of the second; and angel tears are discovered to be falling as well at page 27, as at the conclusion of *The Drama of Exile*. Steam, too, in the shape of Death's White Horse, comes upon the ground, both at page 244 of the first, and 179 of the second volume – and there are multitudinous other repetitions both of phrase and idea – but it is the excessive reiteration of pet *words* which is, perhaps, the most obtrusive of the minor errors of the poet.

'Chrystalline,' 'Apocalypse,' 'foregone,' 'evangel,' ''ware,' 'throb,' 'level,' 'loss,' and the musical term 'minor,' are for ever upon her lips. The chief favourites, however, are 'down' and 'leaning,' which are echoed and re-echoed not only *ad infinitum*, but in every whimsical variation of import. As Miss Barrett certainly cannot be aware of the extent of this mannerism, we will venture to call her attention to a few – comparatively a *very* few examples.

> Pealing *down* the depths of Godhead . . .
> And smiling *down* the stars . . .
> Smiling *down*, as Venus *down* the waves . . .
> Smiling *down* the steep world very purely . . .
> *Down* the purple of this chamber . . .
> Moving *down* the hidden depths of loving . . .
> Cold the sun shines *down* the door . . .
> Which brought angels *down* our talk . . .
> Let your souls behind you *lean* gently moved . . .
> But angels *leaning* from the golden seats . . .
> And melancholy *leaning* out of heaven . . .
> And I know the heavens are *leaning* down . . .
> Then over the casement she *leaneth* . . .
> Forbear that dream, too near to heaven it *leaned* . . .
> I would *lean* my spirit o'er you . . .
> Thou, O sapient angel, *leanest o'er* . . .
> Shapes of brightness *overlean* thee . . .
> They are *leaning* their young heads . . .
> Out of heaven shall o'er you *lean* . . .
> While my spirit *leans* and reaches . . .
> etc., etc., etc.

In the matter of grammar, upon which the Edinburgh critic insists so pertinaciously, the author of *The Drama of Exile* seems to us even peculiarly without fault. The nature of her studies has, no doubt, imbued her with a very delicate instinct of constructive accuracy. The occasional use of phrases so questionable as 'from whence' and the far-fetchedness and involution of which we have already spoken, are the only noticeable blemishes of an exceedingly chaste, vigorous, and comprehensive style.

In her inattention to rhythm, Miss Barrett is guilty of an error that might have been fatal to her fame – that *would* have been fatal to any reputation less solidly founded than her own. We do not allude, so particularly, to her multiplicity of inadmissible rhymes. We would wish, to be sure, that she had not thought proper to couple Eden and succeeding – glories and floorwise – burning and morning – thither and æther – enclose me and across me – misdoers and flowers – centre and winter – guerdon and pardon – conquer and anchor – desert and unmeasured – atoms and fathoms – opal and people – glory and doorway – trumpet and accompted – taming and overcame him – coming and woman – is and trees – off and sun-proof – eagles and vigils – nature and satire – poems and interflowings – certes and virtues – pardon and burden – thereat and great – children and bewildering – mortal and turtle – moonshine and sunshine. It would have been better, we say, if such apologies for rhymes as these had been rejected. But deficiencies of *rhythm* are more serious. In some cases it is nearly impossible to determine what metre is intended. *The Cry of the Children* cannot be scanned: we *never saw* so poor a specimen of verse. In imitating the rhythm of *Locksley Hall*, the poetess has preserved with accuracy (so far as mere syllables are concerned) the forcible line of seven trochees with a final cæsura. The 'double rhymes' have only the force of a single long syllable – a cæsura; but the natural rhythmical division, occurring at the close of the fourth trochee, should never be forced to occur, as Miss Barrett constantly forces it, in the middle of a word, or of an indivisible phrase. If it do so occur, we must sacrifice, in perusal, either the sense or the rhythm. If she will consider, too, that this line of seven trochees and a cæsura is nothing more than two lines written in one – a line of four trochees, succeeded by one of three trochees and a cæsura – she will at once see how unwise she has been in composing her poem in quatrains of the long line with alternate rhymes, instead of immediate ones, as in the case of *Locksley Hall.* The result is, that the ear, expecting the rhymes before they occur, does not appreciate them when they do. These points, however, will be best exemplified by transcribing one of the quatrains in its *natural* arrangement. That actually employed is addressed only to the eye.

Oh, she fluttered like a tame bird
  In among its forest brothers
Far too strong for it, then, drooping,
  Bowed her face upon her hands –
And I spake out wildly, fiercely,
  Brutal truths of her and others!
I, she planted in the desert,
  Swathed her 'wind-like, with my sands.

Here it will be seen that there is a paucity of rhyme, and that it is expected at closes where it does not occur. In fact, if we consider the eight lines as two independent quatrains (which they are,) then we find them *entirely rhymeless.* Now so unhappy are these metrical defects – of so much importance do we take them to be, that we do not hesitate in declaring the general inferiority of the poem to its prototype to be altogether chargeable to *them.* With equal rhythm *Lady Geraldine* had been far – very far the superior poem. Inefficient rhythm is inefficient poetical expression; and expression, in poetry, – what is it? – what is it not? No one living can better answer these queries than Miss Barrett.

We conclude our comments upon her versification by quoting (we will not say whence – from what one of her poems) – a few verses without the linear division as it appears in the book. There are many readers who would never suspect the passage to be intended for metre at all. – 'Ay! – and sometimes, on the hillside, while we sat down on the gowans, with the forest green behind us, and its shadow cast before, and the river running under, and, across it from the rowens a partridge whirring near us till we felt the air it bore – there, obedient to her praying, did I read aloud the poems made by Tuscan flutes, or instruments more various of our own – read the pastoral parts of Spencer – or the subtle interflowing found in Petrarch's sonnets; – here's the book! – the leaf is folded down!'

With this extract we make an end of our fault-finding – and *now,* shall we speak, equally in detail, of the *beauties* of this book? Alas! here, indeed, do we feel the impotence of the pen. We have already said that the supreme excellence of the poetess whose works we review is made up of the multitudinous sums of a world of lofty merits. It is the multiplicity – it is the *aggregation* – which excites our most profound enthusiasm, and enforces our most earnest respect. But unless we had space to extract three-fourths of the volumes, how could we convey this aggregation by specimens? We might quote, to be sure, an example of keen insight into our psychal nature, such as this:

I fell flooded with a Dark,
In the silence of a swoon –
When I rose, still cold and stark,
There was night, – I saw the moon;
And the stars, each in its place,
And the May-blooms on the grass,
Seemed to wonder what I was.
And I walked as if apart

From myself when I could stand –
And I pitied my own heart,
As if I held it in my hand
Somewhat coldly, – with a sense
Of fulfilled benevolence.

Or we might copy an instance of the purest and most radiant imagination, such as this:

So, young muser, I sat listening
To my Fancy's wildest word –
On a sudden, through the glistening
Leaves around, a little stirred,
Came a sound, a sense of music, which was rather felt than heard.
Softly, finely, it inwound me –
From the world it shut me in –
Like a fountain falling round me
Which with silver waters thin,
Holds a little marble Naiad sitting smilingly within.

Or, again, we might extract a specimen of wild Dantesque vigour, such as this – in combination with a pathos never excelled:

Ay! be silent – let them hear each other breathing
For a moment, mouth to mouth –
Let them touch each others' hands in a fresh wreathing
Of their tender human youth!
Let them feel that this cold metallic motion
Is not all the life God fashions or reveals –
Let them prove their inward souls against the notion
That they live in you, or under you, O wheels!

Or, still again, we might give a passage embodying the most elevated sentiment, most tersely and musically thus expressed:

And since, Prince Albert, men have called thy spirit high and rare,
And true to truth, and brave for truth, as some at Augsburg were –
We charge thee by thy lofty thoughts and by thy poet-mind,
Which not by glory or degree takes measure of mankind,
Esteem that wedded hand less dear for sceptre than for ring,
And hold her uncrowned womanhood to be the royal thing!

These passages, we say, and a hundred similar ones, exemplifying particular excellences, might be displayed, and we should still fail, as lamentably as the *skolastikos* with his brick, in conveying an idea of the vast *totality*. By no individual stars can we present the constellatory radiance of the book. *To the book*, then, with implicit confidence we appeal.

That Miss Barrett has done more, in poetry, than any woman living or dead, will scarcely be questioned: – that she has surpassed all her poetical contemporaries of either sex (with a single exception,) is our deliberate opinion – not idly entertained, we think, nor founded on any visionary basis. It may not be uninteresting, therefore, in closing this examination of her claims, to determine in what manner she holds poetical relation with these contemporaries, or with her immediate predecessors, and especially with the great exception to which we have alluded – if at all.

If ever mortal 'wreaked his thoughts upon expression,' it was Shelley. If ever poet sang (as a bird sings) – impulsively – earnestly – with utter abandonment – to himself solely – and for the mere joy of his own song – that poet was the author of *The Sensitive Plant*. Of Art – beyond that which is the inalienable instinct of Genius – he either had little or disdained all. He *really* disdained that Rule which is the emanation from Law, because his own soul was law in itself. His rhapsodies are but the rough notes – the stenographic memoranda of poems – memoranda which, because they were all-sufficient for his own intelligence, he cared not to be at the trouble of transcribing in full for mankind. In his whole life he wrought not thoroughly out a single conception. For this reason it is that he is the most fatiguing of poets. Yet he wearies in having done too little, rather than too much; what seems in him the diffuseness of one idea, is the conglomerate concision of many; and this concision it is which renders him obscure. With such a man, to imitate was out of the question; it would have answered no purpose – for he spoke to his own spirit alone, which would have comprehended no alien tongue; – he was, therefore, profoundly original. His quaintness arose from intuitive perception of that truth to which Lord Verulam alone has given distinct voice: – 'There is no exquisite beauty which has not some strangeness in its proportion.' But whether obscure, original, or quaint, he was at all times sincere. He had no *affectations*.

From the ruins of Shelley there sprang into existence, affronting the Heavens, a tottering and fantastic pagoda, in which the salient angles, tipped with mad jangling bells, were the idiosyncratic *faults* of the great original – faults which cannot be called such in view of his purposes, but which are monstrous when we regard his works as addressed to mankind. A 'school' arose – if that absurd term must still be employed – a school – a system of rules – upon the basis of the Shelley who had none. Young men innumerable, dazzled with the glare and bewildered with the *bizarrerie* of the divine lightning that flickered through the clouds of the *Prometheus*, had no trouble whatever in heaping up imitative vapours, but, for the lightning, were content, perforce, with its *spectrum*, in which the *bizarrerie* appeared without the fire. Nor were great and mature minds unimpressed by the contemplation of a greater and more mature; and thus gradually were interwoven into this school of all Lawlessness – of obscurity, quaintness, exaggeration – the misplaced didacticism of Wordsworth, and the even more preposterously anomalous metaphysicianism of Coleridge. Matters were now fast verging to their worst, and at length, in Tennyson, poetic inconsistency attained its extreme. But it was precisely this extreme (for the greatest error and the greatest truth are scarcely two points in a circle) – it was this extreme which, following the law of all extremes, wrought in him – in Tennyson – a natural and inevitable revulsion, leading him first to contemn and secondly to investigate his early manner, and, finally, to winnow from its magnificent elements the truest and purest of all poetical styles. But not even yet is the process complete; and for this reason in part, but chiefly on account of the mere fortuitousness of that mental and moral combination which shall unite in one person (if *ever* it shall) the Shelleyan *abandon*, the Tennysonian poetic sense, the most profound instinct of Art, and the sternest Will properly to blend and vigorously to control all; – chiefly, we say, because such combination of antagonisms must be purely fortuitous, has the world never yet seen the noblest of the poems of which it is *possible* that it may be put in possession.

And yet Miss Barrett has narrowly missed the fulfilment of these conditions. Her poetic inspiration is the highest – we can conceive nothing more august. Her sense of Art is pure in itself, but has been contaminated by pedantic study of false models – a study which has the more easily led her astray, because she placed an undue value upon it as rare – as alien to her character of woman. The accident of having been long secluded by ill health from the world has effected, moreover, in her behalf, what an innate recklessness did for Shelley – has imparted to her, if not precisely that *abandon* to which I have referred, at least a something that stands well in its stead – a comparative independence of men and opinions with which she did not come personally in contact – a happy audacity of thought and expression never before known in one of her sex. It is, however, this same accident of ill health, perhaps, which has invalidated her original Will – diverted her from proper individuality of purpose – and seduced her into the sin of imitation. Thus, what she might have done we cannot altogether determine. What she has actually accomplished is before us. With Tennyson's works beside her, and a keen appreciation of them in her soul – appreciation too keen to be discriminative; – with an imagination even more vigorous than his, although somewhat less ethereally delicate; with inferior art and more feeble volition; she has written poems such as he *could not write*, but such as he, under *her* conditions of ill health, and seclusion, *would have written* during the epoch of his pupildom in that school which arose out of Shelley, and from which, over a disgustful gulf of utter incongruity and absurdity, lit only by miasmatic flashes, into the broad open meadows of Natural Art and Divine Genius, he – Tennyson – is at once the bridge and the transition.

NATHANIEL HAWTHORNE[1]

The reputation of the author of *Twice-Told Tales* has been confined, until very lately, to literary society; and I have not been wrong, perhaps, in citing him as *the* example, *par excellence*, in this country, of the privately-admired and publicly-unappreciated man of genius. Within the last year or two, it is true, an occasional critic has been urged, by honest indignation, into very warm approval. Mr Webber, for instance, (than whom no one has a keener relish for that kind of writing which Mr Hawthorne has best illustrated,) gave us, in a late number of *The American Review*, a cordial and certainly a full tribute to his talents; and since the issue of the *Mosses from an Old Manse*, criticisms of similar tone have been by no means infrequent in our more authoritative journals. I can call to mind few reviews of Hawthorne published *before* the *Mosses*. One I remember in *Arcturus* (edited by Matthews and Duyckinck) for May, 1841; another in the *American Monthly* (edited by Hoffman and Herbert) for March, 1838; a third in the ninety-sixth number of the *North American Review*. These criticisms, however, seemed to have little effect on the popular taste – at least, if we are to form any idea of the popular taste by reference to its expression in the newspapers, or by the sale of the author's book. It was never the fashion (until lately) to speak of him in any summary of our best authors.

The daily critics would say, on such occasions, 'Is there not Irving and Cooper, and Bryant, and Paulding, and – Smith?' or, 'Have we not Halleck and Dana, and Longfellow, and – Thompson?' or, 'Can we not point triumphantly to our own Sprague, Willis, Channing, Bancroft, Prescott and – Jenkins?' but these unanswerable queries were never wound up by the name of Hawthorne.

Beyond doubt, this inappreciation of him on the part of the public arose chiefly from the two causes to which I have referred – from the facts that he is neither a man of wealth nor a quack; but these are insufficient to account for the whole effect. No small portion of it is attributable to the very marked idiosyncrasy of Mr Hawthorne himself. In one sense, and in great measure, to be peculiar is to be original, and than the true originality there is no higher literary virtue. This true or commendable originality, however, implies not the

[1] *Twice Told Tales*. By Nathaniel Hawthorne. James Munroe & Co., Boston, 1842.
Mosses from an Old Manse. By Nathaniel Hawthorne. Wiley & Putnam, New York, 1846.

uniform, but the continuous peculiarity – a peculiarity springing from ever-active vigour of fancy – better still if from ever-present force of imagination, giving its own hue, its own character to everything it touches, and, especially, *self-impelled to touch everything*.

It is often said, inconsiderately, that very original writers always fail in popularity – that such and such persons are too original, to be comprehended by the mass. 'Too peculiar,' should be the phrase, 'too idiosyncratic.' It is, in fact, the excitable, undisciplined and child-like popular mind which most keenly feels the original.

The criticism of the conservatives, of the hackneys, of the cultivated old clergymen of the *North American Review*, is precisely the criticism which condemns and alone condemns it. 'It becometh not a divine,' saith Lord Coke, 'to be of a fiery and salamandrine spirit.' Their conscience allowing them to move nothing themselves, these dignitaries have a holy horror of being moved. 'Give us *quietude*,' they say. Opening their mouths with proper caution, they sigh forth the word *'Repose.'* And this is, indeed, the one thing they should be permitted to enjoy, if only upon the Christian principle of give and take.

The fact is, that if Mr Hawthorne were really original, he could not fail of making himself felt by the public. But the fact is, he is *not* original in any sense. Those who speak of him as original, mean nothing more than that he differs in his manner or tone, and in his choice of subjects, from any author of their acquaintance – their acquaintance not extending to the German Tieck, whose manner, in *some* of his works, is absolutely identical with that *habitual* to Hawthorne. But it is clear that the element of the literary originality is novelty. The element of its appreciation by the reader is the reader's sense of the new. Whatever gives him a new and insomuch a pleasurable emotion, he considers original, and whoever frequently gives him such emotion, he considers an original writer. In a word, it is by the sum total of these emotions that he decides upon the writer's claim to originality. I may observe here, however, that there is clearly a point at which even novelty itself would cease to produce the legitimate originality, if we judge this originality, as we should, by the effect designed: this point is that at which *novelty becomes nothing novel*; and here the artist, *to preserve his originality*, will subside into the commonplace. No one, I think, has noticed that, merely through inattention to this matter, Moore has comparatively failed in his *Lalla Rookh*. Few readers, and indeed few critics, have commended this poem for originality – and, in fact, the effect, originality, is not produced by it – yet no work of equal size so abounds in the happiest originalities, individually considered. They are so excessive as, in the end, to deaden in the reader all capacity for their appreciation.

These points properly understood, it will be seen that the critic (unacquainted with Tieck) who reads a single tale or essay by Hawthorne, may be justified in thinking him original; but the tone, or manner, or choice of subject, which induces in this critic the sense of the new, will – if not in a second tale, at least in a third and all subsequent ones – not only fail of inducing it, but bring about an exactly antagonistic impression. In concluding a volume, and more especially in concluding all the volumes of the author, the critic will abandon his first design of calling him 'original,' and content himself with styling him 'peculiar.'

With the vague opinion that to be original is to be unpopular, I could, indeed, agree, were I to adopt an understanding of originality which, to my surprise, I have known adopted by many who have a right to be called critical. They have limited, in a love for mere words, the literary to the metaphysical originality. They regard as original in letters, only such combinations of thought, of incident, and so forth, as are, in fact, absolutely novel. It is clear, however, not only that it is the novelty of *effect* alone which is worth consideration, but that this effect is *best* wrought, for the end of all fictitious composition, pleasure, by shunning rather than by seeking the absolute novelty of combination. Originality, thus understood, tasks and startles the intellect, and so brings into undue action the faculties to which, in the lighter literature, we least appeal. And thus understood, it cannot fail to prove unpopular with the masses, who, seeking in this literature amusement, are positively offended by instruction. But the true originality – true in respect of its purposes – is that which, in bringing out the half-formed, the reluctant, or the unexpressed fancies of mankind, or in exciting the more delicate pulses of the heart's passion, or in giving birth to some universal sentiment or instinct in embryo, thus combines with the pleasurable effect of *apparent* novelty, a real egotistic delight. The reader, in the case first supposed, (that of the absolute novelty,) is excited, but embarrassed, disturbed, in some degree even pained at his own want of perception, at his own folly in not having himself hit upon the idea. In the second case, his pleasure is doubled. He is filled with an intrinsic and extrinsic delight. He feels and intensely enjoys the seeming novelty of the thought, enjoys it as really novel, as absolutely original with the writer – *and* himself. They two, he fancies, have, alone of all men, thought thus.

They two have, together, created this thing. Henceforward there is a bond of sympathy between them – a sympathy which irradiates every subsequent page of the book.

There is a species of writing which, with some difficulty, may be admitted as a lower degree of what I have called the true original. In its perusal, we say to ourselves, not 'how original this is!' nor 'here is an idea which I and the author have alone entertained,' but 'here is a charmingly obvious fancy,' or sometimes even, 'here is a thought which I am not sure has ever occurred to myself, but which, of course, has occurred to all the rest of the world.' This kind of composition (which still appertains to a high order) is usually designated as 'the natural.' It has little external resemblance, but strong internal affinity to the true original, if, indeed, as I have suggested, it is not of this latter an inferior degree. It is best exemplified, among English writers, in Addison, Irving and *Hawthorne*. The 'ease' which is so often spoken of as its distinguishing feature, it has been the fashion to regard as ease in appearance alone, as a point of really difficult attainment. This idea, however, must be received with some reservation. The natural style is difficult only to those who should never intermeddle with it – to the unnatural. It is but the result of writing with the understanding, or with the instinct, that the *tone*, in composition, should be that which, at any given point or upon any given topic, would be the tone of the great mass of humanity. The author who, after the manner of the North Americans, is merely at *all* times *quiet*, is, of course, upon *most* occasions, merely silly or stupid, and has no more right to be thought 'easy' or 'natural' than has a cockney exquisite, or the sleeping beauty in the waxworks.

The 'peculiarity,' or sameness, or monotone of Hawthorne, would, in its mere character of 'peculiarity,' and without reference to what *is* the peculiarity, suffice to deprive him of all chance of popular appreciation. But at his failure to be appreciated, we can, *of course*, no longer wonder, when we find him monotonous at decidedly the worst of all possible points – at that point which, having the least concern with Nature, is the farthest removed from the popular intellect, from the popular sentiment, and from the popular taste. I allude to the strain of allegory which completely overwhelms the greater number of his subjects, and which in some measure interferes with the direct conduct of absolutely all.

In defence of allegory, (however, or for whatever object employed,) there is scarcely one respectable word to be said. Its best appeals are made to the fancy – that is to say, to our sense of adaptation, not of matters proper, but of matters improper for the purpose, of the real with the unreal; having never more of intelligible connexion than has something with nothing, never half so much of effective affinity as has the substance for the shadow. The deepest emotion aroused within us by the happiest allegory, *as* allegory, is a very, very imperfectly satisfied sense of the writer's ingenuity in overcoming a difficulty we should have preferred his not having attempted to overcome. The fallacy of the idea that allegory, in any of its moods, can be made to enforce a truth – that metaphor, for example, may illustrate as well as embellish an argument – could be promptly demonstrated; the converse of the supposed fact might be shown, indeed, with very little trouble – but these are topics foreign to my present purpose. One thing is clear, that if allegory ever establishes a fact, it is by dint of overturning a fiction. Where the suggested meaning runs through the obvious one in a *very* profound under-current, so as never to interfere with the upper one without our own volition, so as never to show itself unless *called* to the surface, there only, for the proper uses of fictitious narrative, is it available at all. Under the best circumstances, it must always interfere with that unity of effect which, to the artist, is worth all the allegory in the world. Its vital injury, however, is rendered to the most vitally important point in fiction – that of earnestness or verisimilitude. That *The Pilgrim's Progress* is a ludicrously overrated book, owing its seeming popularity to one or two of those accidents in critical literature which by the critical are sufficiently well understood, is a matter upon which no two thinking people disagree; but the pleasure derivable from it, in any sense, will be found in the direct ratio of the reader's capacity to smother its true purpose, in the direct ratio of his ability to keep the allegory out of sight, or of his *in*ability to comprehend it. Of allegory properly handled, judiciously subdued, seen only as a shadow or by suggestive glimpses, and making its nearest approach to truth in a not obtrusive and therefore not unpleasant *appositeness*, the *Undine* of De la Motte Fouqué is the best, and undoubtedly a very remarkable specimen.

The obvious causes, however, which have prevented Mr Hawthorne's *popularity*, do not suffice to condemn him in the eyes of the few who belong properly to books, and to whom books, perhaps, do not quite so properly belong. These few estimate an author, not as do the public, altogether by what he does, but in great measure – indeed, even in the greatest measure – by what he evinces a capability of doing. In this view, Hawthorne stands among literary people in

America much in the same light as did Coleridge in England. The few, also, through a certain warping of the taste, which long pondering upon books as books merely never fails to induce, are not in condition to view the errors of a scholar as errors altogether. At any time these gentlemen are prone to think the public not right rather than an educated author wrong. But the simple truth is, that the writer who aims at impressing the people, is *always* wrong when he fails in forcing that people to receive the impression. How far Mr Hawthorne has addressed the people at all, is, of course, not a question for me to decide. His books afford strong internal evidence of having been written to himself and his particular friends alone.

There has long existed in literature a fatal and unfounded prejudice, which it will be the office of this age to overthrow – the idea that the mere bulk of a work must enter largely into our estimate of its merit. I do not suppose even the weakest of the Quarterly reviewers weak enough to maintain that in a book's size or mass, abstractly considered, there is anything which especially calls for our admiration. A mountain, simply through the sensation of physical magnitude which it conveys, does, indeed, affect us with a sense of the sublime, but we cannot admit any such influence in the contemplation even of *The Columbiad*. The Quarterlies themselves will not admit it. And yet, what else are we to understand by their continual prating about 'sustained effort'? Granted that this sustained effort has accomplished an epic – let us then admire the effort, (if this be a thing admirable,) but certainly not the epic on the effort's account. Common sense, in the time to come, may possibly insist upon measuring a work of art rather by the object it fulfils, by the impression it makes, than by the time it took to fulfil the object, or by the extent of 'sustained effort' which became necessary to produce the impression. The fact is, that perseverance is one thing and genius quite another; nor can all the transcendentalists in Heathendom confound them.

. . . . .

The pieces in the volumes entitled *Twice-Told Tales*, are now in their third republication, and, of course, are thrice-told. Moreover, they are by no means *all* tales, either in the ordinary or in the legitimate understanding of the term. Many of them are pure essays; for example, *Sights from a Steeple*, *Sunday at Home*, *Little Annie's Ramble*, *A Rill from the Town-Pump*, *The Toll-Gatherer's Day*, *The Haunted Mind*, *The Sister Years*, *Snow-Flakes*, *Night Sketches*, and

Foot-Prints on the Sea-Shore. I mention these matters chiefly on account of their discrepancy with that marked precision and finish by which the body of the work is distinguished.

Of the Essays just named, I must be content to speak in brief. They are each and all beautiful, without being characterized by the polish and adaptation so visible in the tales proper. A painter would at once note their leading or predominant feature, and style it *repose*. There is no attempt at effect. All is quiet, thoughtful, subdued. Yet this repose may exist simultaneously with high originality of thought; and Mr Hawthorne has demonstrated the fact. At every turn we meet with novel combinations; yet these combinations never surpass the limits of the quiet. We are soothed as we read; and withal is a calm astonishment that ideas so apparently obvious have never occurred or been presented to us before. Herein our author differs materially from Lamb or Hunt or Hazlitt – who, with vivid originality of manner and expression, have less of the true novelty of thought than is generally supposed, and whose originality, at best, has an uneasy and meretricious quaintness, replete with startling effects unfounded in nature, and inducing trains of reflection which lead to no satisfactory result. The Essays of Hawthorne have much of the character of Irving, with more of originality, and less of finish; while, compared with the *Spectator*, they have a vast superiority at all points. The *Spectator*, Mr Irving, and Hawthorne have in common that tranquil and subdued manner which I have chosen to denominate *repose*; but, in the case of the two former, this repose is attained rather by the absence of novel combination, or of originality, than otherwise, and consists chiefly in the calm, quiet, unostentatious expression of commonplace thoughts, in an unambitious, unadulterated Saxon. In them, by strong effort, we are made to conceive the absence of all. In the essays before me the absence of effort is too obvious to be mistaken, and a strong under-current of *suggestion* runs continuously beneath the upper stream of the tranquil thesis. In short, these effusions of Mr Hawthorne are the product of a truly imaginative intellect, restrained, and in some measure repressed, by fastidiousness of taste, by constitutional melancholy, and by indolence.

But it is of his tales that I desire principally to speak. The tale proper, in my opinion, affords unquestionably the fairest field for the exercise of the loftiest talent, which can be afforded by the wide domains of mere prose. Were I bidden to say how the highest genius could be most advantageously employed for the best display of its own powers, I should answer, without hesitation – in the composition of a rhymed poem, not to exceed in length what might be perused in an hour. Within this limit alone can the highest order of true poetry exist. I need only here say, upon this topic, that, in almost all classes of composition, the unity of effect or impression is a point of the greatest importance. It is clear, moreover, that this unity cannot be thoroughly preserved in productions whose persual cannot be completed at one sitting. We may continue the reading of a prose composition, from the very nature of prose itself, much longer than we can persevere, to any good purpose, in the perusal of a poem. This latter, if truly fulfilling the demands of the poetic sentiment, induces an exaltation of the soul which cannot be long sustained. All high excitements are necessarily transient. Thus a long poem is a paradox. And, without unity of impression, the deepest effects cannot be brought about. Epics were the offspring of an imperfect sense of Art, and their reign is no more. A poem *too* brief may produce a vivid, but never an intense or enduring impression. Without a certain continuity of effort – without a certain duration or repetition of purpose – the soul is never deeply moved. There must be the dropping of the water upon the rock. De Béranger has wrought brilliant things – pungent and spirit-stirring – but, like all immassive bodies, they lack *momentum*, and thus fail to satisfy the Poetic Sentiment. They sparkle and excite, but, from want of continuity, fail deeply to impress. Extreme brevity will degenerate into epigrammatism; but the sin of extreme length is even more unpardonable. *In medio tutissimus ibis.*

Were I called upon, however, to designate that class of composition which, next to such a poem as I have suggested, should best fulfil the demands of high genius – should offer it the most advantageous field of exertion – I should unhesitatingly speak of the prose tale as Mr Hawthorne has here exemplified it. I allude to the short prose narrative, requiring from a half-hour to one or two hours in its perusal. The ordinary novel is objectionable, from its length, for reasons already stated in substance. As it cannot be read at one sitting, it deprives itself, of course, of the immense force derivable from *totality*. Worldly interests intervening during the pauses of perusal, modify, annul, or counteract, in a greater or less degree, the impressions of the book. But simple cessation in reading would, of itself, be sufficient to destroy the true unity. In the brief tale, however, the author is enabled to carry out the fullness of his intention, be it what it may. During the hour of perusal the soul of the reader is at the writer's control. There are no external or extrinsic influences – resulting from weariness or interruption.

A skilful literary artist has constructed a tale. If wise, he has not fashioned his thoughts to accommodate his incidents; but having conceived, with deliberate care, a certain unique or single *effect* to be wrought out, he then invents such incidents – he then combines such events as may best aid him in establishing this preconceived effect. If his very initial sentence tend not to the outbringing of this effect, then he has failed in his first step. In the whole composition there should be no word written, of which the tendency, direct or indirect, is not to the one pre-established design. And by such means, with such care and skill, a picture is at length painted which leaves in the mind of him who contemplates it with the kindred art, a sense of the fullest satisfaction. The idea of the tale has been presented unblemished, because undisturbed; and this is an end unattainable by the novel. Undue brevity is just as exceptionable here as in the poem; but undue length is yet more to be avoided.

We have said that the tale has a point of superiority even over the poem. In fact, while the *rhythm* of this latter is an essential aid in the development of the poem's highest idea – the idea of the Beautiful – the artificialities of this rhythm are an inseparable bar to the development of all points of thought or expression which have their basis in *Truth*. But Truth is often, and in very great degree, the aim of the tale. Some of the finest tales are tales of ratiocination. Thus the field of this species of composition, if not in so elevated a region on the mountain of Mind, is a tableland of far vaster extent than the domain of the mere poem. Its products are never so rich, but infinitely more numerous, and more appreciable by the mass of mankind. The writer of the prose tale, in short, may bring to his theme a vast variety of modes or inflections of thought and expression – (the ratiocinative, for example, the sarcastic or the humorous) which are not only antagonistical to the nature of the poem, but absolutely forbidden by one of its most peculiar and indispensable adjuncts; we allude, of course, to rhythm. It may be added, here, *par parenthèse*, that the author who aims at the purely beautiful in a prose tale is labouring at a great disadvantage. For Beauty can be better treated in the poem. Not so with terror, or passion, or horror, or a multitude of such other points. And here it will be seen how full of prejudice are the usual animadversions against those *tales of effect*, many fine examples of which were found in the earlier numbers of *Blackwood*. The impressions produced were wrought in a legitimate sphere of action, and constituted a legitimate although sometimes an exaggerated interest. They were relished by every man of genius: although there were found many men of genius who condemned them without just ground. The true critic will but demand that the design intended be accomplished, to the fullest extent, by the means most advantageously applicable.

We have very few American tales of real merit – we may say, indeed, none, with the exception of *The Tales of a Traveller* of Washington Irving, and these *Twice-Told Tales* of Mr Hawthorne. Some of the pieces of Mr John Neal abound in vigour and originality: but in general, his compositions of this class are excessively diffuse, extravagant, and indicative of an imperfect sentiment of Art. Articles at random are, now and then, met with in our periodicals which might be advantageously compared with the best effusions of the British Magazines; but, upon the whole, we are far behind our progenitors in this department of literature.

Of Mr Hawthorne's Tales we would say, emphatically, that they belong to the highest region of Art – an Art subservient to genius of a very lofty order. We had supposed, with good reason for so supposing, that he had been thrust into his present position by one of the impudent *cliques* which beset our literature, and whose pretensions it is our full purpose to expose at the earliest opportunity; but we have been most agreeably mistaken. We know of few compositions which the critic can more honestly commend than these *Twice-Told Tales*. As Americans, we feel proud of the book.

Mr Hawthorne's distinctive trait is invention, creation, imagination, originality – a trait which, in the literature of fiction, is positively worth all the rest. But the nature of the originality, so far as regards its manifestation in letters, is but imperfectly understood. The inventive or original mind as frequently displays itself in novelty of *tone* as in novelty of matter. Mr Hawthorne is original in *all* points.

It would be a matter of some difficulty to designate the best of these tales; we repeat that, without exception, they are beautiful. *Wakefield* is remarkable for the skill with which an old idea – a well-known incident – is worked up or discussed. A man of whims conceives the purpose of quitting his wife and residing *incognito*, for twenty years, in her immediate neighbourhood. Something of this kind actually happened in London. The force of Mr Hawthorne's tale lies in the analysis of the motives which must or might have impelled the husband to such folly, in the first instance, with the possible causes of his perseverance. Upon this thesis a sketch of singular power has been constructed. *The Wedding Knell* is full of the boldest imagination – an imagination fully controlled by taste. The most captious critic could find no flaw in this production. *The Minister's Black Veil* is a masterly composition of which the sole defect is that to the rabble its exquisite skill will be *caviare*. The *obvious* meaning of this article will be found to smother its insinuated one. The *moral* put into the mouth of the dying minister will be supposed to convey the *true* import of the narrative; and that a crime of dark dye (having reference to the 'young lady') has been committed, is a point which only minds congenial with that of the author will perceive. *Mr Higginbotham's Catastrophe* is vividly original and managed most dexterously. *Dr Heidegger's Experiment* is exceedingly well imagined, and executed with surpassing ability. The artist breathes in every line of it. *The White Old Maid* is objectionable, even more than the *Minister's Black Veil*, on the score of its mysticism. Even with the thoughtful and analytic, there will be much trouble in penetrating its entire import.

The Hollow of the Three Hills we would quote in full, had we space; – not as evincing higher talent than any of the other pieces, but as affording an excellent example of the author's peculiar ability. The subject is commonplace. A witch subjects the Distant and the Past to the view of a mourner. It has been the fashion to describe, in such cases, a mirror in which the images of the absent appear; or a cloud of smoke is made to arise, and thence the figures are gradually unfolded. Mr Hawthorne has wonderfully heightened his effect by making the ear, in place of the eye, the medium by which the fantasy is conveyed. The head of the mourner is enveloped in the cloak of the witch, and within its magic folds there arise sounds which have an all-sufficient intelligence. Throughout this article also, the artist is conspicuous – not more in positive than in negative merits. Not only is all done that should be done, but (what perhaps is an end with more difficulty attained) there is nothing done which should not be. Every word *tells*, and there is not a word which does *not* tell.

In *Howe's Masquerade* we observe something which resembles a plagiarism – but which *may be* a very flattering coincidence of thought. We quote the passage in question.

> *With a dark flush of wrath* upon his brow they saw the general *draw his sword*, and *advance to meet* the figure *in the cloak* before the latter had stepped one pace upon the floor.
>
> '*Villain, unmuffle yourself*,' cried he, 'you pass no farther!'

> The figure, without blenching a hair's breadth from the sword which was pointed at his breast, made a solemn pause, and *lowered the cape of the cloak* from his face, yet not sufficiently for the spectators to catch a glimpse of it. But Sir William Howe had evidently seen enough. The sternness of his countenance gave place to a look of wild amazement, if not horror, while he recoiled several steps from the figure, *and let fall his sword* upon the floor. – See vol. 2, p. 20.

The idea here is, that the figure in the cloak is the phantom or reduplication of Sir William Howe; but in an article called *William Wilson*, one of the *Tales of the Grotesque and Arabesque*, we have not only the same idea, but the same idea similarly presented in several respects. We quote two paragraphs, which our readers may compare with what has been already given. We have italicized, above, the immediate particulars of resemblance.

> The brief moment in which I averted my eyes had been sufficient to produce, apparently, a material change in the arrangement at the upper or farther end of the room. A large mirror, it appeared to me, now stood where none had been perceptible before: and as I stepped up to it in extremity of terror, mine own image, but with features all pale and dabbled in blood, *advanced* with a feeble and tottering gait to meet me. Thus it appeared I say, but was not. It was Wilson, who then stood before me in the agonies of dissolution. Not a line in all the marked and singular lineaments of that face which was not even identically mine own. *His mask and cloak lay where he had thrown them, upon the floor*. – Vol. 2, p. 57.

Here, it will be observed that, not only are the two general conceptions identical, but there are various *points* of similarity. In each case the figure seen is the wraith or duplication of the beholder. In each case the scene is a masquerade. In each case the figure is cloaked. In each there is a quarrel – that is to say, angry words pass between the parties. In each the beholder is enraged. In each the cloak and sword fall upon the floor. The 'villain, unmuffle yourself,' of Mr H. is precisely paralleled by a passage at page 56 of *William Wilson*.

. . . . . .

I must hasten to conclude this paper with a summary of Mr Hawthorne's merits and demerits.

He is peculiar and *not* original – unless in those detailed fancies and detached thoughts which his want of general originality will deprive of the appreciation due to them, in preventing them for ever reaching the *public* eye. He is infinitely too fond of allegory, and can never hope for popularity so long as he persists in it. This he will not do, for allegory is at war with the whole tone of his nature, which disports itself never so well as when escaping from the mysticism of his Goodman Browns and White Old Maids into the hearty, genial, but still Indian-summer sunshine of his Wakefields and Little Annie's Rambles. Indeed, *his* spirit of 'metaphor run-mad' is clearly imbibed from the phalanx and phalanstery atmosphere in which he has been so long struggling for breath. He has not half the material for the exclusiveness of authorship that he possesses for its universality. He has the purest style, the finest taste, the most available scholarship, the most delicate humour, the most touching pathos, the most radiant imagination, the most consummate ingenuity; and with these varied good qualities he has done *well* as a mystic. But is there any one of these qualities which should prevent his doing doubly as well in a career of honest, upright, sensible, prehensible and comprehensible things? Let him mend his pen, get a bottle of visible ink, come out from the Old Manse, cut Mr Alcott, hang (if possible) the editor of *The Dial*, and throw out of the window to the pigs all his odd numbers of *The North American Review*.

FROM *MARGINALIA*

INTRODUCTION

In getting my books, I have been always solicitous of an ample margin; this not so much through any love of the thing in itself, however agreeable, as for the facility it affords me of pencilling suggested thoughts, agreements, and differences of opinion, or brief critical comments in general. Where what I have to note is too much to be included within the narrow limits of a margin, I commit it to a slip of paper, and deposit it between the leaves; taking care to secure it by an imperceptible portion of gum tragacanth paste.

All this may be whim; it may be not only a very hackneyed, but a very idle practice; – yet I persist in it still; and it affords me pleasure; which is profit, in despite of Mr Bentham with Mr Mill on his back.

This making of notes, however, is by no means the making of mere *memoranda* – a custom which has its disadvantages, beyond doubt. '*Ce que je mets sur papier*,' says Bernardin de St Pierre, '*je remets de ma mémoire, et par conséquence je l'oublie*' – and, in fact, if you wish to forget anything on the spot, make a note that this thing is to be remembered.

But the purely marginal jottings, done with no eye to the Memorandum Book, have a distinct complexion, and not only a distinct purpose, but none at all; this it is which imparts to them a value. They have a rank somewhat above the chance and desultory comments of literary chit-chat – for these latter are not unfrequently 'talk for talk's sake,' hurried out of the mouth; while the *marginalia* are deliberately pencilled, because the mind of the reader wishes to unburthen itself of a *thought* – however flippant – however silly – however trivial – still a thought indeed, not merely a thing that might have been a thought in time, and under more favourable circumstances. In the *marginalia*, too, we talk only to ourselves; we therefore talk freshly – boldly – originally – with *abandonnement* – without conceit – much after the fashion of Jeremy Taylor, and Sir Thomas Browne, and Sir William Temple, and the anatomical Burton, and that most logical analogist, Butler, and some other people of the old day, who were too full of their matter to have any room for their manner, which being thus left out of question, was a capital manner, indeed – a model of manners, with a richly marginalic air.

The circumscription of space, too, in these pencillings has in it something more of advantage than inconvenience. It compels us (whatever diffuseness of idea we may clandestinely entertain) into Montesquieu-ism, into Tacitus-ism, (here I leave out of view the concluding portion of the *Annals*,) – or even into Carlyle-ism – a thing which, I have been told, is not to be confounded with your ordinary affectation and bad grammar. I say 'bad grammar,' through sheer obstinacy, because the grammarians (who should know better) insist upon it that I should not. But then grammar is not what these grammarians will have it; and, being merely the analysis of language, with the result of this analysis, must be good or bad just as the analyst is sage or silly – just as he is a Horne Tooke or a Cobbett.

But to our sheep. During a rainy afternoon, not long ago, being in a mood too listless for continuous study, I sought relief from *ennui* in dipping here and there, at random, among the volumes of my library – no very large one, certainly, but sufficiently miscellaneous; and, I flatter myself, not a little *recherché*.

Perhaps it was what the Germans call the 'brain-scattering' humour of the moment; but, while the picturesqueness of the numerous pencil-scratches arrested my attention, their helter-skelteriness of commentary amused me. I found myself, at length, forming a wish that it had been some other hand than my own which had so bedevilled the books, and fancying that in such case, I might have derived no inconsiderable pleasure from turning them over. From this the transition-thought (as Mr Lyell, or Mr Murchison, or Mr Featherstonhaugh would have it) was natural enough: – there might be something even in *my* scribblings which, for the mere sake of scribbling, would have interest for others.

The main difficulty respected the mode of transferring the notes from the volumes – the context from the text – without detriment to that exceedingly frail fabric of intelligibility in which the context was imbedded. With all appliances to boot, with the printed pages at their back, the commentaries were too often like Dodona's oracles – or those of Lycophron Tenebrosus – or the essays of the pedant's pupils, in Quintillian, which were 'necessarily excellent, since even he (the pedant) found it impossible to comprehend them': – what, then, would become of it – this context – if transferred? – if translated? Would it not rather be *traduit* (traduced), which is the French synonym, or *overzezet* (turned topsy-turvy), which is the Dutch one?

I concluded, at length, to put extensive faith in the acumen and imagination of the reader: – this as a general rule. But, in some instances, where even faith would not remove mountains, there seemed no safer plan than so to remodel the note as to convey at least a ghost of a conception as to what it was all about. Where, for such conception, the text itself was absolutely necessary, I could quote it; where the title of the book commented upon was indispensable, I could name it. In short, like a novel hero dilemma'd, I made up my mind 'to be guided by circumstances,' in default of more satisfactory rules of conduct.

As for the multitudinous opinion expressed in the subjoined *farrago* – as for my present assent to all, or dissent from any portion of it – as to the possibility of my having, in some instances, altered my mind – or as to the impossibility of my not having altered it often – these are points upon which I say nothing, because upon these there can be nothing cleverly said. It may be as well to observe, however, that just as the goodness of your true pun is in the direct ratio of its intolerability, so is nonsense the essential sense of the Marginal Note.

ARISTOCRACY AND DEMOCRACY

The sense of high birth is a moral force whose value the democrats, albeit compact of mathematics, are never in condition to calculate. '*Pour savoir ce qu'est Dieu,*' says the Baron de Bielfeld, '*il faut être Dieu même.*'

A SOMNAMBULE

One of the happiest examples, in a small way, of the carrying-one's-self-in-a-hand-basket logic, is to be found in a London weekly paper, called *The Popular Record of Modern Science; a Journal of Philosophy and General Information*. This work has a vast circulation, and is respected by eminent men. Sometime in November, 1845, it copied from the *Columbian Magazine*, of New York, a rather adventurous article of mine, called 'Mesmeric Revelation.' It had the impudence, also, to spoil the title by improving it to 'The Last Conversation of a Somnambule' – a phrase that is nothing at all to the purpose, since the person who 'converses' is *not* a somnambule. He is a sleep-waker – *not* a sleep-walker; but I presume that the *Record* thought it was only the difference of an *l*. What I chiefly complain of, however, is that the London editor prefaced my paper with these words: – 'The following is an article communicated to the *Columbian Magazine*, a journal of respectability and influence in the United States, by Mr Edgar A. Poe. *It bears internal evidence of authenticity*'! There is no subject under heaven about which funnier ideas are, in general, entertained than about this subject of internal evidence. It is by 'internal evidence,' observe, that we decide upon the mind. But to the *Record*: – On the issue of my 'Valdemar Case,' this journal copies it as a matter of course, and (also as a matter of course) improves the title, as in the previous instance. But the editorial comments may as well be called profound. Here they are:

> The following narrative appears in a recent number of the *American Magazine*, a respectable periodical in the United States. It comes, it will be observed, from the narrator of the 'Last Conversation of a Somnambule,' published in the *Record* of the 29th of November. In extracting this case the *Morning Post*, of Monday last, takes what it considers the safe side, by remarking – 'For our own parts we do not believe it; and there are several statements made more especially with regard to the disease of which the patient died, which at once prove the case to be either a fabrication, or the work of one little acquainted with consumption. The story, however, is wonderful, and we therefore give it.' The editor, however, does not point out the especial statements which are inconsistent with what we know of the progress of consumption, and as few scientific persons would be willing to take their pathology any more than their logic from the *Morning Post*, his caution, it is to be feared, will not have much weight. The reason assigned by the *Post* for publishing the account is quaint, and would apply equally to an adventure from *Baron Munchausen*: – 'it is wonderful and we therefore give it' . . . The above case is obviously one that cannot be received except on the strongest testimony, and it is equally clear that the testimony by which it is at present accompanied, is not of that character. The most favourable circumstances in support of it, consist in the fact that credence is understood to be given to it at New York, within a few miles of which city the affair took place, and where consequently the most ready means must be found for its authentication or disproval. The initials of the medical men and of the young medical student must be sufficient in the immediate locality, to establish their identity, especially as M. Valdemar was well known, and had been so long ill as to render it out of the question that there should be any difficulty in ascertaining the names of the physicians by whom he had been attended. In the same way the nurses and servants under whose cognizance the case must have come during the seven months which it occupied, are of course accessible to all sorts of

inquiries. It will, therefore, appear that there must have been too many parties concerned to render prolonged deception practicable. The angry excitement and various rumours which have at length rendered a public statement necessary, are also sufficient to show that *something* extraordinary must have taken place. On the other hand there is no strong point for disbelief. The circumstances are, as the *Post* says, 'wonderful'; but so are all circumstances that come to our knowledge for the first time – and in Mesmerism everything is new. An objection may be made that the article has rather a Magazinish air; Mr Poe having evidently written with a view to effect, and so as to excite rather than to subdue the vague appetite for the mysterious and the horrible which such a case, under any circumstances, is sure to awaken – but apart from this there is nothing to deter a philosophic mind from further inquiries regarding it. It is a matter entirely for testimony. [So it is.] Under this view we shall take steps to procure from some of the most intelligent and influential citizens of New York all the evidence that can be had upon the subject. No steamer will leave England for America till the 3rd of February, but within a few weeks of that time we doubt not it will be possible to lay before the readers of the *Record* information which will enable them to come to a pretty accurate conclusion.

Yes; and no doubt they came to one accurate enough, in the end. But all this rigmarole is what people call testing a thing by 'internal evidence.' The *Record* insists upon the truth of the story because of certain facts – because 'the initials of the young men *must* be sufficient to establish their identity' – because 'the nurses *must* be accessible to all sorts of inquiries' – and because the 'angry excitement and various rumours which at length rendered a public statement necessary, are sufficient to show that *something* extraordinary *must* have taken place.' To be sure! The story is proved by these facts – the facts about the students, the nurses, the excitement, the credence given the tale at New York. And now all we have to do is to prove these facts. Ah! – *they* are proved *by the story*. As for the *Morning Post*, it evinces more weakness in its disbelief than the *Record* in its credulity. What the former says about doubting on account of inaccuracy in the detail of the phthisical symptoms, is a mere *fetch*, as the Cockneys have it, in order to make a very few little children believe that it, the *Post*, is not quite so stupid as a post proverbially is. It knows nearly as much about pathology as it does about English grammar – and I really hope it will not feel called upon to blush at the compliment. I represented the symptoms of

M. Valdemar as 'severe,' to be sure. I put an extreme case; for it was necessary that I should leave on the reader's mind no doubt as to the certainty of death without the aid of the Mesmerist – but such symptoms *might* have appeared – the identical symptoms *have appeared*, and will be presented again and again. Had the *Post* been only half as honest as ignorant, it would have owned that it disbelieved for no reason more profound than that which influences all dunces in disbelieving – it would have owned that it doubted the thing merely because the thing was a 'wonderful' thing, and had never yet been printed in a book.

PUNCTUATION

That punctuation is important all agree; but how few comprehend the extent of its importance! The writer who neglects punctuation, or mispunctuates, is liable to be misunderstood – this, according to the popular idea, is the sum of the evils arising from heedlessness or ignorance. It does not seem to be known that, even where the sense is perfectly clear, a sentence may be deprived of half its force – its spirit – its point – by improper punctuations. For the want of merely a comma, it often occurs that an axiom appears a paradox, or that a sarcasm is converted into a sermonoid. There is *no* treatise on the topic – and there is no topic on which a treatise is more needed. There seems to exist a vulgar notion that the subject is one of pure conventionality, and cannot be brought within the limits of intelligible and consistent *rule*. And yet, if fairly looked in the face, the whole matter is so plain that its *rationale* may be read as we run. If not anticipated, I shall hereafter, make an attempt at a magazine paper on 'The Philosophy of Point.' In the meantime let me say a word or two of *the dash*. Every writer for the press, who has any sense of the accurate, must have been frequently mortified and vexed at the distortion of his sentences by the printer's now general substitution of a semicolon, or comma, for the dash of the MS. The total or nearly total disuse of the latter point, has been brought about by the revulsion consequent upon its excessive employment about twenty years ago. The Byronic poets were *all* dash. John Neal, in his earlier novels, exaggerated its use into the grossest abuse – although his very error arose from the philosophical and self-dependent spirit which has always distinguished him, and which will even yet lead him, if I am not greatly mistaken in the man, to do something for the literature of the country which the country 'will not willingly,' and cannot possibly 'let die.' Without entering now into the *why*, let me observe that the printer may always ascertain when the dash of the MS. is properly and when improperly employed, by bearing in mind that this point represents *a second thought – an emendation*. In using it just above I have exemplified its use. The words 'an emendation' are, speaking with reference to grammatical construction, put in *ap*position with the words 'a second thought.' Having written these latter words, I reflected whether it would not be possible to render their meaning more distinct by certain other words. Now, instead of erasing the phrase 'a second thought,' which is of *some* use – which *partially* conveys the idea intended – which advances me *a step toward* my full purpose – I suffer it to remain, and merely put a dash between it and the phrase 'an emendation.' The dash gives the reader a choice between two, or among three or more expressions, one of which may be more forcible than another, but all of which help out the idea. It stands, in general, for these words – *or, to make my meaning more distinct*. This force *it has* – and this force no other point can have; since all other points have well-understood uses quite different from this. Therefore, the dash *cannot* be dispensed with. It has its phases – its variation of the force described; but the one principle – that of second thought or emendation – will be found at the bottom of all.

RHYME

The effect derivable from well-managed rhyme is very imperfectly understood. Conventionally 'rhyme' implies merely close similarity of sound at the ends of verse, and it is really curious to observe how long mankind have been content with their limitation of the idea. What, in rhyme, first and principally pleases, may be referred to the human sense or appreciation of *equality* – the common element, as might be easily shown, of all the gratification we derive from music in its most extended sense – very especially in its modifications of metre and rhythm. We see, for example, a crystal, and are immediately interested by the equality between the sides and angles of one of its faces – but, on bringing to view a second face, in all respects similar to the first, our pleasure seems to be *squared* – on bringing to view a third, it appears to be *cubed*, and so on: I have no doubt, indeed, that the delight experienced, if measurable, would be found to have exact mathematical relations, such, or nearly such, as I suggest – that is to say, as far as a certain point, beyond which there would be a decrease, in similar relations. Now here, as the ultimate result of analysis, we reach the sense of mere *equality*, or rather the human delight in this sense; and it was an instinct, rather than a clear comprehension of this delight as a principle, which, in the first instance, led the poet to attempt an increase of the effect arising from the mere similarity (that is to say equality) between two sounds – led him, I say, to attempt increasing this effect by making a secondary equalization, in placing the rhymes at equal distances – that is, at the ends of lines of equal length. In this manner, rhyme and the termination of the line grew connected in men's thoughts – grew into a conventionalism – the principle being lost sight of altogether. And it was simply because Pindaric verses had, before this epoch, existed – *i.e.* verses of unequal length – that rhymes were subsequently found at unequal distances. It was for this reason solely, I say – for none more profound. Rhyme had come to be regarded as of right appertaining to the *end* of verse – and here we complain that the matter has finally rested. But it is clear that there was much more to be considered. So far, the sense of *equality* alone, entered the effect; or if this equality was slightly varied, it was varied only through an accident – the accident of the existence of Pindaric metres. It will be seen that the rhymes were always *anticipated*. The eye, catching the end of a verse, whether long or short, expected, for the ear, a rhyme. The great element of unexpectedness was not dreamed of – that is to say, of novelty – of originality. 'But,' says Lord Bacon, (how justly!) 'there is no exquisite beauty without some *strangeness* in the proportions.' Take away this element of strangeness – of unexpectedness – of novelty – of originality – call it what we will – and all that is *ethereal* in loveliness is lost at once. We lose – we miss the *unknown* – the vague – the uncomprehended because offered before we have time to examine and comprehend. We lose, in short, all that assimilates the beauty of earth with what we dream of the beauty of Heaven. Perfection of rhyme is attainable only in the combination of the two elements. Equality and Unexpectedness. But as evil cannot exist without good, so unexpectedness must arise from expectedness. We do not contend for mere *arbitrariness* of rhyme. In the first place, we must have equidistant or regularly recurring rhymes, to form the basis, expectedness, out of which arises the element, unexpectedness, by the introduction of rhymes, not arbitrarily, but with an eye to the greatest amount of unexpectedness. We should not introduce them, for example, at such points that the entire line is a multiple of the syllables preceding the points. When, for instance, I write –

And the silken, sad, uncertain rustling of each purple curtain,

I produce more, to be sure, but not remarkably more than the ordinary effect of rhymes regularly recurring at the ends of lines; for the number of syllables in the whole verse is merely a multiple of the number of syllables preceding the rhyme introduced at the middle, and there is still left, therefore, a certain degree of expectedness. What there is of the element, unexpectedness, is addressed, in fact, to the eye only – for the ear divides the verse into two ordinary lines, thus:

And the silken, sad, uncertain
Rustling of each purple curtain

I obtain, however, the whole effect of unexpectedness, when I write –

Thrilled me, *filled* me with fantastic terrors never felt before.

N.B. – It is very commonly supposed that rhyme, as it now ordinarily exists, is of modern invention – but see the *Clouds* of Aristophanes. Hebrew verse, however, did *not* include it – terminations of the lines, where most distinct, never showing anything of the kind.

SCHWARMEREI

The German '*Schwarmerei*' – not exactly 'humbug,' but 'sky-rocketing' – seems to be the only term by which we can conveniently designate that peculiar style of criticism which has lately come into fashion, through the influence of certain members of the *Fabian* family – people who live (upon beans) about Boston.

THOUGHTS AND WORDS

Some Frenchman – possibly Montaigne – says: 'People talk about thinking, but for my part I never think, except when I sit down to write.' It is this never thinking, unless when we sit down to write, which is the cause of so much indifferent composition. But perhaps there is something more involved in the Frenchman's observation than meets the eye. It is certain that the mere act of inditing, tends, in a great degree, to the logicalization of thought. Whenever, on account of its vagueness, I am dissatisfied with a conception of the brain, I resort forthwith to the pen, for the purpose of obtaining, through its aid, the necessary form, consequence and precision.

How very commonly we hear it remarked, that such and such thoughts are beyond the compass of words! I do not believe that any thought, properly so called, is out of the reach of language. I fancy, rather, that where difficulty in expression is experienced, there is, in the intellect which experiences it, a want either of deliberateness or of method. For my own part, I have never had a thought which I could not set down in words with even more distinctness than that with which I conceived it: – as I have before observed, the thought is logicalized by the effort at (written) expression. There is, however, a class of fancies, of exquisite delicacy, which are *not* thoughts, and to which, *as yet*, I have found it absolutely impossible to adapt language. I use the word *fancies* at random, and merely because I must use *some* word; but the idea commonly attached to the term is not even remotely applicable to the shadows of shadows in question. They seem to me rather psychal than intellectual. They arise in the soul (alas, how rarely!) only at its epochs of most intense tranquillity – when the bodily and mental health are in perfection – and at those mere points of time where the confines of the waking world blend with those of the world of dreams. I am aware of these 'fancies' only when I am upon the very brink of sleep, with the consciousness that I am so. I have satisfied myself that this condition exists but for an inappreciable *point* of time – yet it is crowded with these 'shadows of shadows'; and for absolute *thought* there is demanded time's *endurance*. These 'fancies' have in them a pleasurable ecstasy, as far beyond the most pleasurable of the world of wakefulness, or of dreams, as the heaven of the Northman theology is beyond its hell. I regard the visions, even as they arise, with an awe which, in some measure, moderates or tranquillizes the ecstasy – I so regard them, through a conviction (which seems a portion of the ecstasy itself) that this ecstasy, in itself, is of a character supernal to the human nature – is a glimpse of the spirit's outer world; and I arrive at this conclusion if this term is at all applicable to instantaneous intuition by a perception that the delight experienced has, as its element, but *the absoluteness of novelty*. I say the absoluteness – for in these fancies – let me now term them psychal impressions – there is really nothing even approximate in character to impressions ordinarily received. It is as if the five senses were supplanted by five myriad others alien to mortality.

Now, so entire is my faith in the *power of words*, that, at times, I have believed it possible to embody even the evanescence of fancies such as I have attempted to describe. In experiments with this end in view, I have proceeded so far as, first, to control (when the bodily and mental health are good) the existence of the condition: – that is to say, I can now (unless when ill) be sure that the condition will supervene, if I so wish it, at the point of time already described: – of its supervention, until lately, I could never be certain, even under the most favourable circumstances. I mean to say, merely, that now I can be sure, when all circumstances are favourable, of the supervention of the condition, and feel even the capacity of inducing or compelling it: – the favourable circumstances, however, are not the less rare – else had I compelled, already, the heaven into the earth.

I have proceeded so far, secondly, as to prevent the lapse from *the point* of which I speak – the point of blending between wakefulness and sleep – as to prevent at will, I say, the lapse from this border-ground into the dominion of sleep. Not that I can *continue* the condition – not that I can render the point more than a point – but that I can startle myself from the point into wakefulness; *and thus transfer the point itself into the realm of Memory*; convey its impressions, or more properly their recollections, to a situation where (although still for a very brief period) I can survey them with the eye of analysis. For these reasons – that is to say, because I have been enabled to accomplish thus much – I do not altogether despair of embodying in words at least enough of the fancies in question to convey, to certain classes of intellect, a shadowy conception of their character. In saying this I am not to be understood as supposing that the fancies, or psychal impressions, to which I allude, are confined to my individual self – are not, in a word, common to all mankind – for on this point it is quite impossible that I should form an opinion – but nothing can be more certain than that even a partial record of the impressions would startle the universal intellect of mankind, by the *supremeness of the novelty* of the material employed, and of its consequent suggestions. In a word – should I ever write a paper on this topic, the world will be compelled to acknowledge that, at last, I have done an original thing.

MAGAZINES

Whatever may be the merits or demerits, generally, of the Magazine Literature in America, there can be no question as to its extent or influence. The Topic – Magazine Literature – is therefore an important one. In a few years its importance will be found to have increased in geometrical ratio. The whole tendency of the age is

Magazine-ward. The Quarterly Reviews have *never* been popular. Not only are they too stilted, (by way of keeping up a due dignity,) but they make a point, with the same end in view, of discussing only topics which are *caviare* to the many, and which, for the most part, have only a conventional interest even with the few. Their issues, also, are at too long intervals; their subjects get cold before being served up. In a word, their ponderosity is quite out of keeping with the *rush* of the age. We now demand the light artillery of the intellect; we need the curt, the condensed, the pointed, the readily diffused – in place of the verbose, the detailed, the voluminous, the inaccessible. On the other hand, the lightness of the artillery should not degenerate into popgunnery – by which term we may designate the character of the greater portion of the newspaper press – their sole legitimate object being the discussion of ephemeral matters in an ephemeral manner. Whatever talent may be brought to bear upon our daily journals, and in many cases this talent is very great, still the imperative necessity of catching, *currente calamo*, each topic as it flits before the eye of the public, must of course materially narrow the limits of their power. The bulk and the period of issue of the monthly magazines, seem to be precisely adapted, if not to all the literary wants of the day, at least to the largest and most imperative, as well as the most consequential portion of them.

IMAGINATION

The *pure Imagination* chooses, from *either Beauty or Deformity*, only the most combinable things hitherto uncombined; the compound, as a general rule, partaking, in character, of beauty, or sublimity, in the ratio of the respective beauty or sublimity of the things combined – which are themselves still to be considered as atomic – that is to say, as previous combinations. But, as often analogously happens in physical chemistry, so not unfrequently does it occur in this chemistry of the intellect, that the admixture of two elements results in a something that has nothing of the qualities of one of them, or even nothing of the qualities of either . . . Thus, the range of Imagination is unlimited. Its materials extend throughout the universe. Even out of deformities it fabricates that *Beauty* which is at once its sole object and its inevitable test. But, in general, the richness of force of the matters combined; the facility of discovering combinable novelties worth combining; and, especially, the absolute 'chemical combination' of the completed mass – are the particulars to be regarded in our estimate of Imagination. It is this thorough harmony of an imaginative work which so often causes it to be undervalued by the thoughtless, through the character of *obviousness* which is superinduced. We are apt to find ourselves asking *why* it is that these combinations have never been imagined before.

EMERSON

When I consider the true talent – the real force of Mr Emerson, I am lost in amazement at finding in him little more than a respectful imitation of Carlyle. Is it possible that Mr E. has ever seen a copy of Seneca? Scarcely – or he would long ago have abandoned his model in utter confusion at the parallel between his own worship of the author of *Sartor Resartus* and the aping of Sallust by Aruntius, as described in the 114th Epistle. In the writer of the *History of the Punic Wars* Emerson is portrayed to the life. The parallel is close; for not only is the imitation of the same character, but the things imitated are identical. Undoubtedly it is to be said of Sallust, far more plausibly than of Carlyle, that his obscurity, his unusuality of expression, and his Laconism (which had the effect of diffuseness, since the time gained in the mere perusal of his pithinesses is trebly lost in the necessity of cogitating them out) – that these qualities bore the impress of his genius, and were but a portion of his unaffected thought. If there is any difference between Aruntius and Emerson, this difference is clearly in favour of the former, who was in some measure excusable, on the ground that he was as great a fool as the latter *is not*.

'UNDINE'

How radically has *Undine* been misunderstood! Beneath its obvious meaning there runs an under-current, simple, quite intelligible, artistically managed, and richly philosophical.

From internal evidence afforded by the book itself, I gather that the author suffered from the ills of a mal-arranged marriage – the bitter reflections thus engendered, inducing the fable.

In the contrast between the artless, thoughtless, and careless character of Undine before possessing a soul, and her serious, enwrapt, and anxious yet happy condition after possessing it, – a condition which, with all its multiform disquietudes, she still feels to be preferable to her original state, – Fouqué has beautifully painted the difference between the heart unused to *love*, and the heart which has received its inspiration.

The jealousies which follow the marriage, arising from the conduct of Bertalda, are but the natural troubles of love; but the persecutions of Kuhleborn and the other water-spirits who take umbrage at Huldbrand's treatment of his wife, are meant to picture certain difficulties from the interference of relations in conjugal matters – difficulties which the author has himself experienced. The warning of Undine to Huldbrand – 'Reproach me not upon the waters, or we part forever' – is intended to embody the truth that quarrels between man and wife are seldom or never irremediable unless when taking place in the presence of third parties. The second wedding of the knight with his gradual forgetfulness of Undine, and Undine's intense grief beneath the waters – are dwelt upon so pathetically – so passionately – that there can be no doubt of the author's personal opinions on the subject of second marriages – no doubt of his deep personal interest in the question. How thrillingly are these few and simple words made to convey his belief that the mere death of a beloved wife does not imply a separation so final or so complete as to justify an union with another!

> The fisherman had loved Undine with exceeding tenderness, and it was a doubtful conclusion to his mind that the mere disappearance of his beloved child could be properly viewed as her death.

This is where the old man is endeavouring to dissuade the knight from wedding Bertalda.

I cannot say whether the novelty of the conception of *Undine*, or the loftiness and purity of its ideality, or the intensity of its pathos, or the rigour of its simplicity, or the high artistical ability with which all are combined into a well-kept, well-*motivirt* whole of absolute unity of effect – is the particular chiefly to be admired.

How delicate and graceful are the transitions from subject to subject! – a point severely testing the autorial power – as, when, for the purposes of the story, it becomes necessary that the knight, with Undine and Bertalda, shall proceed down the Danube. An ordinary novelist would have here tormented both himself and his readers, in his search for a sufficient motive for the voyage. But, in a fable such as *Undine*, how all-sufficient – how well in keeping – appears the simple motive assigned! –

> In this grateful union of friendship and affection, winter came and passed away; and spring, with its foliage of tender green, and its

heaven of softest blue, succeeded to gladden the hearts of the three inmates of the castle. *What wonder, then, that its storks and swallows inspired them also with a disposition to travel?*

SUE'S 'MYSTERIES OF PARIS'

I have just finished the *Mysteries of Paris* – a work of unquestionable power – a museum of novel and ingenious incident – a paradox of childish folly and consummate skill. It has this point in common with all the 'convulsive' fictions – that the incidents are *consequential* from the premises, while the premises themselves are laughably incredible. Admitting, for instance, the possibility of such a man as Rodolphe, and of such a state of society as would tolerate his perpetual interference, we have no difficulty in agreeing to admit the possibility of his accomplishing all that is accomplished. Another point which distinguishes the Sue school, is the total want of the *ars celare artem*. In effect the writer is always saying to the reader, 'Now – in one moment – you shall see what you shall see. I am about to produce on you a remarkable impression. Prepare to have your imagination, or your pity, greatly excited.' The wires are not only not concealed, but displayed as things to be admired, equally with the puppets they set in motion. The result is, that in perusing, for example, a pathetic chapter in the *Mysteries of Paris* we say to ourselves, without shedding a tear – 'Now, here is something which will be sure to move every reader to tears.' The philosophical motives attributed to Sue are absurd in the extreme. His first, and in fact his sole object, is to make an exciting, and therefore saleable book. The cant (implied or direct) about the amelioration of society, etc., is but a very usual trick among authors, whereby they hope to add such a tone of dignity or utilitarianism to their pages as shall gild the pill of their licentiousness. The *ruse* is even more generally employed by way of engrafting a meaning upon the otherwise unintelligible. In the latter case, however, this *ruse* is an after-thought, manifested in the shape of a moral, either appended (as in Æsop) or dove-tailed into the body of the work, piece by piece, with great care, but never without leaving evidence of its after-insertion.

AMERICA AND THE CRITICS

No doubt, the association of idea is somewhat singular – but I never can hear a crowd of people singing and gesticulating, all together, at an Italian opera, without fancying myself at Athens, listening to that particular tragedy, by Sophocles, in which he introduces a full chorus of turkeys, who set about bewailing the death of Meleager. It is noticeable in this connexion, by the way, that there is not a goose in the world who, in point of sagacity, would not feel itself insulted in being compared with a turkey. The French seem to feel this. In Paris, I am sure, no one would think of saying to Mr F——, 'What a goose you are!' – Quel *dindon* tu es!' would be the phrase employed as equivalent.

Alas! how many American critics neglect the happy suggestion of M. Timon – '*que le ministre de L'Instruction Publique doit lui-même savoir parler Français.*'

It is folly to assert, as some at present are fond of asserting, that the Literature of any nation or age was ever injured by plain speaking on the part of the Critics. As for American Letters, plain-speaking about *them* is, simply, the one thing needed. They are in a condition of absolute quagmire – a quagmire, to use the words of Victor Hugo, *d'où on ne peut se tirer par des périphrases – par des quemadmodums et des verumenimveros.*

AMERICAN NATIONALITY IN LITERATURE

Much has been said, of late, about the necessity of maintaining a proper *nationality* in American Letters; but what this nationality *is*, or what is to be gained by it, has never been distinctly understood. That an American should confine himself to American themes, or even prefer them, is rather a political than a literary idea – and at best is a questionable point. We would do well to bear in mind that 'distance lends enchantment to the view.' *Ceteris paribus*, a foreign theme is, in a strictly literary sense, to be preferred. After all, the world at large is the only legitimate stage for the autorial *histrio*.

But of the need of *that* nationality which defends our own literature, sustains our own men of letters, upholds our own dignity, and depends upon our own resources, there cannot be the shadow of a doubt. Yet here is the very point at which we are most supine. We complain of our want of an International Copyright, on the ground that this want justifies our publishers in inundating us with British opinion in British books; and yet when these very publishers, at their own obvious risk, and even obvious loss, do publish an American book, we turn up our noses at it with supreme contempt (this as a general thing) until it (the American book) has been dubbed 'readable' by some illiterate Cockney critic. Is it too much to say that, with us, the opinion of Washington Irving – of Prescott – of Bryant – is a mere nullity in comparison with that of any anonymous sub-sub-editor of the *Spectator*, the *Athenæum*, or the London *Punch*? It is *not* saying too much, to say this. It is a solemn – an absolutely awful fact. Every publisher in the country will admit it to be a fact. There is not a more disgusting spectacle under the sun than our subserviency to British criticism. It is disgusting, first, because it is truckling, servile, pusillanimous – secondly, because of its gross irrationality. We *know* the British to bear us little but ill will – we know that, in no case, do they utter unbiased opinions of American books – we know that in the few instances in which our writers have been treated with common decency in England, these writers have either openly paid homage to English institutions, or have had lurking at the bottom of their hearts a secret principle at war with Democracy: – we *know* all this, and yet, day after day, submit our necks to the degrading yoke of the crudest opinion that emanates from the fatherland. Now if we *must* have nationality, let it be a nationality that will throw off this yoke.

The chief of the rhapsodists who have ridden us to death like the Old Man of the Mountain, is the ignorant and egotistical Wilson. We use the term rhapsodists with perfect deliberation; for, Macaulay, and Dilke, and one or two others, excepted, there is not in Great Britain a critic who can be fairly considered worthy the name. The Germans, and even the French, are infinitely superior. As regards Wilson, no man ever penned worse criticism or better rodomontade. That he is 'egotistical' his works show to all men, running as they read. That he is 'ignorant' let his absurd and continuous schoolboy blunders about Homer bear witness. Not long ago we ourselves pointed out a series of similar inanities in his review of Miss Barrett's poems – a series, we say, of gross blunders, arising from sheer ignorance – and we defy him or anyone to answer a single syllable of what we then advanced.

And yet this is the man whose simple *dictum* (to our shame be it spoken) has the power to make or to mar any American reputation! In the last number of *Blackwood*, he has a continuation of the dull 'Specimens of the British Critics,' and makes occasion wantonly to insult one of the noblest of our poets, Mr Lowell. The point of the whole attack consists in the use of slang epithets and phrases of the most ineffably vulgar description. 'Squabashes' is a pet term. 'Faugh!' is another. 'We are Scotsmen to *the spine!*' says Sawney – as if the thing were not more than self-evident. Mr Lowell is called 'a magpie,' an 'ape,' a 'Yankee cockney,' and his name is intentionally miswritten *John* Russell Lowell. Now were these indecencies perpetrated by an American critic, that critic would be sent to Coventry by the whole press of the country, but since it is Wilson who insults, we, as in duty bound, not only submit to the insult, but echo it, as an excellent jest, throughout the length and breadth of the land. *Quamdiu Catilina?* We do indeed demand the nationality of self-respect. In Letters as in Government we require a Declaration of Independence. A better thing still would be a Declaration of War – and that war should be carried forthwith 'into Africa.'

THE ELDER POETS

It cannot, we think, be a matter of doubt with any reflecting mind, that at least one-third of the *reverence*, or of the *affection*, with which we regard the elder poets of Great Britain, should be credited to what is, in itself, a thing apart from poetry – we mean to the simple love of the antique – and that again a third and even the proper *poetic sentiment* inspired by these writings should be ascribed to a fact which, while it has a strict connexion with poetry in the abstract, and also with the particular poems in question, must not be looked upon as a merit appertaining to the writers of the poems. Almost every devout reader of the old English bards, if demanded his opinion of their productions, would mention vaguely, yet with perfect sincerity, a sense of dreamy, wild, indefinite, and, he would perhaps say, undefinable delight. Upon being required to point out the source of this so shadowy pleasure, he would be apt to speak of the quaint in phraseology and of the grotesque in rhythm. And this quaintness and grotesqueness are, as we have elsewhere endeavoured to show, very powerful, and, if well managed, very admissible adjuncts to ideality. But in the present instance they arise independently of the author's will, and are matters altogether apart from his intention.

MEN OF GENIUS

Men of genius are far more abundant than is supposed. In fact, to appreciate thoroughly the work of what we call genius, is to possess all the genius by which the work was produced. But the person appreciating may be utterly incompetent to reproduce the work, or anything similar, and this solely through lack of what may be termed the constructive ability – a matter quite independent of what we agree to understand in the term 'genius' itself. This ability is based, to be sure, in great part, upon the faculty of analysis, enabling the artist to get full view of the machinery of his proposed effect, and thus work it and regulate it at will; but a great deal depends also upon properties strictly moral – for example, upon patience, upon concentrativeness, or the power of holding the attention steadily to the one purpose, upon self-dependence and contempt for all opinion which is opinion and no more – in especial, upon energy or industry. So vitally important is this last, that it may well be doubted if anything to which we have been accustomed to give the title of a 'work of genius' was ever accomplished without it, and it is chiefly because this quality and genius are nearly incompatible, that 'works of genius' are few, while mere men of genius are, as I say, abundant. The Romans, who excelled us in acuteness of *observation* while falling below us in induction from facts observed, seem to have been so fully aware of the inseparable connexion between industry and a 'work of genius,' as to have adopted the error that industry, in great measure, was genius itself. The highest compliment is intended by a Roman, when, of an epic, or anything similar, he says that it is written *industriâ mirabili* or *incredibili industriâ*.

BULWER LYTTON

We have long learned to reverence the fine intellect of Bulwer. We take up any production of his pen with a positive certainty that, in reading it, the wildest passions of our nature, the most profound of our thoughts, the brightest visions of our fancy, and the most ennobling and lofty of our aspirations will, in due turn, be enkindled within us. We feel sure of rising from the perusal a wiser if not a better man. In no instance are we deceived. From the brief tale – from the *Monos and Daimonos* of the author – to his most ponderous and laboured novels – all is richly, and glowingly intellectual – all is energetic, or astute, or brilliant, or profound. There *may* be men now living who possess the power of Bulwer – but it is quite evident that very few have made that power so palpably manifest. Indeed we know of *none*. Viewing him as a novelist – a point of view exceedingly unfavourable (if we hold to the common acceptation of 'the novel') for a proper contemplation of his genius – he is unsurpassed by any writer living or dead. Why should we hesitate to say this, feeling, as we do, thoroughly persuaded of its truth? Scott has excelled him in *many* points and *The Bride of Lammermoor* is a better book than any individual work by the author of *Pelham* – *Ivanhoe* is, perhaps, equal to any. Descending to particulars, D'Israeli has a more brilliant, a more lofty, and a more delicate (we do not say a *wilder*) imagination. Lady Dacre has written *Ellen Wareham*, a more forcible tale of passioin. In some species of wit Theodore Hook rivals, and in broad humour our own Paulding surpasses him. The writer of *Godolphin* equals him in energy. Banim is a better sketcher of character. Hope is a richer colourist. Captain Trelawney is as original – Moore is as fanciful, and Horace Smith is as learned. But who is there, uniting in one person the imagination, the passion, the humour, the energy, the knowledge of the heart, the artist-like eye, the originality, the fancy, and the learning of Edward Lytton Bulwer? In a vivid wit – in profundity and a Gothic massiveness of thought – in style – in a calm certainty and definitiveness of purpose – in industry – and above all, in the power of controlling and regulating by volition his illimitable faculties of mind, he is unequalled – he is unapproached.

TOM HOOD

'Frequently since his recent death,' says the American editor of Hood, 'he has been called a great author – a phrase used not inconsiderately or in vain.' Yet, if we adopt the conventional idea of 'a great author,' there has lived, perhaps, no writer of the last half century who, with equal notoriety, was less entitled than Hood to be so called. In fact, he was a literary merchant, whose main stock in trade was *littleness*; for, during the larger portion of his life, he seemed to breathe only for the purpose of perpetrating puns – things of so despicable a platitude that the man who is capable of habitually committing them, is seldom found capable of anything else. Whatever merit *may* be discovered in a pun, arises altogether from *unexpectedness*. This is the pun's element and is twofold. First, we demand that the *combination* of the pun be unexpected; and, secondly, we require the most entire unexpectedness in the pun *per se*. A rare pun rarely appearing, is, to a certain extent, a pleasurable effect; but to no mind, however debased in taste, is a continuous effort at punning otherwise than unendurable. The man who maintains that he derives gratification from any such chapters of punnage as Hood was in the daily practice of committing to paper, should not be credited upon oath.

The puns of the author of *Fair Inez*, however, are to be regarded as the weak points of the man. Independently of their ill effect, in a literary view, as mere puns, they leave upon us a painful impression; for too evidently they are the hypochondriac's struggles at mirth – the grinnings of the death's-head. No one can read his *Literary Reminiscences* without being convinced of his habitual despondency: – and the species of false wit in question is precisely of that character which would be adopted by an author of Hood's temperament and cast of intellect, when compelled to write at an emergency. That his heart had no interest in these *niaiseries*, is clear. I allude, of course, to his *mere* puns for the pun's sake – a class of letters by which he attained his widest renown. That he did *more* in this way than in any other, is but a corollary from what I have already said, for, generally, he was unhappy, and almost continually he wrote *invitâ Minerva*. But his true province was a very rare and ethereal *humour*, in which the mere pun was left out of sight, or took the character of the richest *grotesquerie*; impressing the imaginative reader with remarkable force, as if by a new phase of the ideal. It is in this species of brilliant, or, rather, *glowing* grotesquerie, uttered with a rushing *abandon* vastly heightening its effect, that Hood's marked originality mainly consisted: – and it is this which entitles him, at times, to the epithet 'great': for *that* undeniably may be considered great (of whatever seeming littleness in itself) which is capable of inducing intense emotion in the minds or hearts of those who are themselves undeniably great.

The field in which Hood is *distinctive* is a borderland between Fancy and Fantasy. In this region he reigns supreme. Nevertheless, he has made successful and frequent incursions, although vacillatingly, into the domain of the true Imagination. I mean to say that he is never truly or purely imaginative for more than a paragraph at a time. In a word, his peculiar genius was the result of vivid *Fancy* impelled by Hypochondriasis.

LORD BYRON AND MARY CHAWORTH

'*Les anges*,' says Madame Dudevant, a woman who intersperses many an admirable sentiment amid a chaos of the most shapeless and altogether objectionable fiction – '*Les anges ne sont plus pures que le cœur d'un jeune homme qui aime en vérité*.' The angels are not more pure than the heart of a young man who loves with fervour. The hyperbole is scarcely less than true. It would be truth itself were it averred of the love of him who is at the same time young and a poet. The boyish poet-love is indisputably that one of the human sentiments whch most nearly realizes our dreams of the chastened voluptuousness of heaven.

In every allusion made by the author of *Childe Harold* to his passion for Mary Chaworth, there runs a vein of almost spiritual tenderness and purity, strongly in contrast with the gross earthliness pervading and disfiguring his ordinary love-poems. *The Dream*, in which the incidents of his parting with her when about to travel, are said to be delineated, or at least paralleled, has never been excelled (certainly never excelled by him) in the blended fervour, delicacy, truthfulness and ethereality which sublimate and adorn it. For this reason, it may well be doubted if he has written anything so universally popular. That his attachment for this 'Mary' (in whose very name there indeed seemed to exist for him an 'enchantment') was earnest, and long-abiding, we have every reason to believe. There are a hundred evidences of this fact, scattered not only through his own poems and letters, but in the memoirs of his relatives, and contemporaries in general. But that it *was* thus earnest and enduring, does not controvert, in any degree, the opinion that it was a passion (if passion it can properly be termed) of the most thoroughly romantic, shadowy and imaginative character. It was born of the hour, and of the youthful necessity to love, while it was nurtured by the waters and the hills, and the flowers, and the stars. It had no peculiar regard to the person, or to the character, or to the reciprocating affection of Mary Chaworth. Any maiden, not immediately and positively repulsive, he would have loved, under the same circumstances of hourly and unrestricted communion, such as the engravings of the subject shadow forth. They met without restraint and without reserve. As mere children they sported together; in boyhood and girlhood they read from the same books, sang the same songs, or roamed hand in hand through the grounds of the conjoining estates. The result was not merely natural or merely probable, it was as inevitable as destiny itself.

In view of a passion thus engendered, Miss Chaworth, (who is represented as possessed of no little personal beauty and some accomplishments,) could not have failed to serve sufficiently well as the incarnation of the ideal that haunted the fancy of the poet. It is perhaps better, nevertheless, for the mere romance of the love passages between the two, that their intercourse was broken up in early life and never uninterruptedly resumed in after years. Whatever of warmth, whatever of soul-passion, whatever of the truer nare[1] and essentiality of romance was elicited during the youthful association is to be attributed altogether to the poet. If *she* felt at all, it was only while the magnetism of *his* actual presence compelled her to feel. If *she* responded at all, it was merely because the necromancy of *his* words of fire could not do otherwise than exhort a response. In absence, the bard bore easily with him all the fancies which were the basis of his flame – a flame which absence itself but served to keep in vigour – while the less ideal but at the same time the less really substantial affection of his lady-love, perished utterly and forthwith, through simple lack of the element which had fanned it into being. He to her, in brief, was a not unhandsome, and not ignoble, but somewhat portionless, somewhat eccentric and rather lame young man. She to him was the Egeria of his dreams – the Venus Aphrodite that sprang, in full and supernal loveliness, from the bright foam upon the storm-tormented ocean of his thoughts.

'THE LADY OF LYONS'

A hundred criticisms to the contrary notwithstanding, I must regard *The Lady of Lyons* as one of the most successful dramatic efforts of modern times. It is popular, and justly so. It could not fail to be popular so long as the people have a heart. It abounds in sentiments which stir the soul as the sound of a trumpet. It proceeds rapidly and consequentially; the interest not for one moment being permitted to flag. Its incidents are admirably conceived and skilfully wrought into execution. Its *dramatis personæ*, throughout, have the high merit of being natural, although, except in the case of Pauline, there is no marked individuality. She is a creation which would have done no dishonour to Shakespeare. She excites profound emotion. It has been sillily objected to her, that she is weak, mercenary, and at points ignoble. She is; and what then? We are not dealing with Clarissa Harlowe. Bulwer has painted a woman. The chief defect of the play lies in the heroine's consenting to wed Beauseant, while aware of the existence and even the continued love of Claude. As the plot runs, there is a question in Pauline's soul between a comparatively trivial (because merely worldly) injury to her father, and utter ruin and despair inflicted upon her husband. Here there should not have been an instant's hesitation. The audience have no sympathy with any.

[1]This may be a misprint in the original review for 'nature'.

Nothing on earth should have induced the wife to give up the living Melnotte. Only the assurance of his death could have justified her in sacrificing herself to Beauseant. As it is, we hate her for the sacrifice. The effect is repulsive – but I must be understood as calling this effect objectionable solely on the ground of its being at war with the whole genius of the play.

WHAT IS POETRY?

If need were, I should have little difficulty, perhaps, in defending a certain apparent dogmatism to which I am prone, on the topic of versification.

'What is Poetry?' notwithstanding Leigh Hunt's rigmarolic attempt at answering it, is a query that, with great care and deliberate agreement beforehand on the exact value of certain leading words, *may*, possibly, be settled to the partial satisfaction of a few analytical intellects, but which, in the existing condition of metaphysics, never *can* be settled to the satisfaction of the majority; for the question is purely metaphysical, and the whole science of metaphysics is at present a chaos, through the impossibility of fixing the meanings of the words which its very nature compels it to employ. But as regards versification, this difficulty is only partial; for although one-third of the topic may be considered metaphysical, and thus may be mooted at the fancy of this individual or of that, still the remaining two-thirds belong, undeniably, to the mathematics. The questions ordinarily discussed with so much gravity in regard to rhythm, metre, etc., are susceptible of positive adjustment by demonstration. Their laws are merely a portion of the Median laws of form and quantity – of relation. In respect, then, to any of these ordinary questions – these sillily moot points which so often arise in common criticism – the prosodist would speak as weakly in saying 'this or that proposition is *probably* so and so, or *possibly* so and so,' as would the mathematician in admitting that, in his humble opinion, or if he were not greatly mistaken, any two sides of a triangle were, together, greater than the third side. I must add, however, as some palliation of the discussions referred to, and of the objections so often urged with a sneer to 'particular theories of versification binding no one but their inventor' – that there is really extant no such work as a Prosody *Raisonnée*. The Prosodies of the schools are merely collections of vague *laws*, with their more vague exceptions, based upon no principles whatever, but extorted in the most speculative manner from the usages of the ancients, who had *no* laws beyond those of their ears and fingers. 'And these were sufficient,' it will be said, 'since the Iliad is melodious and harmonious beyond anything of modern times.' Admit this: – but neither do we write in Greek, nor has the invention of modern times been as yet exhausted. An analysis based on the natural laws of which the bard of Scios was ignorant, would suggest multitudinous improvements to the best passages of even the Iliad – nor does it in any manner follow from the supposititious fact that Homer found in his ears and fingers a satisfactory system of rules (the point which I have just denied) – nor does it follow, I say, from this, that the rules which *we* deduce from the Homeric *effects* are to supersede those immutable principles of time, quantity, etc. – the mathematics, in short, of music – which must have stood to these Homeric effects in the relation of *causes* – the *mediate* causes of which these 'ears and fingers' are simply the *intermedia*.

'THE OLD CURIOSITY SHOP'

The great feature of the *Curiosity Shop* is its chaste, vigorous, and glorious *imagination*. This is the one charm, all potent, which alone would suffice to compensate for a world more of error than Mr Dickens ever committed. It is not only seen in the conception, and general handling of the story, or in the invention of character; but it pervades every sentence of the book. We recognize its prodigious influence in every inspired word. It is this which induces the reader who is at all ideal, to pause frequently, to re-read the occasionally quaint phrases, to muse in uncontrollable delight over thoughts which, while he wonders he has never hit upon them before, he yet admits that he never has encountered. In fact, it is the wand of the enchanter.

Had we room to particularize, we would mention as points evincing most distinctly the ideality of the *Curiosity Shop* – the picture of the shop itself – the newly-born desire of the worldly old man for the peace of green fields – his whole character and conduct in short – the schoolmaster, with his desolate fortunes, seeking affection in little children – the haunts of Quilp among the wharf-rats – the tinkering of the Punch-men among the tombs – the glorious scene where the man of the forge sits poring, at deep midnight, into that dread fire – again the whole conception of this character; and, last and greatest, the stealthy approach of Nell to her death – her gradual sinking away on the journey to the village, so skilfully indicated rather than described – her pensive and prescient meditation – the fit of strange musing which came over her when the house *in which she was to die* first broke upon her sight – the description of this house, of the old church, and of the churchyard – everything in rigid consonance with the one impression to be conveyed – that deep meaningless well – the comments of the Sexton upon death, and upon his own secure life – this whole world of mournful yet peaceful idea merging, at length, into the decease of the child Nelly, and the uncomprehending despair of the grandfather. These concluding scenes are so drawn that human language, urged by human thought, could go no farther in the excitement of human feelings. And the pathos is of that best order which is relieved, in great measure, by ideality. Here the book has never been equalled, – never approached except in one instance, and that is in the case of the *Undine* of De la Motte Fouqué. The imagination is perhaps as great in this latter work, but the pathos, although truly beautiful and deep, fails of much of its effect through the material from which it is wrought. The chief character, being endowed with purely fanciful attributes, cannot command our full sympathies, as can a simple denizen of earth. In saying, a page or so above, that the death of the child left too painful an impression, and should therefore have been avoided, we must, of course, be understood as referring to the work as a whole, and in respect to its general appreciation and popularity. The death, as recorded, is, we repeat, of the highest order of literary excellence – yet while none can deny this fact, there are few who will be willing to read the concluding passages a second time.

Upon the whole we think the *Curiosity Shop* very much the best of the works of Mr Dickens. It is scarcely possible to speak of it too well. It is in all respects a tale which will secure for its author the enthusiastic admiration of every man of genius.

TENNYSON

I am not sure that Tennyson is not the greatest of poets. The uncertainty attending the public conception of the term 'poet' alone prevents me from demonstrating that he *is*. Other bards produce effects which are, now and then, otherwise produced than by what we call poems; but Tennyson an effect which only a poem does. His alone are idiosyncratic poems. By the enjoyment or non-enjoyment of the *Morte d'Arthur*, or of the *Œnone*, I would test any one's ideal sense. There are passages in his works which rivet a conviction I had long entertained, that the *indefinite* is an element in the true ποιησις. Why do some persons fatigue themselves in attempts to unravel such fantasy-pieces as the *Lady of Shalott?* As well unweave the '*ventum textilem*.' If the author did not deliberately propose to himself a suggestive indefinitiveness of meaning, with the view of bringing about a definitiveness of vague and therefore of spiritual *effect* – this, at least, arose from the silent analytical promptings of that poetic genius which, in its supreme development, embodies all orders of intellectual capacity. I *know* that indefinitiveness is an element of the true music – I mean of the true musical expression. Give to it any undue decision – imbue it with any very determinate tone – and you deprive it, at once, of its ethereal, its ideal, its intrinsic and essential character. You dispel its luxury of dream. You dissolve the atmosphere of the mystic upon which it floats. You exhaust it of its breath of faery. It now becomes a tangible and easily appreciable idea – a thing of the earth, earthy. It has not, indeed, lost its power to please, but all which I consider the distinctiveness of that power. And to the uncultivated talent, or to the unimaginative apprehension, this deprivation of its most delicate nare[1] will be, not unfrequently, a recommendation. A determinateness of expression is sought – and often by composers who should know better – is sought as a beauty rather than rejected as a blemish. Thus we have, even from high authorities, attempts at absolute *imitation* in music. Who can forget the silliness of the *Battle of Prague*? What man of taste but must laugh at the interminable drums, trumpets, blunderbuses, and thunder? '*Vocal* music,' says l'Abbate Gravina, who would have said the same thing of instrumental, 'ought to imitate the natural language of the human feelings and passions, rather than the warblings of Canary birds, which our singers, nowadays, affect so vastly to mimic with their quaverings and boasted cadences.' This is true only so far as the 'rather' is concerned. If any music must imitate anything, it were assuredly better to limit the imitation as Gravina suggests. Tennyson's shorter pieces abound in minute rhythmical lapses sufficient to assure me that – in common with all poets living or dead – he has neglected to make precise investigation of the principles of metre; but, on the other hand so perfect is his rhythmical instinct in general, that, like the present Viscount Canterbury, he seems *to see with his ear*.

[1]This may be a misprint for 'nature'. At least one other edition of this essay has the word 'grace' here.

DEFOE

While Defoe would have been fairly entitled to immortality had he never written *Robinson Crusoe*, yet his many other very excellent writings have nearly faded from our attention, in the superior lustre of the Adventures of the Mariner of York. What better possible species of reputation could the author have desired for that book than the species which it has so long enjoyed? It has become a household thing in nearly every family in Christendom. Yet never was admiration of any work – universal admiration – more indiscriminately or more inappropriately bestowed. Not one person in ten – nay, not one person in five hundred, has, during the perusal of *Robinson Crusoe*, the most remote conception that any particle of genius, or even of common talent, has been employed in its creation! Men do not look upon it in the light of a literary performance. Defoe has none of their thoughts – Robinson all. The powers which have wrought the wonder have been thrown into obscurity by the very stupendousness of the wonder they have wrought! We read, and become perfect abstractions in the intensity of our interest – we close the book, and are quite satisfied that we could have written as well ourselves. All this is effected by the potent magic of verisimilitude. Indeed, the author of *Crusoe* must have possessed, above all other faculties, what has been termed the faculty of *identification* – that dominion exercised by volition over imagination which enables the mind to lose its own, in a fictitious, individuality. This includes, in a very great degree, the power of abstraction; and with these keys we may partially unlock the mystery of that spell which has so long invested the volume before us. But a complete analysis of our interest in it cannot be thus afforded. Defoe is largely indebted to his subject. The idea of man in a state of perfect isolation, although often entertained, was never before so comprehensively carried out. Indeed, the frequency of its occurrence to the thoughts of mankind argued the extent of its influence on their sympathies, while the fact of no attempt having been made to give an embodied form to the conception, went to prove the difficulty of the undertaking. But the true narrative of Selkirk in 1711, with the powerful impression it then made upon the public mind, sufficed to inspire Defoe with both the necessary courage for his work and entire confidence in its success. How wonderful has been the result!

MAGAZINE LITERATURE

The increase, within a few years, of the magazine literature, is by no means to be regarded as indicating what some critics would suppose it to indicate – a downward tendency in American taste or in American letters. It is but a sign of the times – an indication of an era in which men are forced upon the curt, the condensed, the well-digested – in place of the voluminous – in a word, upon journalism in lieu of dissertation. We need now the light artillery rather than the Peace-makers of the intellect. I will not be sure that men at present think more profoundly than half a century ago, but beyond question they think with more rapidity, with more skill, with more tact, with more of method and less of excrescence in the thought. Besides all this, they have a vast increase in the thinking material; they have more facts, more to think about. For this reason, they are disposed to put the greatest amount of thought in the smallest compass and disperse it with the utmost attainable rapidity. Hence the journalism of the age; hence, in especial, magazines. Too many we cannot have, as a general proposition; but we demand that they have sufficient merit to render them noticeable in the beginning, and that they continue in existence sufficiently long to permit us a fair estimation of their value.

LISTENERS' LURE

One half the pleasure experienced at a theatre arises from the spectator's sympathy with the rest of the audience, and, especially, from his belief in their sympathy with him. The eccentric gentleman who not long ago, at the Park, found himself the solitary occupant of box, pit, and gallery, would have derived but little enjoyment from his visit, had he been suffered to remain. It was an act of mercy to turn him out. The present absurd rage for lecturing is founded in the feeling in question. Essays which we would not be hired to read – so trite is their subject – so feeble is their execution – so much easier is it to get better information on similar themes out of any encyclopædia in Christendom – we are brought to tolerate, and alas, even to applaud in their tenth and twentieth repetition, through the sole force of our sympathy with the throng. In the same way we listen to a story with greater zest when there are others present at its narration beside ourselves. Aware of this, authors without due reflection have repeatedly attempted, by supposing a circle of listeners, to imbue their narratives with the interest of sympathy. At a cursory glance the idea seems plausible enough. But, in the one case, there is an actual, personal, and palpable sympathy, conveyed in looks, gestures and brief comments – a sympathy of real individuals, all with the matters discussed to be sure, but then especially, *each with each*. In the other instance, we, alone in our closet, are required to sympathize *with* the sympathy of fictitious listeners, who, so far from being present in body, are often studiously kept out of sight and out of mind for two or three hundred pages at a time. This is sympathy double-diluted – the shadow of a shade. It is unnecessary to say that the design invariably fails of its effect.

EXPLANATORY NOTES

POEMS

Tamerlane

Poe took little from the historical sources concerning Tamerlane (1336–1405). His poem is more of a lyric allegory, based on his love for Sarah Elmira Royster. Engaged to her, Poe left for the University of Virginia. Although he wrote home to her, her father intercepted the letters; and Poe returned to Richmond to find her engaged to someone else and therefore 'dead' to him.

To——

This evidently refers to the marriage of Sarah Elmira Royster to someone else.

Dreams

This early poem reveals Poe's poetic debt to Byron.

Spirits of the Dead

An earlier version of this poem was entitled 'Visit of the Dead'. This is an early example of one of Poe's favourite subjects, the 'imaginative landscape'.

Evening Star

This poem anticipates 'Ulalume'.

A Dream Within a Dream

This was originally entitled 'Imitation', possibly in acknowledgement of its indebtedness to Byron.

Stanzas

This relatively difficult poem describes how in youth the poet communed with nature but did not understand its 'power'. He questions if this is madness but believes it is visionary. Finding deep meaning in commonplace things, he declares that beauty, anticipating heaven, draws him away from a fall threatened by pride. The epigraph is from Byron's *The Island*, II, xvi, 13–16.

A Dream

This poem probably alludes to the poet's loss of Mrs Stanard ('Helen') and Sarah Elmira Royster.

'The Happiest Day, the Happiest Hour'

Also indebted to Byron (as are so many of Poe's verses), this poem may refer to the 'happiest day' when, privately at least, Poe became engaged to Sarah Elmira Royster.

The Lake: To —

This is based on a visit Poe made at sunset to the Lake of the Dismal Swamp in Virginia.

Sonnet – To Science

This sonnet, in which Poe declares his aim of disregarding scientific fact when imaginative fantasy seems more compelling, was first used as an introduction to *Al Aaraaf, Tamerlane, and Minor Poems* (1829) and then served as a motto to the prose fantasy, *The Island of Fay.*

Al Aaraaf

In the Koran, Al Aaraaf is the name Mohammedans give to the middle kingdom between heaven and hell (cf. limbo). Its inhabitants were tantalized by being offered glimpses of paradise. The main theme of the poem concerning the nature and divinity of beauty is supplemented by a subsidiary theme highlighting the power of knowledge to spoil human appreciation of that beauty.

Romance

A declaration of the poet's dedication to romance in the voice of nature (a voice speaking to him through a parakeet), this poem was originally titled 'Preface'.

To —

This poem may be seen as an early version of 'A Dream Within a Dream'. It is not certain who the subject of the poem is, although Poe's cousin, Elizabeth Herring, has been suggested.

To the River —

There is a concealed joke here, in that the poem alludes to Byron's 'Stanza to the Po', with 'Po' (a river in Italy) being a play on the author's name.

To —

Originally entitled 'To M —' (in a different version), the subject of this poem is unknown.

Fairy-Land

Another example of Poe's interest in imaginative landscapes, this poem mixes fantasy with touches of arch humour.

To Helen

Poe took twelve years to perfect this poem, often regarded as the finest of his lyrics. In a letter written in 1848, he confessed that it was inspired by 'the first purely ideal love of my soul': Mrs Jane Stith Stanard whom he had known during his youth in Richmond. Poe uses this personal memory as the basis for celebrating beauty and the spiritual love that leads us to that beauty, guiding us out of the mundane and commonplace and into 'the regions which/Are Holy Land!'

Israfel

This poem is inspired by a passage from the Koran: 'And the angel Israfel, whose heart-strings are a lute, and who has the sweetest voice of all God's creatures'.

The City in the Sea

One of the most famous of Poe's poems, this is discussed in the introduction. An earlier version was entitled 'The Doomed City'.

The Sleeper

The original version of this poem was entitled 'Irene'. It illustrates Poe's interest in the death of beautiful women, which in *The Philosophy of Composition* he termed 'the most poetical topic in the world'.

Lenore

The very earliest version of this was entitled *Pæan.*

The Valley of Unrest

Entitled in its original version 'The Valley of Nis', this poem is another example of the subject he made his own, the imaginative landscape. 'Distant subjects,' Poe wrote in his notes for a projected book on American writers, 'are in fact the most desirable . . . The true poet is less affected by the absolute contemplation than the imagination of a great landscape.'

The Coliseum

For Poe, in this poem, the Colosseum in Rome is both a memorial to the sources of our civilization and an inspiration for the present and future.

To One in Paradise

In his tale *The Visionary*, subsequently entitled 'The Assignation', Poe presents this poem as the composition of the protagonist whose beloved is married to an older nobleman.

Hymn

Addressed to the Virgin Mary, this is Poe's most overtly religious poem.

To F—

This is one of three poems to Mrs Francis Sargent Osgood, the other two being *To F—s S. O—d* and *A Valentine*. Mrs Osgood was one of the women with whom Poe had a close relationship in the later part of his life.

To F—s S. O—d

An earlier version of this poem was entitled 'Lines Written in an Album'.

Scenes from Politian

The plot of *Politian* is drawn from a sensational series of events occurring in Kentucky in 1825 and 1826. Jeroboam O. Beauchamp murdered the man who betrayed Beauchamp's wife, a Colonel Solomon P. Sharp. Beauchamp was tried and convicted; Beauchamp's wife committed suicide; and Beauchamp then attempted to commit suicide on the day scheduled for his execution. The names of Poe's dramatic personæ are drawn from Italian history: characteristically, he distanced what became known as 'the Kentucky tragedy' by situating it in a different time and place.

Bridal Ballad

This poem may refer to the marriage of Sarah Elmira Royster to someone else, and to her distress at learning that Poe had not, as she had believed, been disloyal while away from her.

Sonnet to Zante

Zante is a modern form of Zacynthus, an island whose name has associations with the hyacinth, 'fairest of all flowers'. The occasion of this poem may have been a meeting between Poe and his new wife Virginia, with an old sweetheart of Poe's, Elmira Shelton, now married to another.

The Haunted Palace

This poem is clearly an allegory, describing a person with golden hair, bright eyes, fine teeth and lips, full of intelligent and poetic utterances, who is seized by madness; his eyes consequently become bloodshot, his whole physical being deteriorates, and only insane laughter issues from his lips. In *The Fall of the House of Usher*, the poem is attributed to Roderick Usher who is, by this means, alluding to his own strange decline.

Sonnet – Silence

A poem that explores the silences of nature in its apparently virgin state, this also contrasts death of the body, which is inevitable, with death of the soul, which is not.

The Conqueror Worm

In its second version, this poem was included in the tale *Ligeia*. One commentator has suggested that its five stanzas represent or correspond to the five acts of a tragedy.

Dream-Land

As a variation on the theme of the imaginative landscape, this is close to some earlier poems, like 'Spirits of the Dead', 'Valley of Unrest', and 'Fairy-Land'. In its constant use of a refrain, however, it is close to some later poems, such as 'Eulalie – A Song', 'The Raven', and 'Ulalume'.

The Raven

Poe regarded this poem as his masterpiece and discussed it at length in 'The Philosophy of Composition'. For further details see both that essay and the introduction.

Eulalie – A Song

It is not known if there was any specific woman to whom this poem was addressed. It may have been written for Virginia Poe; the name was probably chosen for its musicality.

A Valentine

The name of the person to whom this poem is addressed is concealed in the lines. By combining the first letter of the first line with the second letter of the second line, and so on, the reader will come up with the name, Frances Sargent Osgood.

To M.L.S—

This is a tribute to Mrs Marie Louise Shaw, who nursed Poe and his wife Virginia when they were ill.

Ulalume

This poem, probably written only a few weeks before Poe's death, belongs to a genre of dialogues between body and soul that were popular during the Middle Ages. It describes how, in October of a year when recollection is difficult, in the imaginary world of music and painting the protagonist and his soul walk through a mysterious landscape. It is

Hallowe'en, when the dead have power, and as dawn draws near they see the planet of love in the sky: that planet is seen as warmer than the moon and as having escaped from the turmoil of lust. The soul does not trust Venus but is soothed by reasoning until they stop at a tomb, which is that of the protagonist's lost love. A question is posed as to whether the ghouls, friendly to living people, have summoned up a phantom of hope to rescue the walkers from memory of a terrible loss.

The title of the poem may be taken from the Latin verb *ululare* (to wail); and the details of the journey may recall walks taken by Poe to visit the grave of his wife Virginia.

An Enigma

The name of Sarah Anna Lewis, a close friend of Poe's, can be constructed by combining the first letter of the first line with the second letter of the second line, and so on.

To ——

The subject of this poem is Marie Louise Shaw (see 'To M.L.S—') whose forenames are 'two foreign soft dissyllables'.

The Bells

This poem has often been praised for its use of onomatopœia, repetition, assonance, and alliteration and, in general, for its attempt to turn language into music.

To Helen

This poem describes Poe's romantic love affair with Sarah Helen Whitman. Poe claimed that he first saw Sarah Whitman in 1845. Later, he proposed marriage to her; and she agreed, it seems, on the understanding that he would abstain from alcohol. The banns were read: but, on the day before the wedding, Sarah Whitman heard that Poe had not kept his pledge and broke off the engagement.

Eldorado

Sometimes described as Poe's last poem, this takes the legendary realm of Eldorado, a land of gold that is sought but never found, and links it with the occasion of the 1849 Gold Rush to California. Characteristically, Poe attempts to transform a historical moment into a spiritual legend.

For Annie

This is addressed to a close and long-time friend of Poe's, Mrs Annie Richmond, from whom, Poe claimed, he had extracted the promise that she would come to him on his 'bed of death'.

To My Mother

This poem is, in fact, addressed to Poe's mother-in-law, Mrs Maria Clemm.

Annabel Lee

Although there have been several different claims as to the subject of this poem, it is commonly accepted that it refers to Virginia, Poe's wife.

ESSAYS

Letter to Mr ——

This letter introduced the second edition of Poe's poems (1831) and demonstrates Poe's debt to the two great English poets of the time, Coleridge and Wordsworth, as well as his attempts to establish his independence from them. The ellipses in the text are apparently Poe's device for suggesting that parts of his treatise have been omitted.

The Philosophy of Composition

For a discussion of this essay, see the introduction. The title could be paraphrased as 'The Theory of Writing'.

The Rationale of Verse

This essay reveals Poe's preoccupation with poetry as a craft as well as an art.

The Poetic Principle

Probably the most intensive and sustained discussion of the poetic art that Poe ever wrote, this essay is discussed in the introduction.

Georgia Scenes

'I am a Southerner', Poe liked to claim; and this brief review reveals his preoccupation with regional interests and themes.

Fancy and Imagination

This review is another illustration of Poe's debt to and differences from Coleridge as far as aesthetic theory is concerned.

Charles Dickens

This and the following three reviews show Poe's involvement in the literary controversies of the day, his interest in contemporary literature, and his attempt to formulate a critical approach that was both provocative and analytical.

from Marginalia

The origin and aims of the *Marginalia* are explained in Poe's introduction, included here. The selection is intended to illustrate something of the range of Poe's literary, cultural, and social interests.

POE AND HIS CRITICS

THE FRENCH RESPONSE TO POE[1]

'Edgar Poe, who isn't much in America, *must* become a great man in France – at least that is what I want.' When Baudelaire wrote those words to Sainte-Beuve in 1856, he had already given nine years to a task that was to preoccupy him for seven years more. It was only when a paralytic stroke shattered him in 1866 that Baudelaire abandoned, along with all lesser interests, this one which had dominated most of his mature life. One of the results of this remarkable devotion is that of the twelve volumes of Baudelaire's works in the definitive Crépet edition, five are translations from the work of Poe. This simple arithmetic involves a fact of major significance. For in Baudelaire there was a great creative genius, a writer who had, and knew he had, one of the rarest of all gifts: the power to alter and revivify his own country's literature. And yet this man, for nearly twenty years, gave himself with an almost ascetic energy and ardour to the wearisome and specifically uncreative work of sedulous translating. Certainly this was no pastime for him, nor was it simply the means of obtaining an income, although it did serve that end, too. One is almost tempted to go so far as to say that Baudelaire's life work, his great achievement, was not so much *Les Fleurs du mal* as it was his Poe translations. However this may be, the five Poe volumes fulfilled and surpassed all that Baudelaire had hoped for them. Not only did Poe become a great man in France; he has become, thanks to Baudelaire, a world figure, and this despite the fact that his reputation as a major writer in America has hardly been better than precarious. Let us examine this astonishing paradox.

Although it is a commonplace that in American literature there are few writers of really major rank, it is perilous to offer an opinion as to just who these writers are. Whatever the list, the objection will be made that the prizes were not fairly awarded. But it seems fairly

[1] From *The French Face of Edgar Poe* by Patrick F. Quinn (Southern Illinois UP, 1957).

certain that if the list is a brief one Poe's claims for inclusion in it are by no means considered self-evident in this country, and have seldom been convincingly sponsored. The general reading public, which might be expected to show a warm interest in Poe, or at least a dutiful respect for him, has shown neither. Some forty years after his death, when a poll was taken to discover which ten books were generally considered the best to be written in America, Emerson's *Essays* and Hawthorne's *Scarlet Letter* reached the top of the list. Nothing by Poe was voted to rank among the first ten, or the first thirty! No doubt Poe would fare better today if a similar competition were arranged, but it seems true nonetheless that his status as a classic American author exists, in the mind of the general public, rather by default than acclaim.

. . . . .

His American contemporaries were reluctant to pay him merely conventional homage; for his French admirers the problem was to find a language of praise sufficiently sublime. Baudelaire, of course, carried away by his missionary zeal, was not one to hesitate on this subject. In *L'Art romantique* he calls Poe simply 'the most powerful writer of the age'. Make what allowances we will for this as a statement intended for public consumption, the sincerity underlying it may be inferred from the allusion, in *Journaux intimes*, to his morning prayers to God and to Edgar Poe as his intercessor in heaven. For Mallarmé also, Poe was a writer altogether unique, *the* poet, as we know from 'Le Tombeau d'Edgar Poe'. For him as for Baudelaire the stature of Poe was evidently that of a literary deity. Thus when Mallarmé sent to his friend Cazalis a copy of his sonnet 'L'Azur', the first in which he had completely succeeded in the style that was to be distinctively his own, he remarked in his letter: 'The more I continue in this direction the more faithful shall I be to those severe ideas which I owe to my great master Edgar Poe.' And for Valéry in the next generation Poe was also to be a great master: 'Poe is the only impeccable writer. He was never mistaken.' In the first letter he wrote to Mallarmé, in 1890, Valéry was careful to underline their common admiration of Poe; and fifty years later he was to specify Poe, along with Leonardo da Vinci, as the major influences in his literary and philosophical career.

That an enthusiasm for Poe should have been shared by the three most influential poets in modern French literature, that this American writer should have become the pivot on which for the past century

French literature has turned, this by itself is sufficiently extraordinary. But even this statement of the case does no more than suggest the force of Poe's impact. There is scarcely one French writer from the time of Baudelaire to the present who has not in one way or another paid his respects to Poe. Villiers de l'Isle Adam, Verlaine and Rimbaud, Huysmans, Claudel, Gide, Edmond Jaloux – these are names at random, but they will serve to indicate the scope of the interest Poe has had for France. Indeed the only *short* list of French writers that would be relevant to this subject would consist of those men, like Barbey d'Aurevilly and Sainte-Beuve, who did not join the pilgrimage to the Poe shrine. For this interest became something very like a religious cult. If Baudelaire was unique in actually praying to Edgar Poe, some of Baudelaire's successors were not far behind him in their fervent devotion. For the adherents to this cult Poe becomes immense, transcendent, to be associated, as he is by Jules Lemaître, only with the very greatest figures, Plato and Shakespeare. The Poe text, accordingly, is conned with the fanatic zeal appropriate to sacred books. Thus Jean Moréas, in an article in *Le Symboliste*, could assume that the readers of that journal would appreciate a reference to one of Poe's least known stories, 'The Devil in the Belfry'. And what if not religious awe is this, registered by Albert Samain in his *Carnets intimes*?

> Have read Edgar Poe, *Eureka*. Overwhelming sensation, especially towards the end. The grandeur of the hypotheses, the limitless nature of the concept, terrify me. I wanted to read it through in one night, and this dizzy flight through the incommensurable makes me collapse on my bed, my body aching, my head splitting.

No matter how the chart is read, therefore, whether we attend to such men as Baudelaire and Mallarmé or to writers of secondary and tertiary importance, the results are identical: Baudelaire made Poe a great figure in France, and not for his own time only but for the next hundred years. This apotheosis is probably unmatched in literature.

. . . . .

As Poe's translator, Baudelaire gave his attention almost entirely to the stories. But in his essays he had something suggestive to say of every aspect of Poe's work. 'His poetry, profound and plaintive, is nevertheless wrought and pure, correct and brilliant as a crystal jewel.' Inspired? That too; but in addition the work of a man of will, master of himself, who realized that in art there can be no minutiae.

Mallarmé was fascinated by hints such as these and took up a task which Baudelaire had thought impossible, the translating of Poe's poems. Poe's aesthetic, exacting and disciplined, calling for a union of inspiration and method – this was to be the focus of Valéry's interest. Of Poe's *Eureka* Baudelaire had said that it would require an essay all to itself; in 'A Propos d'Eureka' Valéry wrote that essay.

Baudelaire's successors thus found in the articles on Poe a number of hints which they acted on according to their own interests and predilections. For Baudelaire himself it was Poe's work in fiction that chiefly mattered, and it is not surprising that his most illuminating remarks are those he made on this subject. In general, he indicated that the stories were not to be read as mechanical melodramas, as contrived exercises in the horror genre. The 'new literature' which Poe had created would be devoid of all novelty if they were merely that. Consequently, Baudelaire took care to underscore the psychological context of these stories as their distinguishing feature. Much as he admired Poe's talent for ratiocination, and the 'impeccable' quality of his style, the real Poe, for him, was 'the writer of the nerves', who in exploring mental and moral disease had opened up for literature an order of experience that seemed to have been effectively sealed off. In his preface to *Tales of the Grotesque and Arabesque* (1840), Poe hinted that the terror he was writing about was 'not of Germany but of the soul'. In substance, that is what Baudelaire had to say about the spirit in which Poe's stories should be read.

Here again we find no more than a direction given. It was something, however, to make this point clearly, to define Poe's characteristic subject matter as belonging to the psychological order, and, if only by implication, to warn against the superficiality of seeing his work as the imitative productions of a sensational journalist who had some skill at writing weird tales. Baudelaire succeeded in setting up a strong barrier against such a misconception. It is chiefly as a result of this that subsequent French commentary on Poe has been so fecund. In this country, on the other hand, the prevailing view has been at best an uneasy one, unsure whether Poe's tales should not be dismissed as so much claptrap. In American criticism, ancient or modern, the treatment Poe has received has as a rule been either lean with censure or fat with platitude, and thus has generally failed to give a satisfactory account of his undeniable permanence and power.

. . . . .

Like almost all the discussions of Poe that have been written in France since the appearance of the Bonaparte volumes,[1] those of Gaston Bachelard are indebted to her analysis. Bachelard's readings of Poe cannot be treated, however, as if they were merely an extension of her theories. They must be seen in the light of the rather special work he has been concerned with during the past twenty years, and on this intricate subject I shall attempt a word of explanation here.

For some years prior to his recent retirement at the age of seventy, Bachelard was professor of philosophy and head of the Institute of the History of Science and Techniques at the University of Paris. Encyclopedic in his interests, at home in physics, chemistry, and mathematics, and apparently as widely read in literature as any man in France, this extraordinary figure is above all a philosopher, creative, seminal, original. Original, and therefore iconoclastic. It was this bent that led him, in the course of his research into the work of the alchemists and pre-scientific 'scientists' of the seventeenth and eighteenth centuries, to go beyond merely descriptive cataloguing. Granted, he seems to have said, that these men were not really scientists and so gave us nothing that we recognize as scientific knowledge; yet neither were they merely stupid men. What, then, is the lesson their pre-scientific experience contains? In his analysis of this problem Bachelard developed the thesis that a psychology could be worked out for subjective knowledge, for intuition and reverie, the realm midway between dream and conscious thought. This is, precisely, the realm of the imagination. It was accordingly to the evidence of imaginative literature that he turned for the detailed demonstration of this theory. Resurrecting the ancient intuition that correspondences exist between the four elements and the human temperaments, Bachelard has presented in five volumes – from *La Psychanalyse du feu* (1938) to *La Terre et les rêveries du repos* (1948) – his amazing studies in the psychology of the imagination.

The rich suggestiveness of these books may be gauged from the fact that although relatively few pages deal with Poe those pages present some of the most illuminating commentary Poe has ever received. For Bachelard, Poe is, in general terms, a poet of water. That is the element towards which he was orientated and which polarized, so to speak, his imagination. This insight makes possible, among other

[1]Marie Bonaparte, author of the two-volume study *Edgar Poe* (Paris, 1933). The importance of her study was that it was one of the first to apply psychoanalytical theory to an analysis of Poe's life and work. In particular, Bonaparte argued that Poe was obsessed with his mother and sexually impotent, and used these arguments to 'explain' recurrent themes in his writing.

things, a clear-cut demarcation between Poe and a writer with whom he is often associated, E. T. A. Hoffmann. A study of their imagery of water and fire shows how different they are: Hoffmann fascinated by flame, Poe recoiling compulsively from it, so that, as in 'Ulalume', a volcano image is given in the form of 'scoriac rivers', even though this fluvial effect weakens the figure Poe must have intended. More specifically, Poe is the poet of darkened water, water which is stagnant, heavy, and dead. It absorbs life, drains it away. In a word, the water which fascinated Poe and which, in 'Ulalume', 'The City in the Sea,' 'Usher', and so on, is a dominant image, is no longer the 'real' water which is drunk, but *that which drinks*. In an essay of thirty pages in *L'Eau et les rêves*, Bachelard examines the stories and poems of Poe, bringing into relief the great attraction the symbol of the dank tarn and the sullen, melancholy pool had for the imagination of this writer.

In Poe's best work there is both a manifest and a latent content. Beneath the surface account of more or less credible incident there is a subcurrent which flows from the world of dreams. Bachelard defines Poe's special quality in these terms. He admires Poe as one of the few writers who have been able to work along the frontier between the real and the dream worlds, a shadowy frontier where the writer's experience is strangely blended of elements drawn from both those realms.

Thus, in his comments on Poe, Bachelard accomplishes two important things. For one, he directs attention to the particular element-symbol in terms of which the Poe imagination was frequently aligned; and in addition he indicates and illustrates the technique of the double reading, through which alone, in his opinion, we can become aware of the kind of life that sustains Poe's melodramas. It is true, then, that although Bachelard treats Poe incidentally, as simply one exemplification of a recondite hypothesis, his discussion refines the exhaustive critique of Marie Bonaparte. Making a subtler use of some of the assumptions of psychoanalysis, less dogmatic and systematic in method, he nonetheless retains the essence of her theory (it was Baudelaire's as well): that Poe's singular gift was to probe into the caverns of the psyche and to bring up to the level of imaginative literature the dark scrolls – of fear, guilt, and obsession – that those caverns contain.

VULGARITY IN LITERATURE[1]

Eulalie, Ulalume, Raven and Bells, Conqueror Worm and Haunted Palace . . . Was Edgar Allan Poe a major poet? It would surely never occur to any English-speaking critic to say so. And yet, in France, from 1850 till the present time, the best poets of each generation – yes, and the best critics, too; for, like most excellent poets, Baudelaire, Mallarmé, Paul Valéry are also admirable critics – have gone out of their way to praise him. Only a year or two ago M. Valéry repeated the now traditional French encomium of Poe, and added at the same time a protest against the faintness of our English praise. We who are speakers of English and not English scholars, who were born into the language and from childhood have been pickled in its literature – we can only say, with all due respect, that Baudelaire, Mallarmé and Valéry are wrong and that Poe is not one of our major poets. A taint of vulgarity spoils, for the English reader, all but two or three of his poems – the marvellous 'City in the Sea' and 'To Helen', for example, whose beauty and crystal perfection make us realize as we read them, what a very great artist perished on most of the occasions when Poe wrote verse. It is to this perished artist that the French poets pay their tribute. Not being English, they are incapable of appreciating those finer shades of vulgarity that ruin Poe for us, just as we, not being French, are incapable of appreciating those finer shades of lyrical beauty which are, for them, the making of La Fontaine.

The substance of Poe is refined; it is his form that is vulgar. He is, as it were, one of Nature's Gentlemen, unhappily cursed with incorrigible bad taste. To the most sensitive and high-souled man in the world we should find it hard to forgive, shall we say, the wearing of a diamond ring on every finger. Poe does the equivalent of this in his poetry; we notice the solecism and shudder. Foreign observers do not notice it; they detect only the native gentlemanliness in the poetical intention, not the vulgarity in the details of execution. To them, we seem perversely and quite incomprehensibly unjust.

It is when Poe tries to make it too poetical that his poetry takes on its peculiar tinge of badness. Protesting too much that he is a gentleman, and opulent into the bargain, he falls into vulgarity. Diamond rings on every finger proclaim the parvenu.

[1]From 'Vulgarity in Literature', in *Music at Night and Other Essays* by Aldous Huxley (Chatto & Windus, 1958).

Consider, for example, the first two stanzas of 'Ulalume.'

> The skies they were ashen and sober;
> The leaves they were crisped and sere –
> The leaves they were withering and sere:
> It was night in the lonesome October
> Of my most immemorial year:
> It was hard by the dim lake of Auber,
> In the misty mid region of Weir:–
> It was down by the dank tarn of Auber,
> In the ghoul-haunted woodland of Weir.
>
> Here once, through an alley Titanic,
> Of cypress, I roamed with my Soul –
> Of cypress, with Psyche, my Soul.
> These were days when my heart was volcanic
> As the scoriac rivers that roll –
> As the lavas that restlessly roll
> Their sulphurous currents down Yaanek,
> In the ultimate climes of the Pole –
> That groan as they roll down Mount Yaanek,
> In the realms of the Boreal Pole.

These lines protest too much (and with what a variety of voices!) that they are poetical, and, protesting, are therefore vulgar. To start with, the walloping dactyllic metre is all too musical. Poetry ought to be musical, but musical with tact, subtly and variously. Metres whose rhythms, as in this case, are strong, insistent and practically invariable offer the poet a kind of short cut to musicality. They provide him (my subject calls for a mixture of metaphors) with a ready-made, reach-me-down-music. He does not have to create a music appropriately modulated to his meaning; all he has to do is to shovel the meaning into the moving stream of the metre and allow the current to carry it along on waves that, like those of the best hairdressers, are guaranteed permanent.

. . . . .

Of the versification of 'The Raven' Poe says, in his 'Philosophy of Composition':

> My first object (as usual) was originality. The extent to which this has been neglected, in versification, is one of the most unaccountable things in the world. Admitting that there is little possibility of variety in mere *rhythm*, it is still clear that the possible varieties of metre and

> stanza are absolutely infinite – and yet, *for centuries, no man, in verse, has ever done, or ever seemed to think of doing, an original thing.*

This fact, which Poe hardly exaggerates, speaks volumes for the good sense of the poets. Feeling that almost all strikingly original metres and stanzas were only illegitimate short cuts to a music which, when reached, turned out to be but a poor and vulgar substitute for individual music, they wisely stuck to the less blatantly musical metres of tradition. The ordinary iambic decasyllable, for example, is intrinsically musical enough to be just able, when required, to stand up by itself. But its musical stiffness can easily be taken out of it. It can be now a chasuble, a golden carapace of sound, now, if the poet so desires, a pliant, soft and, musically speaking, almost neutral material, out of which he can fashion a special music of his own to fit his thoughts and feelings in all their incessant transformations. Good landscape painters seldom choose a 'picturesque' subject; they want to paint their own picture, not have it imposed on them by nature. In the thoroughly paintable little places of this world you will generally find only bad painters. (It's so easy to paint the thoroughly paintable.) The good ones prefer the unspectacular neutrality of the Home Counties to those Cornish coves and Ligurian fishing villages, whose picturesqueness is the delight of all those who have no pictures of their own to project on to the canvas. It is the same with poetry: good poets avoid what I may call, by analogy, 'musicesque' metres, preferring to create their own music out of raw materials as nearly as possible neutral. Only bad poets, or good poets against their better judgment, and by mistake, go to the Musicesque for their material. 'For centuries no man, in verse, has ever done, or ever seemed to think of doing, an original thing.' It remained for Poe and the other nineteenth-century metrists to do it; Procrustes-like, they tortured and amputated significance into fitting the ready-made music of their highly original metres and stanzas. The result was, in most cases, as vulgar as a Royal Academy Sunrise on Ben Nevis (with Highland Cattle) or a genuine hand-painted sketch of Portofino.

How could a judge so fastidious as Baudelaire listen to Poe's music and remain unaware of its vulgarity? A happy ignorance of English versification preserved him, I fancy, from this realization. His own imitations of mediaeval hymns prove how far he was from understanding the first principles of versification in a language where the stresses are not, as in French, equal, but essentially and insistently uneven. In his Latin poems Baudelaire makes the ghost of Bernard of

Cluny write as though he had learned his art from Racine. The principles of English versification are much the same as those of mediaeval Latin. If Baudelaire could discover lines composed of equally stressed syllables in Bernard, he must also have discovered them in Poe. Interpreted according to Racinian principles, such verses as

> It was down by the dank tarn of Auber,
> In the ghoul-haunted woodland of Weir

must have taken on, for Baudelaire, heaven knows what exotic subtlety of rhythm. We can never hope to guess what that ghoul-haunted woodland means to a Frenchman possessing only a distant and theoretical knowledge of our language.

Returning now to 'Ulalume', we find that its too-poetical metre has the effect of vulgarizing by contagion what would be otherwise perfectly harmless and refined technical devices. Thus, even the very mild alliterations in 'the ghoul-haunted woodland of Weir' seem to protest too much. And yet an iambic verse beginning 'Woodland of Weir, ghoul-haunted', would not sound in the least over-poetical. It is only in the dactylic environment that those two w's strike one as protesting too much.

And then there are the proper names. Well used, proper names can be relied on to produce the most thrilling musical-magical effects. But use them without discretion, and the magic evaporates into abracadabrical absurdity, or becomes its own mocking parody; the over-emphatic music shrills first into vulgarity and finally into ridiculousness. Poe tends to place his proper names in the most conspicuous position in the line (he uses them constantly as rhyme words), showing them off – these magical-musical jewels – as the *rastacouaire* might display the twin cabochon emeralds at his shirt cuffs and the platinum wrist watch, with his monogram in diamonds. These proper-name rhyme-jewels are particularly flashy in Poe's case because they are mostly dissyllabic. Now, the dissyllabic rhyme in English is poetically so precious and so conspicuous by its richness that, if it is not perfect in itself and perfectly used, it emphatically ruins what it was meant emphatically to adorn. Thus, sound and association make of 'Thule' a musical-magical proper name of exceptional power. But when Poe writes,

> I have reached these lands but newly
> From an ultimate dim Thule,

he spoils the effect which the word ought to produce by insisting too much, and incompetently, on its musicality. He shows off his jewel as conspicuously as he can, but only reveals thereby the badness of its setting and his own Levantine love of display. For 'newly' does not rhyme with 'Thule' – or only rhymes on condition that you pronounce the adverb as though you were a Bengali, or the name as though you came from Whitechapel. The paramour of Goethe's king rhymed perfectly with the name of his kingdom; and when Laforgue wrote of that 'roi de Thulé, Immaculé' his *rime riche* was entirely above suspicion. That dank tarn of Auber is only very dubiously a fit poetical companion for the tenth month, and though Mount Yaanek is, *ex hypothesi*, a volcano, the rhyme with volcanic is, frankly, impossible. On other occasions Poe's proper names rhyme not only well enough, but actually, in the particular context, much too well. Dead D'Elormie, in 'The Bridal Ballad', is prosodically in order, because Poe had brought his ancestors over with the conqueror (as he also imported the ancestors of that Guy de Vere who wept his tear over Lenore) for the express purpose of providing a richly musical-magical rhyme to 'bore me' and 'before me'. Dead D'Elormie is first cousin to Edward Lear's aged Uncle Arly, sitting on a heap of Barley – ludicrous; but also (unlike dear Uncle Arly) horribly vulgar, because of the too musical lusciousness of his invented name and his display, in all tragical seriousness, of an obviously faked Norman pedigree. Dead D'Elormie is a poetical disaster.

THE CONSCIOUS ART OF EDGAR ALLAN POE[1]

I am convinced that all of Poe's poems were composed with conscious art. How else can we account for his frequent and meticulous revision? Most if not all of them had their origin in thought and express or suggest clearly-formed ideas. 'Al Aaraaf' was written with the conscious purpose of suggesting Poe's aesthetic theory: that beauty is the province of art, that the artist reveals truth through beauty, and that he must keep his art free of passion. 'To Helen' tells how an artist who has been lost on the turbulent seas of passion is restored to his artistic home through the beauty of woman. 'Israfel' reminds us that in this imperfect world the poet can approach truth only through the veil of beautiful forms. 'The Sleeper' and 'The City in the Sea' present a series of images all developed from the trivial

[1]From 'The Conscious Art of Edgar Allan Poe' by Floyd Stovall, *College English* (March 1963), 417–21.

idea, or superstition, that those who die rest comfortably in their graves only so long as their surviving friends remember them and mourn. 'Dream-Land' is just what the title promises: a description of the topsy-turvy world of dreams. 'The Raven' describes the inconsolable grief of a bereaved lover unable to believe in life after death.

Poe did not tell us how he wrote 'The Sleeper' and 'The City in the Sea', but the several surviving versions of the poems record pretty fully the process of their development. In the earliest version of 'The Sleeper' the initial idea was clearly stated, but the passage in which it appeared was later deleted, and so the idea remains only in the images that grew out of it. Certainly all the details were not preformed in his mind before he composed the first draft, but the overall pattern of the poem might well have been. I think it quite possible that 'The Raven' was planned in advance of composition very much as Poe says it was in 'The Philosophy of Composition'. The difference between the early and late poems is chiefly in the technique of composition. The former are predominantly the lyric expression of moods in the style of the English romantic poets, particularly Coleridge; the latter are more dramatic in form, and characterized in style by novelties of rhyme, repetition, metre, and stanza structure, with elements of the fantastic not common before 1840. These novelties of style give the later poems the effect of seeming contrived; and indeed they may have been more completely the work of the deliberate craftsman than the earlier ones.

. . . . .

Poe's criticism is less difficult than his tales and poems. His theory of the short story is stated, in essence, in the well-known paragraph of his review of Hawthorne's *Twice-Told Tales*, where he says the writer first deliberately conceives the single effect to be wrought, and then invents such incidents, arranges them in such order, and presents them in such a tone as will produce in the reader the preconceived effect. He adds that for fullest satisfaction, the story must be read with an art akin to that of its creator.

Poe's theory of poetry is similar, though less simply stated. According to this theory, every person is endowed by nature with the Poetic Sentiment, or Sentiment of Beauty, an insatiable desire to experience that Supernal Beauty which Poe conceived in Platonic terms as beyond the power of finite man wholly to possess. In this sense, Beauty is an effect, not an attribute. Sensuous beauty, the beauty of natural objects and artistic creations, though it is not an effect but only an attribute, is yet capable of evoking the Sentiment of Beauty, which is an effect, and thus furthering the soul's progress toward Supernal Beauty. Those who have found fault with Poe's definition of Beauty as an effect, not a quality, have failed to weigh sufficiently the sentence in 'The Poetic Principle' in which Poe describes man's sense of the beautiful in language reminiscent of Plato as the 'struggle, by multiform combinations among the things and thoughts of Time, to attain a portion of that Loveliness whose very elements, perhaps, appertain to eternity alone'.

Though Poe denies the poet the use of the didactic method of inculcating the truths of the intellect and the moral sense, he insists that the true poet can and must suggest Truth through Beauty. He believes, with Emerson, that the Good, the True, and the Beautiful are aspects of one divine Unity; that though they are approached by different means, they are identical under the aspect of eternity. As he says in 'Eureka', a work of art is necessarily true, and an intellectual structure, because of the harmony of its elements, is necessarily beautiful. Indeed, as stated above, the imaginative and analytic faculties work best when they work together. The scientist uses intuitive reasoning, and the poet requires constructive skill. In 'Eureka' he calls Kepler a greater man than Newton because Kepler imagined, or 'guessed', the physical laws which Newton later demonstrated rationally to be true. This is not to say that Newton had no imagination, but only that Kepler had more.

If modern sceptics would read 'Eureka' carefully and without prejudice, as Paul Valéry did, they might not be so ready to scoff at Poe's account of writing 'The Raven' in 'The Philosophy of Composition'. Poe means that the poem began in the Poetic Sentiment, was shaped by the imagination, and then constructed according to the imagined pattern with deliberate and methodical skill in the manner best calculated to evoke in the reader the mood from which it grew in the mind of the poet. In short, 'The Raven', and with certain necessary individual differences, every other poem Poe wrote, was the product of conscious effort by a healthy and alert intelligence.[1]

[1] Acknowledgements are due to the copyright holders of the extracts reprinted in the above section of this edition.

SUGGESTIONS FOR FURTHER READING

There is no recent scholarly edition of the works of Poe. The principal source used here is the seventeen-volume Virginia Edition of the *Complete Works* edited by James A. Harrison (1902). There are, however, facsimile reprints of early editions; and *The Imaginary Voyages* edited by Burton R. Pollin, the first volume of a projected *Collected Writings*, appeared in 1981. *The Letters of Edgar Allan Poe* edited by John W. Ostrom was published in 1948 with a revised, two-volume edition in 1966. Also of note, as far as collections of Poe's work are concerned, are *Collected Works* edited by Thomas O. Mabbott, in three volumes, 1969 (volume 1), 1978 (volumes 2 and 3) edited by M. C. Mabbott and E. D. Kewer; *Literary Criticism* edited by Robert L. Hough (1965); and *Marginalia* edited by John C. Miller (1981).

The most useful single reference book on Poe is *The Poe Log: A Documentary of the Life of Edgar Allan Poe* edited by Dwight Thomas and David K. Jackson; while a comprehensive listing of works on Poe is Esther F. Hyneman, *Edgar Allan Poe: An Annotated Bibliography of Books and Articles in English, 1827–1973* (1974). Also helpful, as far as bibliographical information is concerned, are John W. Robertson, *Bibliography of the Writings of Poe* (1934); C. R. Heartman and J. R. Canny, *A Bibliography of First Printings of the Writings of Poe* (1941); J. Leslie Dameron and I. B. Cauthen, *Poe: A Bibliography of Criticism 1827–1967* (1974); and Jay B. Hubbell, 'Poe', in *Eight American Authors: A Review of Research and Criticism* edited by Floyd Stovall (1956; revised edition, 1963). Worth referring to, also, are the journal *Poe Studies* and the annual editions of *American Literary Scholarship*, each of which cites published criticism on Poe for the relevant year.

The most reliable scholarly biography is Arthur H. Quinn, *Edgar Allan Poe: A Critical Biography* (1941). However, particular aspects of Poe's life and career are covered more effectively in Sidney P. Moss, *Poe's Literary Battles: The Critic in the Context of his Literary Milieu* (1963) and *Poe's Major Crisis: His Libel Suit and New York's Literary World* (1970); and Robert D. Jacobs, *Poe: Journalist and Critic* (1969). The general reader is also likely to find one of the following more entertaining and, possibly, informative: Vincent Buranelli, *Edgar Allan Poe* (1961); W. Bittner, *Poe: A Biography* (1962); Edward Wagenknecht, *Edgar Allan Poe: The Man Behind the Legend* (1963); Julian Symons, *The Tell-Tale Heart: The Life and Works of Edgar Allan Poe* (1978); Wolf Mankewitz, *A Biography of Edgar Allan Poe* (1978); Kenneth Silverman, *Edgar A. Poe: Mournful and Never-Ending Remembrance* (1992).

The critical writing on Poe is very extensive. Poe's early reputation is traced in Eric Carlson, *The Recognition of Edgar Allan Poe* and Jean Alexander, *Affidavits of Genius: Edgar Allan Poe and the French Critics 1847–1924* (1971). Excellent selections of more recent criticism are to be found in *Poe: A Collection of Critical Essays* edited by Robert Regan (1967), *Twentieth-Century Interpretations of Poe's Tales* edited by William L. Howarth (1977), and *Papers on Poe* edited by Richard P. Veler. Among the most stimulating books on Poe over the last fifty years are N. Bryllion Fagin, *The Histrionic Mr Poe* (1949); Charles Baudelaire, *Baudelaire on Poe: Critical Papers* translated by Lois and Francis E. Hyslop (1952); Edward H. Davidson, *Poe: A Critical Commentary* (1957); Patrick F. Quinn, *The French Face of Edgar Allan Poe* (1957); Floyd Stovall, *Poe the Poet: Essays New and Old on the Man and his Work* (1959); Michael Allen, *Poe and the British Magazine Tradition* (1969); Daniel Hoffman, *Poe, Poe, Poe, Poe, Poe, Poe, Poe* (1972); David Halliburton, *Edgar Allan Poe: A Phenomenological View* (1973); David Sinclair, *Edgar Allan Poe* (1977).

Other seminal discussions of Poe are to be found in D. H. Lawrence, *Studies in Classic American Literature* (1923); William Carlos Williams, *In the American Grain* (1925); Constance Rourke, *American Humor: A Study of the National Character* (1931); Yvor Winters, *Maule's Curse* (1938); Harry Levin, *The Power of Blackness* (1958); Allen Tate, *Collected Essays* (1959); Leslie Fiedler, *Love and Death in the American Novel* (1960); Edwin Fussell, *Frontier: American Literature and the American West* (1965); Barbara Johnson, 'The Frame of Reference: Poe, Lacan, Derrida', *Literature and Psychoanalysis, Yale French Studies* (1977), 55–6; Larzer Ziff, *Literary Democracy* (1981).